CRUMBS FROM THE PASTOR'S TABLE

Reflections on the Catholic Lectionary Three-year cycle

Fr Francis

The author hereby declares that no copyright infringement was intended or knowingly committed in the creation of this literary work. Diligent efforts have been undertaken to ensure the material does not infringe upon any existing copyrights. However, in the unlikely event that any unintentional infringement has occurred, the author sincerely regrets the oversight and commits to promptly addressing and rectifying the issue in subsequent editions.

This work is dedicated to my parents
"The real cost of what we received is what our parents went without so that we could have"

CONTENTS

FOREWORD

Shortly after my first appointment, my parish priest handed me two hard-back notebooks. The bishop will be visiting the parish next year he said, and he will be looking for statistics. So, off you go and do a census of the parish. It meant visiting every home in the parish. That initial experience became a formative influence on my ministry. It convinced me of the value of home visitation. It became a priority for me for the next fifty years. A priest friend once said to me; when you have had tea at the kitchen table, you become accepted as part of the family.!

I have always had a strong sense that the parish is more than a body of people who subscribe to the same set of truths and beliefs. It is far more. It is a community, in relationship with each other, and I believe it is a significant bonus when the priest himself models this relationship with his people. We all know the difference between 'having lots of knowledge' about the Lord and 'knowing' the Lord. I venture to suggest that the same is true in our relationship with our people in the parish. Home visitation builds relationship. Regrettably, our reduced manpower in recent years, has made this practice very difficult, and in so many parishes simply impossible. But that wise parish priest appreciated, that our immersion in the everyday lives of our parishioners, can be at a minimum, helpful in pre-disposing openness to our message.

In what you read here, I have tried to avoid language and concepts, which though very familiar to us, may rarely be part of the everyday dialogue of our parishioners. Not being practiced in the art of the written word, I hope you will forgive me for often just transferring the spoken word to print. We each have our own style of communication. I hope you are not too 'thrown' by mine.

Finally, may I just say that over fifty years, the weekly homily was always the biggest challenge of the week for me. I never felt that mine had to be as good as, or better than anyone else's, but I have always believed that it had to be the very best I could produce at the time. Once I had done that, I could at least feel that I had fulfilled my responsibility. What happens to it, once it has been delivered, becomes someone else's choice, not mine. If we have five hundred people in the congregation and we preach for six minutes, that is fifty hours of other people's time !. Keeping that in mind, has always helped me to take the challenge very seriously.

Thank you for picking up this book. I sincerely hope that in it you may find something helpful. I am hoping someone might get a little inspiration and maybe even a little enjoyment from its pages. As St Bernadette once said to a young novice; 'When assigned to taking care of a sick person, withdraw before they have the opportunity to thank you. Helping the person should be its own reward'. If you find this effort of mine even a little helpful, that will be my reward.

Thank you.

Fr Francis

YEAR A

2nd Sunday in Ordinary Time

This light is entrusted to you to be kept burning brightly

Words can sometimes be the source of misunderstandings. In the English language, the word 'Church' can convey very different things to different people

To some it's the building. 'He's below at the church'. To others, it's the institution, 'The church teaches this, that, or the other'. Not that many, when they hear the word church, think of us the people.

In the Gaelic Language it is clearer. If you want to refer to the building, you call it the 'seipeal' (shea-pale). Referring to the institution you call it the 'Eaglais' (ogg-lish). If you want to refer to the people you speak of 'Pobal De', -God's People; 'See the church assembled here', -God's family, gathered. Today we will be looking at 'Pobal De'; God's family, and how we all became part of this family

I sometimes joke at a Baptism; that when I ring someone's doorbell late in the evening, I visualise the reaction inside; "Who could that be at this hour, and then, would you ever go out and see what they want!" When God's family are gathered and there is a ring at the door, (as when a couple arrive with their child to be baptised), the priest, representing you, goes to the door to welcome them and he asks the question'; Who are you and what do you want ?– translated into,

- What name do you wish to give this little child?
- What do you want for this little child?

The proud parents answer: Baptism, or We would like our little child admitted to 'Pobal De'[God's family] So that's why the priest meets the couple at the door of the church. The celebration of Baptism begins there, not at the font. On your behalf the priest, representing you, Pobal De here, makes a commitment to the new born's parents. We will do all in our power to create here the kind of community in which your child will be immersed in and formed by the values of Jesus. He might even at this point explain that we can't do this, for you. We can only do it with you. So, the celebration of Baptism begins with an invitation to parents to be active, participating members, of this faith community.

There are many beautiful moments in the ceremony. Many of you will remember on Holy Saturday night, when the whole building here is plunged into darkness and a huge candle is brought through the main door. As we see the darkness recede before the light, the whole church begins to light up. That candle represents the Risen Jesus; Light of the World, on Easter Morning overcoming darkness and bringing Light. It is from that Paschal Candle that the Child's candle is lit at Baptism. It symbolises the passing on of the Light of Christ to this little child. These are the words addressed to the parents; 'This light is entrusted to you to be kept burning brightly. This little child is to walk always as a child of Light.' The fragile little flame of faith in the child's heart, has to be minded, nurtured and protected, as it is entrusted to you by God

Immediately the child is baptised with water at the font, two things happen. The priest anoints the little child with the oil of Chrism [used only in Baptism, Confirmation and Ordination]. This child has now become a living tabernacle, where God has taken up residence deep within. He will remain with this little child for the rest of his/her life, walk them in the good days, and carry them on the not so good days.

The little child is wrapped in the white Baptism Shawl, with the beautiful words. 'See in this white garment the outward sign of your Christian dignity. With your family and friends to help you by word and example, bring this unstained into the presence of the Living God.' At the conclusion of the Baptism ceremony, we gather around the altar, the Table of the Lord, as we look forward together to this little child one day joining us there. These are some of the lovely symbols, full of meaning, used in the Baptism Ceremony. They tell us who we are and who we are called to be. The very symbols used as we enter 'Pobal De' for the first time are the symbols that will be used, as we leave for the final time

On both occasions we are brought by the people who love us most. On each occasion, the journey is to the altar. The Paschal Candle that welcomed us on our first arrival, is the Pascal Candle that lights over us on our final farewell

The White Robe given us on the day of our Baptism is wrapped around us now as we complete our journey home. The Water in which we were baptised when we first arrived is the water sprinkled on us as we say our last farewell. The incense is used to emphasise again that our body is a Temple of the Holy Spirit, God's dwelling place, sacred in death as in life

So, as we enter Pobal De at Baptism. God makes His home within each of us.

At the very centre of our journey is the Altar of God, to which our family brought us as we began life's journey, where we meet weekly with our family on the journey, and to which we are brought back at the end of life's journey. The altar at the heart of our church is a symbol of the table that gives meaning to our lives, the table we sit at with the Lord when the journey is complete. That after all, is what gives meaning to the journey we share on life's pilgrimage together.

3rd Sunday Ordinary Time

We are called to be a light that shines for others

Mother Teresa tells a story of once visiting the house of an old man. It was in a terrible state. The furniture was covered with layers of dust. Cobwebs hung from the walls and ceiling. The man lived in almost permanent darkness. The curtains were never open.

She began to clean the room. He protested that it was fine the way it was. After some coaxing, he left her start. She tackled removing the layers of rags and rubbish. Buried in it all she found an oil lamp covered with layers of grit and dust. She took it out, cleaned it and polished it with a rag. It was obvious it hadn't been used in years.

"Why haven't you used it?" she asked. 'Why should I" he said. "I don't need it for myself. I'm perfectly at home in the darkness and no one ever comes to see me." Mother Teresa got him to promise to light it each time her sisters visited him, and he agreed. One of Mother Teresa's sisters began to visit on a regular basis. Each time she came he lit the oil lamp. It was the beginning of a new life for him. Not only did his house brighten up, so also did his heart.

Then one day he said to the sister who had been visiting him: "Sister, I'm okay now. I can manage on my own. But do me a favour. Tell that first sister who came to see me that the light she lit in my life is still burning."

Over the Christmas period the lights were very prominent on our streets, in our churches, and in many of our homes. All those lights were pointing us to the coming of Christ the Light of the World. We opened our hearts to welcome Him. As in the life of that man in Mother Teresa's story, that light can sometimes disturb our inner world. For the old man in that the story the light was hardly welcome. He would have preferred not to know. He had grown accustomed to the darkness. He felt no need to change.

In that at least maybe we can identify with him. Which one of us wants to be challenged to change? But if at Christmas we have really opened our hearts and let the Light of Christ shine into our own lives that light will surely have shown up little areas, where there are darknesses and a few cobwebs to be dealt with.

Just two points we might take away today, to reflect on: We have all welcomed the Light of Christ at Christmas. Exposed to that light, dusty and cobwebbed areas of our lives are quickly exposed. We have two choices. We can accept the challenge to do something about them and be all the better for it or we can pull down the shutters, close the door, keep the curtains pulled, and stay in the darkness because we are uncomfortable with the light

The second point might be this: That sister, by being a light, herself, was able to bring that light into someone else's life. The transformation might not have been possible without her. Each of us is called to bring light into each other's life. But we can only bring it to others if we have welcomed it ourselves. Christmas lights will soon be taken down and packed away

And as they are, the challenge and invitation for all of us is to ensure that the Light that shone in our hearts at Christmas time is kept alight and burning brightly at the heart of our community

We are called to be that Light for each other. We are called to be that person who, like the sister in the story, causes our light to shine into other people's lives. Once we do our little bit, we can be assured that the Lord will do the rest

4th Sunday in Ordinary Time

God has chosen the foolish, the weak, the common and the contemptible

Reflecting on St. Paul's words to the people of Corinth, I found myself coming back again and again to do a little bit of introspection: "Take yourselves, before you were called, how many of you were wise and influential? What had you to offer or to boast about?". And before applying that question to anyone else each of us would have to apply it to ourselves. A priest, answering that question for himself, is good for the humility.

'Who are we anyway and what right have we to be where we are?' . That question, a priest doesn't just face today, confronted with these readings. It's a question he has had to face many times. From the first day he found himself setting eyes on the priesthood and saying, 'yes' to that mysterious call, one of the biggest hurdles he has to face is the mystery of 'why me?" It's a mystery that is compounded as the months and years of seminary life pass by and he sees the ranks of his classmates deplete and the numbers on the journey shrink. In my own case, almost a hundred of us started on the road together as first year students. Seven years later when it came to ordination the figure had dwindled to the mid-thirties, Why me? St. Paul tells us that "It was to shame the wise that God chose what is foolish by human reckoning. To shame what is strong that he chose what is weak by human reckoning. Those whom the world thinks common and contemptible are the ones God has chosen. Those who are nothing at all to show up those who are everything"

There is plenty to reflect on in Paul's words to each of us priests. We have nothing to boast about to God. Everything we have is His gift. A gift is not earned or deserved.

God is telling us Himself in Scripture that He has chosen; the foolish, the weak, the common, and the contemptible. When we discover this to be the case in our own experience, what we have discovered is not a reason to be shocked, disappointed or disillusioned, but rather the truth of God's word. Would it be fair to say that when **we** are disillusioned by human weakness among His chosen, that we're not displaying a marked familiarity with God's word. !!

We priests are often struck by the yawning gap between that which we are called to; to represent God to His people, and the inadequacy and unworthiness of us who are called. Paul's words of course have a much wider application, a universal application to all of us called and chosen in Baptism. We can all ask that question, Why me?.

5th Sunday in Ordinary Time

A light is not to be hidden, but put on the lampstand for all to see

Our Scripture Readings today don't need too many words of further explanation, but they do give all of us plenty of scope for action. The opening words of Jesus in the gospel are a huge compliment to all of you gathered here this morning. Jesus says to you. You are the Salt of the Earth

We might like salt, or we might not like salt, but there are very few who wouldn't recognize it because of its distinctive taste on the plate. The presence of salt is immediately obvious and instantly recognizable. Jesus tells us that 'WE' are the salt of the earth, so our presence should be instantly recognizable and our values immediately obvious. In the circles in which we move, in the community to which we belong, in the way we treat others, would I be the salt that has kept its taste, or the salt that has lost its taste?

The second huge compliment Jesus pays us today is that He says of you here. 'You are the light of the world. A light is not to be hidden under a tub but put on the lampstand for all to see. He wants us to be a beacon of light, that lets our light shine for others

The 1st. Reading of our mass today suggests how we can be that light. "Thus says the Lord, share your bread with the hungry and shelter the homeless poor, clothe the man you see to be naked and turn not from your own kin. Then will your light shine like the dawn."

So, my friends, Jesus tells us in the Gospel that we are the salt of the earth and the light of the world. As salt is instantly recognizable by its taste, so He asks us to be recognizable by our values and our lives. As light exists, not for itself, but to show others the way, so He wants our lives to be the lampstands that guide them

I began by saying today's gospel has little need of words but huge scope for action. Jesus is saying to each of us today: 'You are the salt of the earth, but if salt becomes tasteless, it is good for nothing and can only be thrown out to be trampled underfoot'.

You are the light of the world. No one lights a lamp to put it under a tub. They put it on a lampstand, where it shines for everyone in the house. In the same way your light must shine in the sight of men, so that, seeing your good works, they may give the praise to your Father in heaven.'

6th Sunday in Ordinary Time

Forgiveness is not an option, but a necessary part of belonging.

"Sinners", the Master teacher said, are nearer to God than saints. When asked to explain how this could be, He used an image to make his point. It is he said, as if each of us is connected to God by a piece of string. When we sin, we pull away from God and we break that string. When God forgives, He takes the two broken ends and knots them back together. Each time a knot is made, the string is shortened. So, sinners, because of all the knots on their piece of string, have shortened their connecting string considerably. That the teacher said, is how they have been drawn closer to God by each knot.

When I shared that story with a group one evening, the reaction of one of those in the groups was: 'That story is very unfair'. Well, he had a point, but I still think that little story is a gorgeous image of the God who will do anything to forgive us and bring us close.

Nowadays, I find myself in a house with someone of my age and more, who is as comfortable with their iPad as their parents were with the Radio. We all take modern technology for granted and are comfortable with it, but it wasn't always so. I remember my first painful lessons trying to master it. I know exactly when it was, over thirty years ago. I was leaving a parish, and I got a present of an electronic diary

I had never seen anything like it before and I was mystified by it. But, having got it as a present, I had to make an effort to use it. You could put all the names and address of your telephone book into this thing. And it was so tiny it fitted in my shirt pocket. In those days it was seen as the most amazing invention. So, I took on the challenge and tackled mastering it. Well, the keys on it were so small and my fingers were so big, it was tortuously slow and painstaking, but I got it working. I input about a hundred names, addresses and phone numbers. And then miraculously it sorted them all in alphabetical order. This thing was a mind-boggling little bit of equipment. Now that I had all this done, I wanted to really advance my knowledge. One day I found a tiny little hole, on the back of it and I wanted to find out what this was there for. So, I pushed in the end of a paper click to see what would happen. In that split second, I found out to my cost. I wiped it clear, everything gone, not a solitary trace left behind. My hours of painful inputting wiped off the face of the earth

The image of God I have is of a God who loves experimenting with His computer and of a God who has an endless supply of paper clips. And each time I come to him in the Sacrament to say sorry, He deliberately sticks a pin in that little pinhole on the back. And bang, He wipes the lot! Not a solitary trace left behind. Every record of what I have done is gone.

But there is another side to the coin that He doesn't allow me to forget; God asks me to be His "double". "The Lord has forgiven you. Now you must do the same." And it's not just that I must forgive, but that I must forgive as He forgives. I must be prepared to stick in the pin and wipe the lot. Not a solitary trace to be left. Every record to be destroyed. That is the forgiveness of the gospel. The only person who thinks that's easy must surely be someone who has never tried.

There's a sentence in today's gospel that sends a little shiver down my spine. A sentence that should shock us into realising how radical our call is to forgive

"If you are bringing your gift to the altar and there remember your brother has something against you, leave your offering there before the altar, go and be reconciled with your brother first and then come back and present your offering." Jesus tells us that that kind of radical level of forgiveness, is not just an option for us. It is a condition of belonging. An unforgiving Christian is a contradiction. A Christian, who reserves a place in his heart for a chip on his shoulder, must find it very hard to have room in his heart for Jesus as well

How many of us have really taken that on board? How many of us have done the check before bringing our gift to the altar. They are not my words; they are the words of Jesus in today's gospel. So, my friends, if sinners are closer to God than saints, it is because of the quality of God's forgiveness for us, a forgiveness that obliterates the lot, leaving not a trace behind. But a forgiveness not just to be marveled at, but to be imitated. Forgiveness, that for us, is not an option but a condition of belonging.

Jesus tells us in the gospel today "If you are bringing your gift to the altar and there remember your brother has something against you, leave your offering there before the altar, go and be reconciled with your brother first and then come back and present your offering.".

There's no one at the Church doors tonight to check if anyone has left!. There doesn't need to be, because what humans see is not important, it is what the Lord sees that is. The Lord is not looking at the externals but straight into our heart. Is it worth paying such an outlandish price, just to hold on to that CHIP?

7th Sunday in Ordinary Time

I will never let other people determine how I act!

Alastair, a good Orange Man. Dublin was by now his home for many years. But He hadn't severed all connections with his roots. The 12th. was still a very important day in his Calendar, a time he was back among his own walking in those parades was part of his heritage. Alastair was a creature of habit. Retired now, each day began with his early morning walk. The corner shop, on his way home, was part of his routine. The paper, the milk, his cigarettes, his few odds and ends.

The woman who ran the corner shop was of a very different political persuasion to Alastair. She was staunch Republican, equally proud of her roots. Normally she and Alastair got on pretty well. But those weeks in early July were always a bit tetchy.

Sometimes there was even hostility in the atmosphere. Sometimes he would overhear a cutting remark being passed. He knew it was specifically for his benefit, but Alastair had a calm serenity about his disposition. He did not let such remarks get under his skin. He certainly never allowed himself to be provoked. He seemed more than capable of taking it all in his stride. 'Thank you mam, and good morning, to you', he would say as he picked up his paper and his messages and he was gone.

Others were less comfortable. They could sense the tension in the atmosphere. They felt for him. He must have been feeling hurt and humiliated. One day as Alastair left the shop someone followed him. "I have just seen what went on in there" he said. "I am annoyed at what you are subjected to. I am kind of mad with you for putting up with it. I just wish that someday you would pick up your courage and stand up for yourself, that you would stand back from that woman, look her in the eye and give back as good as you are receiving."

Alastair thanked him for his concern. He appreciated his empathy. He acknowledged the expression of support and then he had this to add, by way of explaining his non reaction, to the unwelcome remarks, "I will never" he said, "allow that woman determine how I act".

I have always found that story very challenging. I often look back and wish I myself could have been like Alastair. I wish I could have his attitude and take his thinking to my heart. When we allow ourselves to be upset or provoked by another, we actually allow others 'determine' how we act. We surrender our own freedom and become subject to them. We hand over control of our lives at that moment to them. We become like a little puppet at the end of 'their' string. When they choose to tug the string, they have power over us. We allow them to throw our emotions into turmoil. We cease to be pro-active and let them make us re-active. We give to another the power to inflict hurt and frustration and let them upset us or ruin our day, all because we have chosen to allow them to determine how we re-act

To be Christian is to be free, not to allow ourselves to be controlled by anyone. To be Christian is to be responsible, not to allow ourselves to be turned into a robot by anyone. To be Christian is to be independent, never just be a puppet on the end of someone else's string.

To be Christian is to refuse; "an eye for an eye, a tooth for a tooth". To be Christian is to be big enough to "turn the other cheek".

Alastair was of a different political persuasion to those around him. But he had one heck of a lot to teach us all and would we all be better humans and Christians if we could adopt his approach in this little area of our lives?. Think of Alastair next time someone is getting under your skin, and you are tempted to stand back and tell that one a few home truths. Succeed in being Alastair. You will not believe the inner peace it brings

1st Sunday of Lent

Central to Lent are fasting, prayer and almsgiving.

The symbol of wearing ashes goes right back to the Old Testament. We find poor Job saying to God. My ears had heard of you. But now my eyes have seen you. Therefore, I repent in dust and ashes. We don't wear ashes to proclaim we are holy. We wear ashes to acknowledge that we sin and that we all need forgiveness. Central to Lent are Fasting; Praying; Almsgiving. Why do we Fast, Pray and Give?

Thomas Merton is quoted as saying that we can be like little kids, who when they want something want it now. Little kids are helped to develop their self-discipline because if we indulge them all the time, soon they'd be running the house! Maybe there is a good bit of the little child in all of us. Sometimes we too want, what we want, when we want it. There is a lot to be said for a self-discipline that helps us ensure our wants, rather than our needs don't run wild and dominate our lives. Self-discipline helps us to ensure that sometimes we can freely choose to go without. As we control our dominant desires, our deeper ones can surface

Second very important element in Lent is prayer. The simplest definition of Prayer is the one my generation learned. Prayer is a raising of the mind and heart to God

If I may quote Thomas Merton

The most important thing about prayer is to take the time. To set time aside to raise my mind and heart to God. We can do this in the simplest of ways. Some people just love the 'Jesus Prayer', simply repeating around the house or in the car or wherever we find ourselves, the words; Lord Jesus Christ, Son of the Living

God, have mercy on me a sinner. Others may like, during Lent to make a point of dropping in to a church, they are passing by, for a few quiet moments with the Lord. The final one I take from a good friend who during Lent makes a point of turning off the radio sometimes when he finds himself travelling in the car and tuning into the presence of the Lord instead. Whichever is your own favourite, go with it.

Finally in Lent, let's not forget our brothers and sisters who are so less blessed than we are. Many take time to think of, and respond to, the needs of those who are struggling against desperate odds, both on our own doorsteps and across the world in our time. It disturbs us all deeply to see how some can amass billions in their personal fortunes while hundreds of thousands of our deprived brothers and sisters go without even the essentials of food, clean water and medical care. Traditionally, Lent is a time we think about them and try to do something to help. Of course, the Trocaire Box has been a great help to keep us sensitised to this area. Hopefully we will have it this Lent at home

So, I leave you with those few thoughts as we begin our Lenten journey together. Prayer, Fasting and sharing we are all invited to work on in the weeks ahead.

2nd Sunday of Lent

Because I saw differently, I felt and behaved differently.

Steve Covey, author of the bestselling book, 'The Seven Habits of Highly Effective People', recalls an experience he had on a New York subway. One Sunday morning. He says that people were sitting quietly. Some were reading newspapers, some were dozing, others were simply miles away with their eyes closed. It was a rather peaceful, calm scene.

At one stop a man and his children entered the car. The children were soon yelling back and forth, throwing things, even grabbing people's newspapers. It was all very disturbing and yet the father just sat there. It was not difficult to feel irritated. Steve could not believe the man could be so insensitive, as to let his children run wild and do nothing about it. It was easy to see that everyone else in the car was annoyed as well. So finally, with what he thought was admirable restraint and patience, Steve said to the man, "Sir, your children are really disturbing a lot of people. I wonder if you couldn't control them a little bit more?". The man lifted his gaze. As if jumping into consciousness for the first time and said, "Oh, you are right he said, I guess I should do something about it. We just came from the hospital, where their mother died about an hour ago. I do not know what to think. And I guess they do not know how to handle it either."

Steve says, "Can you imagine what I felt at that moment? Suddenly I saw things differently. Because I saw differently, I felt differently, I behaved differently. My irritation vanished. My heart was filled with this man's pain. Feelings of compassion and sympathy flowed freely. 'Your wife just died?' Oh, I am so sorry. Can you tell me about it? What can I do to help?"

Nothing 'changed' in that subway car; the same people, the same irritation, the same kids. What did change was a way of 'seeing' it all. And, with that, a change of attitude, a change of behaviour. It was Steve Covey's "moment of Transfiguration"

For Peter, James and John their Moment of Transfiguration was on the Mountain. That moment changed forever how they saw Jesus. That moment on the train described by Steve, was for everyone their moment of Transfiguration, from seeing a family as a nuisance and an irritation, to taking them to their hearts in caring and concern.

Life constantly throws us into situations, where it can be very easy or tempting to jump into judgement. As we go forward in life, it might be helpful to bring that picture from the train with us.

As we make judgements in life, we too need to be sure we have the full story. We need to be very sure we see the full picture. Even one little missing detail can change everything. The missing bit, the bit that we are not privy to, is so often the bit that makes all the difference. And if we had that little missing bit maybe our attitude, our behaviour and our judgements might be very different. The Transfiguration is not just about what happened on a mountain, it is about what we all need to ensure is happening in our hearts

3rd Sunday of Lent - Trocaire

Half of all the food produced in the world ends up in the waste bin.

Some years ago, someone, who I think was working for Trocaire, came up with a striking image to drive home their message. The image was of ten people in a room. These ten people represent the entire human family on earth. There is a large table in the middle of the room, with an abundance of food piled on it, that represents all the food in the world today

The ten people in the room are about to have dinner. This is how the scene unfolded. The three healthiest people first approach the table. They fill up their plates with the finest food on the table, meat, fish, fowl, vegetables, milk and eggs. They take a lot more than they can eat. So, when they're finished eating, they have a lot left over. What happens that? Oh, they dump it in the garbage bin

Now the next two of the ten, step over to the table. As they share out the food for themselves, they take just enough to meet their needs. The eat their share, are happy and leave the table. There are five others, who have still to get their food. The next three of them come to the table. There's still a lot of food there; plenty bread and rice. So, they fill themselves up with bread and rice. It's not very attractive, but it has one thing going for it, it staves off the hunger.

So that's 'eight' of the Ten in the Room taken care of. There are still two left, who never got to the table at all, but all the food is now gone. So, the two at the end of the pecking order get nothing. So, what happens to these two who get nothing? They die from disease. The food needed to keep them alive was taken by the 1st group. No, they did not need it, they did not eat it. What might have kept these last two alive, was dumped

Half of all the food produced in the world, billions of tons end up in the waste. Almost half of the food that is bought in richer countries is 'thrown away' by those who bought it. They tell us that the amount of food wasted in our world would feed all those hungry in the world today.

By God's grace we were born into a place and time where we do not have first-hand experience of famine in our time. But sharing that human table with us at the moment are people in Southern Sudan, in Gaza and in so many countries, facing horrendous famine. To the victims it matters not, whether the famine is due to natural calamities, warring factions or plain greed. The are equally helpless in face of all three.

But we are blessed that, certainly by comparison. We live in a land of plenty and can make a difference. We remember that picture of the ten people in the room. Which group do we want to belong to? And regarding those billions of tons of food that go into waste every year, am I a contributor? Before I put it in the trolley can I ask myself, will this be eaten or be thrown away?

4th Sunday of Lent

Jesus opened the heart of the blind man, not just his eyes

Can you imagine what it would be like to be blind? Close your eyes. Now think about all the things you have already done today. You got out of bed. You put on your clothes and shoes. You washed your teeth, had your breakfast. What would it be like if you had to do all those, eyes closed? Would it be a lot harder to do them if you could not, see?

In today's Gospel story, Jesus meets a man who was born blind. So, it was like that for him the whole time. Everything he did, he had to do in the dark. What did Jesus do for the blind Man? He cured Him. How did He do it?. - with clay. Did the blind man have to do something? And when He did, what happened?

Did the blind man know who cured him? He knew, the man called Jesus, put clay on my eyes, and I washed, and now I can see." So, he knew it was Jesus who cured Him. But he also knew that Jesus was 'no ordinary man'. Unless this man was sent by God, He could not have done such a marvellous thing.' So, Jesus did two things at the same time. He opened the man's eyes and let him see all the wonderful things around him. But he also opened his heart and let him see in his heart that Jesus was the Son of God. But Jesus opens our eyes every day to see. Here he opens our heart to recognise Him as our friend

5th Sunday of Lent

About dying we have no choice, but about our final destination, we do.

To go inside the gospel story of today, we need to go inside a house in Bethany. It might not be an exaggeration to say that it was His second home for Jesus, where He switched off, where Martha made the tea; where He was at home when He dropped in. A little haven away from the pressures of the demanding crowds. It was in today's terms where He could unwind. Where he could take time out with his closest friends. The gospel says it well. Jesus loved Martha, Mary and Lazarus.

But there was panic in Bethany. Martha and Mary had sent an urgent message to Jesus. The man you love is ill. You would have expected that Jesus would have downed tools, that He would have headed straight for Bethany. I mean he was only a couple of miles away. In our terms He was only up the road. Instead of dropping everything and heading straight for Bethany, the gospel says: Jesus stayed where He was two more days. When He turns up Martha confronts Him. If you had been here my brother would not have died. Mary threw herself on the ground in front of Him and repeated the accusation, if you had been here, my brother would not have died.

Well, how would you feel if there was a tragedy in your family. You sent an emergency call for the doctor, who happened to be your family's special friend also. He was just two miles away. He turns up on your doorstep days after the funeral is over. We can see that they were annoyed He had not come. But was His non-coming an accident or was it deliberate? Was it to convey a message?

Physical death is the tragic end and breakdown of life. It brings with it great sadness. That sadness is all over the gospel story today. The panic that preceded it, the heartbreak and tears that accompanied it, the regrets that followed it. 'If you had been here...,the sympathisers that tried to soften it, the tomb that tried to contain it. But their best friend seemed to have ignored it. Death stops the clock for a family. Everything, however important, is put on hold. When it hits our family, we find it very hard to see beyond it; It takes a shock like the one Mary and Martha got, to jolt us into seeing beyond it to its meaning

About dying we have no choice, but about what comes afterwards we do.

Each day by the choices we make, we are becoming a particular kind of person, more loving or less loving, more generous or less generous. One day the 'becoming' will stop, the day the biological clock stops. We will then be as we enter eternity the kind of person we have become, the kind of person we have made ourselves to be, by the choices we are making today.

In the choice we make, each day, we are saying yes or no to God

Most of the time, we are trying our best to say yes. Death becomes the moment all our life's choices are drawn together into one. That one, becoming our Final Choice, our final irreversible yes or no to God. We will then be. in eternity, the person we have become, by the choices we have made in our lives. There are many choices we each make, that we, afterwards, have regrets about, choices that would make us into the kind person we certainly don't want to be for all eternity

God knew we would get it wrong sometimes. He knew we would be sorry when we do and wish we could undo the damage. He gave us a Special Sacrament to enable us to do just that, or more correctly to allow Him to do it for us. Holy Week is a time to review the choices we have been making, the kind of person we are becoming, to face the question, is this the kind of person I want for all eternity to be. Holy Week has always been a time to start that road again. The Sacrament of Reconciliation is an excellent way to start. The Sacrament of Reconciliation points us in a new direction

We invite you all to come this week. Easter is about Resurrection, Joy and new Life, celebrating it by sharing in it. It is about leaving the past behind and setting out on a new road. 'If you had been here Martha said to Jesus, my brother would not have died'. You weren't here. He died. Can we see that as the story of all our lives. If Jesus is not in them, something very important in them has died

But there is another side to the story too, however disappointed with myself I may have been, however let down by my behaviour I may have felt, however regretful I am about that incident that happened, however stupid the mistakes I have made, if I invite the Lord and welcome Him back into my life, it can be transformed, and I get a new start again

To the believer, death is the beginning of what I will be for eternity. Death is God paying me the compliment of accepting and respecting the choices I have made in life. Think of an artist on the hill of Barna looking out over the Golden Vale meticulously transferring it all to canvass. With each stroke of the artist's brush, the picture is becoming what it one day 'will be'. Then at last there comes the 'final' stroke. The artist lays down her brush. The picture will forever be what it has now become. That is the story of you and me. The choices we make, each day, are the strokes of the artist's brush, shaping me into the kind of person I am becoming. The final portrait will forever hang on Eternity's wall

Unlike the artist, once it is hanged on the wall, I do not have the choice to take it down again and do it differently the next time. Today, the brush is still in my hands.

2nd Sunday of Easter

It was by His wounds that they recognised Him.

They had seen Him feed the thousands. They had seen Him raise Lazarus from the dead. They had been astounded the night of the storm when even the wind and sea obeyed Him. But when, on that hillside outside Jerusalem, they saw Him hanged between two criminals, the 1,000s that had followed Him, quickly scattered. All that was left of them now was a little remnant, huddled together in fear in an Upper Room

Many of you joining us today, can remember the days of the 1,000s and the days of the packed churches. Many remember when at Christmas or Easter, you would have to be there a half hour early to be sure you could even get a seat in the church. In the days when everyone went to mass, an empty seat or two in the church, would have been a rarity. Well, if the disciples, who had seen the cripples stand and the lame walk, who had even witnessed Jesus raise people from the dead, if they lost heart when it all went wrong, it's hardly surprising that we would lose heart a bit, when things seemed to go so wrong in our lifetime

In that little Upper Room in Jerusalem were gathered those who had left everything and followed Him, those who had invested everything in His message. When the disaster of Calvary struck, their whole world collapsed around them. Their Hero been discredited and been crucified. They knew the soldiers who had come to the garden for Him, would shortly come for them. Those who had not already run away, had locked themselves behind closed doors, in a little upper room waiting for the worst

In our own times too, we have seen Him battered and betrayed, discredited and let down terribly. And it is not a big surprise that many have walked away. Maybe that is why today's gospel is really worth taking a closer look at. When the Risen Jesus appeared in the Upper Room, how did He identify Himself to His disciples?. 'He showed them His hands and His side'. It was by His wounds that they recognised Him. What is more, it was by His wounds, He wanted to be recognised. And when

He appeared to them sometime later, what was it that convinced the doubting Thomas, not His glory, but His wounds! "Thomas: Put your finger here, look here are my hands. Give me your hand, put it into my side. Doubt no longer but believe "

And on the darkest hour on Calvary, how did the good thief recognise Him? Was it not by His battered body on the Cross? And what was his reward for that? This day you will be with me in Paradise and let us not forget that it was after they had recognised Him in 'His wounded-ness', that Jesus gave His Apostles the power to heal the wounded-ness in the rest of us. "Whose sins you shall forgive, they are forgiven", He told them

Like the Apostles, we have been part of the thousands who were with Him. We were once part of the huge crowds, who had to be in the church early to even get a seat! But we have been with Him through His Good Fridays too, and for His Passion, in our own times. We have been with Him in His 'Good Times'. We've been with Him through some of His bad ones too

And you, who gather around the altar in this church today, are the ones who have not walked away, despite all you have been through, despite everything that has happened in your time. Despite everything, you have remained faithful. Because like the Good thief on his Cross on Calvary, you have been able to see beyond His Battered Body and recognise Jesus by His Wounds in our time. I'm sure there have been times for you, when your faith has been shaken. I'm sure you have felt your faith challenged. But to you today, as to His disciples in that Upper Room that night, the words of Jesus are addressed Receive the Holy Spirit: As the Father sent me, I am now sending you. Blessed are you, who despite all you have been through, still believe. To you are addressed the Words and Promise of the Risen Jesus. Receive the Holy Spirit I will be with you all days even to the end of time. Welcome to the Upper Room!

3rd Sunday of Easter

We recognise Jesus in the Eucharist. May He help us to recognise Him in each other.

Two of the disciples of Jesus are walking along the road. A stranger joins them. He becomes engrossed in their story as they describe all that happened in

Jerusalem, about Jesus of Nazareth who had been put to death. They arrive at the place they were heading for. It is late, so the disciples invite this stranger to stay the night with them. He can continue his journey in the morning. And as they are at table this stranger takes bread, blesses it, breaks it and shares it with them. And their eyes are opened, and they recognise that this is 'Jesus', – Risen from the Dead

They had walked the roads of Galilee with him for three years. They had been with Him when He raised Lazarus from the dead. They had seen his Miracles of multiplying loaves and curing the sick. They had the life frightened out of them on Calvary, when their whole world collapsed around them. And now just a couple of days later, this same Jesus, whom they had lived with for three years, joins them on the road, walks for miles beside them, and they do not even recognise Him. Hard to get your head around it, is it not ?

And it was only when they sat around the table with Him and He broke bread with them, that the penny dropped. As the gospel says, their eyes were opened. They recognised this was Jesus who had been crucified and that He had risen. It seems unbelievable that they had not recognised Him earlier on the road. Well, is it really as unbelievable, as it seemed to us on first reading

Let us start where the story finishes. They are sitting around the table together in Emmaus. And instantly they recognise Jesus in the breaking of the bread, but at that stage, they had walked about six miles together. They had been chatting all along the road. They had been sharing stories with Him about all that had been going on in Jerusalem. But it had never even dawned on them who it was that was walking beside them all that time. We might think that is unbelievable, that that could never happen to us. But hang on, a minute. Can we ourselves fall into the same trap as they did? All of us here recognise Jesus too in the Eucharist. All of us here recognise Jesus in the Tabernacle. But, like them, do we recognise Him in the flesh walking beside us, in the person we met on the road yesterday, in the person behind the checkout counter, in the neighbour who needs a visit, in someone who could have done with our help in the past week, but we were busy ourselves at the time

Shortly now, Jesus will take bread on this Altar. He will break it and share it with all of us, as He did with the Disciples that evening in Emmaus. Like them, we will instantly recognise Him present here on the Altar. We will instantly recognise Him in the Eucharist. We will instantly recognise Him in Holy Communion, but do we find it very challenging to recognise Him, when He walks beside us in the people we meet every day. Of course, Jesus wants us to recognise Him in the Eucharist, but does He not also want us to recognise and meet Him in each other. "As often as you do it to one of these the least of my brothers – you do it to Me."

Sometimes, or should I say most times, it can be a lot easier to recognise and love Jesus in the Eucharist and in the Tabernacle, but it is a far greater challenge for us to recognise and to love Jesus in each other, in the stranger who joins us along the road, in the refugee who wants a roof over his or her head, indeed His presence in every person we meet

Today we are those disciples walking on that road, the stranger we meet is the same person that they met. The disciples wondered how they could have been so blind not to recognise Jesus, when he walked beside them on that 1st Easter Sunday. Would it not be a great pity if we, His disciples today, were making the very same mistake today?

4th Sunday of Easter

If the church were only for saints, none of us would be here

There is a lovely story told about Pope Pius X. On the day he was being ordained a Bishop, as the people, queued up to receive his blessing, he spotted a familiar face kneeling at the altar rails. As he blessed her, she reached to kiss his ring. He stooped low and whispered in her ear. Mom, he said, but for that wedding ring on your finger, this Bishop's ring could never have been on mine. His single sentence said it all. You cannot speak about vocations without speaking about homes

The first seminary any young man goes to is his own home. His first Spiritual Directors are his own parents. They are also the best he will ever have. They teach and inspire by their example. Example is not just the best teacher. It is the only one that works. Without good

Christian homes, it is very hard to see where vocations will come from in the future. It is in the atmosphere of a Christian home, where Christian values are learned from being lived, that son or daughter can hear the gentle whispering Call of the Lord 'Come Follow Me'

God calls whom He wills. We do not know why God calls some and does not call others. Maybe we do not always agree with His choice. Sometimes to our eyes it is a total mystery. God works in strange ways. He does not choose the most suitable, to human eyes. He does not choose the most gifted or the most brilliant. Simply, He chooses whom He wills. God uses human instruments to achieve His goal. That is all we are just instruments, awkward and imperfect ones, fragile human instruments in the mighty hand of God. His Church is home to sinners and saints alike. Just as well, because if the church were only for saints, none of us might qualify for membership.

In praying for vocations today, we pray not for perfect instruments. Jesus did not find them, Himself. We are unlikely to. Jesus himself chose twelve. One of them betrayed Him. Another denied He ever knew the

Man. Most of His disciples disappeared like scalded cats, when they saw Him hanging on a Cross. The mystery of God's choice has always baffled people. Who would, on that First Good Friday evening, with their founder hanging disgraced on a cross, and His followers scattered and dispirited, who would have given this crazy sect any chance of survival. Yet 2,000 years later, over a billion people across the world commit themselves to following His Way of Living

5th Sunday of Easter

"Look, follow me", he said "and I will lead you there"

Most people go to Lourdes by air. About forty years ago myself and a couple of colleagues, decided that it would be an adventure to do it by car instead. We took the Ferry from Rosslare to Le Havre, heading for the Irish College in Paris, where we had arranged a bed for the first night, before taking on the five hundred plus miles to the South. Driving on French roads was intimidating. The sheer volume of traffic, the speed at which it moved, the challenge of driving on the other side of the road. Within a few hours we were on the verge of Paris. The 'Boulevard De Periferique', the great ring road around Paris, beckoned. For what was ahead nothing could have prepared us

From all sides streams of traffic converged on us, like rivers in swell rushing headlong to the sea. Into that current we disappeared. In that swell we were swallowed up. What began as a mission to find the Irish College, quickly became a mission to survive, and not finish up squashed under a giant tourist coach or an articulated truck. Engulfed in a sea of vehicles, we were swept along, with little control of our destiny, just waiting to see where the swell would deposit us. Finally, as it had swept us in, it dumped us out, like flotsam or jetsam deposited on the shore by crashing waves. We made it to the safety of some back street, where we could pull in, park the car, and draw a breath

Relieved to be alive, totally lost, without an earthly clue where we were, incapable of even 'attempting' to find our destination. It was there on that side street we met an angel, a two legged one! He understood English, which was a great help. He took a good look at us. He saw the desperation on our faces and took pity on us.

Look, follow me, he said, and I will bring you there. We latched on to that car, we stuck to him like glue. Wherever he turned we followed, with no idea where we were going, but totalling trusting our guide. True to his word, he landed us at the door of the Irish College, flashed his indicator, beeped his horn at us, and he was gone.

At some time or other, most of us have had the experience of feeling totally lost and helpless. What a relief, when we turn to someone for help and they say, "look, follow me, I am going that way. I will drop you there"

The biggest journey we all make on this earth, is the journey of life. The most important destination we all want to reach is our final home, the one Jesus has told us He has prepared for each of us. Thomas the Apostle, in today's gospel asked Jesus for directions to get Him there. Jesus said to him, "I am the way, and the truth, and the life. No one comes to the Father except through me". In Jesus we have a Saviour who is waiting for us when we have lost our way, who picks us up when we're left stranded on a side street. Like that Angel we met on a

Paris side street that evening, He takes a good look at us, reads the message on our faces and says to us, Look, just follow me and will bring you there, because no one can come to the Father except through me. If we cling to Him, and if we totally focus on, and follow His directions, not always knowing where we are going, but totalling trusting in our guide. If we do that on the most important journey of all, life's journey, He guarantees us that He will drop us at the door of our Final Home

6th Sunday of Easter

Move over and let God's Spirit do what He wants to do!

When I was in national school, which was not today or yesterday, one of the questions I remember from the old Catechism was, what is Prayer. Not only do I remember the question, but I remember the answer

Prayer is, a raising up of the mind and heart to God, to adore and praise Him, to thank Him for His favours, to beg His grace and blessings and to obtain pardon for our sins. The first line of that answer told us that Prayer was a raising of the mind and heart to God. And if you wanted to pray that is where you started, by raising of the mind and heart to God. So, it follows logically that, it is good prayer if we do it well, or it is bad prayer if we do it badly

In our gospel today Jesus presents another and different way of looking at prayer. "I will not leave you orphans." He says I will ask the Father and He will send you an 'Advocate'. An Advocate is someone who represents us. Someone who pleads our case. Someone who speaks on our behalf. Jesus tells us that the Advocate that He has chosen for each of us, is already with us now, and will be with us forever. And that advocate who is within each of us, is constantly representing each of us before God. He is constantly speaking up on our behalf to His father, His Holy Spirit which He has given each of us. He has told us that when we want to pray but cannot find the right words ourselves, not to worry, because God's Spirit within us already knows what we want to say, and our prayers expressed by Holy Spirit on our behalf are in accordance with the mind of God

So, we can see prayer, not just as our raising our mind and heart to God, but as our giving God's Spirit within us, the freedom to speak on our behalf to God

So, if I really want God's Spirit who is deep within me, to represent me and speak to God on my behalf, what I need to do is to create the space for Him to work in, by removing the obstacles by getting rid of the distractions. For prayer to happen, obstacles must be put on the shelf for the moment

In our busy pressurised world today, this form of prayer comes highly recommended. Finding a quiet place where there are no distractions. Taking just a minute or so at the beginning to place myself in God's presence. Let me correct that, we are always in God's presence. This minute or so is, just to become steeped in awareness of it. Actively aware of His presence within us, to do two very simple things. First, tell Him that this period of time is going to be totally His, my gift to him and I am not going to take any of it back or allow it to be wasted or robbed from Him, by distractions. Then tell him, that what will happen in this prayer time will not be what I do but what His Holy Spirit, deep within me will do in me and through me. So, the real challenge in prayer is to get out of the Holy Spirit's way and take the distractions with me. Just, steeped in the presence of God who is all around us, allow God's Spirit who is at the very core of each of our being, to do what He is there for, to represent us and speak on our behalf to the Father. No words we could use, no thoughts we could have, could be as powerful as the prayer of God's Spirit rising from within us, to the Father

The Advocate, the Holy Spirit, whom Jesus promised in the gospel, is praying on our behalf, representing us before the Father, expressing our needs, cares, worries, in a language and with a power we could never hope to match. What is asked of me in this form of prayer is, move over and let God's Spirit do what He wants to do in us. All I am asked to do is be there. Put aside the time. Unclutter the cluttered mind for fifteen minutes. Put away the thoughts, worries and cares. Just be in God's Presence. Just allow God's Spirit within do the job Jesus gave him to do, to be our Advocate with the Father. In doing this, in praying in this way, we will be holding

Jesus to His Promise. No one who holds Jesus to His promises Is ever disappointed.

Ascension of the Lord

When we have done all we can, the Lord does the rest.

The eleven disciples set out for Galilee to the mountain where Jesus had arranged to meet them. Who were these eleven? They were the closest friends Jesus had, the ones who had been with Him from the beginning. What had they seen? They had seen Him walk on water. They had seen the wind and sea obey Him. They had seen sickness disappear before His touch. They had seen the wake of the Centurion's daughter, transformed into the party for her return to life. They had seen a funeral cortege stopped in its tracks at the village of Naim and the widow's son step off the bier and return home with his ecstatic mother. They had made the journey to Bethany, days after they had heard of the death of Lazarus and had watched Him walk out alive from His tomb. They had watched helplessly as Jesus was betrayed and crucified as a criminal outside the city. They had seen the empty tomb on Easter morning. Some of them had walked the road to Emmaus with Him, the very day of His Resurrection. They recognised Him later in the breaking of bread.

The first reading tells us that for forty days after the Resurrection He had continued to appear to them and tell them about the Kingdom of God.

But that forty day of Easter is now over, Matthew today turns the camera on their final meeting. He says, the eleven set out for Galilee to the mountain where Jesus had arranged to meet them. This was to be their final meeting on this earth, the most important meeting they ever had. To leave them in no doubt about its importance. To leave them in no doubt about the gravity of the message. To make it clear He was speaking to them, not only for himself but also for His father, Jesus prefaced His remarks with a remarkable statement; All authority in heaven and on earth, He said, is given to me and then he then handed out to the eleven their job description

'Go therefore, make disciples of all nations, baptise them in the name of the father and of the Son and of the

Holy Spirit and teach them to observe all the commands that I gave you'

Those eleven were the foundation of the church that was to continue the mission of Jesus for the next two thousand years at least. This was their job description. In giving their job description to the Eleven, who were the foundation of His church, Jesús was giving its job description to His church. In giving its job description to the church, Jesus was giving our job description to each of us, who are His church today. It is not just the job description for bishops or priests, because it is not ordination that makes us members of Christ's church. It is our Baptism. So, this is the job description for all the baptised, for all of us

So now let us look at it again and more closely. Jesus, this morning, is saying to each of us, Go make disciples, then baptise them, then teach them. But what is hugely significant in the job description Jesus gives to each of us is, that the first thing He asks us to do is to go and make disciples. We make disciples by attracting people to follow us. We attract people to follow us by our example. Followers are drawn not driven. Followers are attracted not compelled. So, the first thing Jesus asks of each of us is that we live in such a way that people will be attracted by our values, by our honesty, by our integrity, by our transparency, by our truthfulness, by our caring for the less well off, by our support of those in need and by our refusal to judge and to condemn. People will be attracted by our values, rather than by our words. It is a big challenge for all of us. The future of the church in this parish does not depend on the sermons preached. It does not depend on the quality of our buildings or the size of our offertory collection. It does not even ultimately depend on the permanent presence of a priest. The future of the church in this parish depends on how each of us live the values we profess. None of us can do it alone. We need the support of each other. That is why each of our presence is important here. It is a formidable challenge in today's world, to live by the gospel values and to pass them on. But we are not asked do it on our own. The last sentence of our gospel is 'Know that I am with you always, to the end of time'

During the week I was reading a commentary written by a Benedictine monk on today's gospel. He suggested that we take a single sentence from that gospel today; 'I will be with you always to the end of time', that we learn it off, that we repeat it to ourselves many times each day. When we find the challenge to live those Christian values tough, that we remember that promise, that we repeat that sentence; I will be with you always, yes to the end of time

We will sometimes feel discouraged. We will sometimes feel it is all falling apart around us. That is the time to realise it is God's church not ours and, in the confusion, and our darkness His promise holds true; 'I am with you always, yes to the end of time'

We do our very best to live our values. We do our level best to lead by example. We try to be truthful and transparent. He will do the rest.

There are many things the Lord will never do to you. One of them certainly is to break His Promise. 'I am with you always, yes to the end of time'. When the evidence seems absent, remember we see the externals, but the Lord sees the heart. When we've done all we can, the time comes to leave the rest to Him

Pentecost Sunday

As God chose to depend on them then, He has chosen to depend on us now

Today we celebrate the Feast of Pentecost. Jesus promised He would not leave us alone, that He would send us the Holy Spirit. Pentecost marks the fulfilment of that promise. You all know the story of the First Pentecost. The disciples huddled in the upper room. They were confused and frightened. They had seen what happened to Jesus. They feared the same awaited them

Then, there came what sounded like a powerful wind. Something appeared like tongues of fire, that separated and came to rest on each one of them. They were filled with the Holy Spirit. In that instant, they were utterly transformed. Peter, who had been so scared, He had denied that he ever even knew Jesus, was now openly preaching about Him in the streets, with total disregard for what might happen to him. Other disciples fanned out across the Land, preaching the message of Jesus. Many of them not only died as martyrs but saw it as a privilege to have the opportunity. The Holy Spirit that descended on the disciples on that First Pentecost, is the same Holy Spirit you and I received in Baptism and Confirmation

That Holy Spirit is in each of our hearts today. Otherwise, none of us would be here because Scripture tells us, No one can say 'Jesus is Lord', unless God's spirit is within them. That Spirit of God within us; The Holy Spirit is the spirit of wisdom, the light that guides us, that keeps us on the right road, even as those around us choose another way. God's spirit helps us to choose the good and the right in preference to the attractive and the wrong

That group in the Upper Room on that First Pentecost were chosen, not for what they could do for God, individually or collectively, they were chosen for what God could do through them. As God chose to depend on them then, the same God chooses to depend on us now. Today on the Feast of Pentecost we are called to say Yes to God's Spirit in our hearts in faith, Yes to God's spirit in our lives, Yes to God's spirit in our world by our values, Yes to God's spirit in our community by our gifts

If God's spirit is to shine in today's world, it can only do so, from our hearts. If God's spirit is to change today's world, it must do so through our lives

It will be done, by very ordinary people like you and me, trying our best, to live the values of the gospel in our hearts, transmit the values of the gospel in our homes, and reflect the values of the Gospel in our lives and by sharing our God-given gifts in our community. Never ever, whatever happens, underestimate the power of your example or the witness of your lives; both of which are the fruits of Gods Spirit at work in your hearts

The Most Holy Trinity

"What we know is the drop. What we do not know is the ocean."

They tell me that there was a time, when the bishop on Confirmation Day, before confirming each child, would ask them a question from the Catechism. The question he asked one little girl was; What is the Holy Trinity? She answered in a very soft voice; the Holy Trinity is three persons in one God. The bishop was a bit hard of hearing, leaning forward, he said; 'I didn't understand what you said'. To which the little girl in beautiful innocence answered, 'you are not supposed to understand it, it is a mystery!'

A mystery the Trinity may be, but it is a mystery that is much more part of our lives than we realise. Leaving home, we dip our fingers in the Holy Water Font, and we bless ourselves, In the Name of the Father, of the Son of the Holy Spirit. Every time we go into a Church, we bless ourselves, In the name of the Father, Son and Holy Spirit. As the priest begins mass each time, he begins; In the name of the Father, Son and Holy Spirit. As we finish our mass today, I will pray May Almighty God bless you, In the name of the Father, Son and Holy Spirit. When we arrived into the world, at Baptism the priest said; I baptize you in the name of the Father and of the Son and of the Holy Spirit. When we kneel in Confession, the priest says; I absolve you from your sins, in the name of the Father and of the Son and of the Holy Spirit. When the time comes for my final exit from here, I hope a priest will bend over me and say; Through the power the Apostolic See has given me, I grant you a

Plenary Indulgence and full remission of all your sins; In the Name of the Father and the Son and the Holy Spirit. As I said at the beginning, the Trinity Is much more part of our lives, than we realize.

That little girl at Confirmation said that Trinity is a Mystery that we are not meant to understand. But we live every day with many things we do not understand. I cannot get my head around the mystery of how the swallows who built their nest in our old cowhouses at home, migrate down through France and Spain into Morocco, before crossing the Sahara Desert and the Congo rainforest, finally reaching South Africa and Namibia. And having found their way to the other side of the world, return the next year to the same nest, in the same rafter, in the same cowhouse in our backyard at home

Or how the newborn Salmon, who first saw life in Loughfouder, find their way back through the Atlantic Ocean years later, swing in the mouth of the Cashen, navigate up the Feale, take a sharp right when they reach Glaishe Cheann Comhair (a tiny little river) and head back six to eight miles upstream to where they were born, to spawn, having clocked up thousands of miles, but returning with 'pin point' accuracy to the place of their birth

Those who reject religion or faith on the basis that in this age of technology and science there is no place for mystery, might revisit the words of Isaac Newton in the 18th Century; "What we know is the drop". "What we do not know is the ocean." As we celebrate the Feast of the Holy Trinity today, the challenge is not to understand the doctrine, but to live consciously in the presence of, the father who made us, The Son who redeemed us and The Holy Spirit who protects and guides us. We experience God in the Mysteries of Nature and in the mysteries of Creation all around us every day, but He wants to be experienced too in the mystery of His Presence within us; Father who created us, Son who redeemed us, Holy Spirit who guides us.

As St. Augustine told us, we will never understand the Trinity. As that little girl told the bishop at her Confirmation, you are not expected to, it is a Mystery. But if we really do believe Trinity is within us, we will certainly find time to spend being together. That time we devote to being consciously together is what in our Christian Tradition we call prayer. So, if I can leave you with a thought for the day. We worship God best when we offer to Him what He most wants. Such is the generosity of God, that what He most wants is not that we do something great for Him, but that we give Him the space to do great things for us. Prayer is creating and giving Him space, during which He can deliver His gifts to us. Prayer is not about understanding the mystery of the Trinity but about the space we make in each day to live 'consciously' in its presence

11th Sunday; Corpus Christi

"When we face the sun, we get a tan... but when we stand before Jesus in the Eucharist we become saints." "The Millennial Saint", Blessed Carlo Acutis

As we celebrate the Feast of Corpus Christi this weekend, I would like to introduce you to a little boy, whose Faith in, and love for, the Eucharist, has made an amazing impact on people across the world. Carlo Acutis was born in London of Italian parents in May 1991. Shortly after his birth his family relocated to Italy, where they settled in Milan

As a child Carlo developed a remarkable devotion to, and love of, the Eucharist, which became the centre point of his life. Here is a lovely quote from the very young Carlo -"If we stand in front of the sun, we get a tan, but if we spend time before the Blessed Sacrament, we become saints".

Still a child Carlo was known to his friends and community, as a computer genius. As a young teenager Carlo married his extraordinary love of the Eucharist and his talents at computer programming, creating a special website documenting almost two hundred true stories of Eucharistic Miracles, across the world. That website is available today in seventeen different languages on the internet. In his early teens Carlo was diagnosed with advanced Leukaemia. He died in 2006 at the tender age of fifteen. A short number of years after being laid to rest, dressed in his jeans and tennis shoes, fifteen-year-old Carlo was beatified. His body lies in a church in Assisi, which I was privileged to visit

Among the Miracles of the Eucharist, which Carlo has documented is the Miracle of the Eucharist at Lanciano, a town southwest of Assisi. It is an appropriate story to share as we celebrate the Feast of Corpus Christi, the great Feast of the Eucharist this weekend. A priest, who was plagued with doubts about the Eucharist, was celebrating mass one day and as He spoke the Words of Consecration, the host in his hand miraculously changed into human flesh and the wine in the Chalice miraculously changed into the precious Blood. Word of the 'Extraordinary Miracle' spread rapidly and investigation was immediately set up. Extensive scientific investigations have taken place through the centuries. The results have continued to verify the Amazing Miracle. The Flesh was found to be human flesh, with the structure of the heart wall. The Blood was also of human origin with the type 'AB'.

Proteins in the clotted Blood were found in the make-up of normal, 'fresh' human blood. In 1973 the Chief Advisory Board of the World Health Organization set up a Special Commission of Investigation. After fifteen months and 500 different tests, it declared that science, [aware of its limitations], had come to a halt, face to face with the impossibility of giving an explanation. In the words of the Parish Priest of Lourdes during the apparitions there; "For those who believe no explanation is necessary. For those who do not believe no explanation is possible". To this day the Sacred Host is in the Franciscan Church in Luciano. I was privileged to visit and pray there some years ago

But amazing and extraordinary as the verified Miracle of Lanciano is, we do not base our Faith in the Eucharist on this Miracle or on any of the 100s of other documented Eucharistic Miracles. We base our Faith in the Eucharist on the Words of Jesus; Take and Eat this is My Body. Take and Drink this is My Blood. My Flesh is real food and my Blood real drink. He who eats my Flesh and drinks my Blood has life eternal and I will raise him up on the last day.

If we want to witness the Miracle of Lanciano, we don't have to get a plane ticket or a train ticket. The Miracle of Lanciano takes place on the altar here each time the priest says the Words of Consecration. The Miracle of Lanciano is here in your church every day, as your church is open to visit Jesus in the Blessed Sacrament. Jesus is present in the Tabernacle here in your own church as truly as it is in that Monstrance in Lanciano today. Each time we come to Mass; we witness that miracle. On this the Feast of Corpus Christi, the Body and Blood of Christ, may we too take a page from the life of Carlo Acutis and may the Mass and the Eucharist be the centre of our lives too

12th Sunday in Ordinary Time

Even though Hell may be, it holds no fear for those who follow Jesus

We live in an age when opinion polls, surveys and statistics are part of our daily diet. They measure people's attitudes and values and can even sometimes have a big influence in shaping them. While from time to time they take a battering in their predictions, overall, it's probably broadly true to say that when scientifically carried out and operating within their areas of competence, they can sometimes produce amazingly accurate results. But of course, the opposite can also be true. When either of the above is missing, their results carry little weight

If a poll were done today as we left the church, on the kind of summer weather we would like to have, overwhelmingly we would probably go for the best summer ever. But however big the majority, it would have little influence on the summer we get

Some time back there was a survey on our attitudes to Hell. It found that 70% of Catholics today do not believe in Hell and the results were accurate, when properly understood. They reflected the true opinions of the people surveyed, but I'm afraid, if presented as a conclusion that Hell had been abolished, we might be in for a bit of a shock if we based our life on it. If all the people of the parish were surveyed on whether your house was ever likely to go on fire or not, and the result was overwhelmingly that it was not, I do not think too many would act on it and cancel their fire insurance

We may or may not like the fact that there is a Hell. Indeed, we may have little understanding of what it is. We may prefer to think it is not there or should not be. We may even get annoyed at those who dare to mention it. But the issue is not whether we like the idea or not. The issue is not whether it should be there or not. The issue is not the size of the majority who believe. The only issue is whether there actually is a Hell. That is independent of our views about it, independent even of what the majority believe or do not believe.

May I quote you a sentence from our gospel today? . "Do not be afraid of those who kill the body but cannot kill the soul, fear him rather who can destroy both body and soul in Hell". Those are the words of Jesus Christ. We do have the choice; whether to believe His Words to us, or believe the Son of God is lying when He says this. I will leave you to come to your own conclusion on that

It has been said that one of the great gifts of Jesus is the gift of being able to say hard things but always speak them in love. He spoke the truth, not to frighten us, but to protect us. In that short gospel today, he doesn't shrink from identifying the reality of Hell and naming it as it is. But He twice tells us not to be afraid. And a third time in that short gospel reading, He reassures us: "There is no need to be afraid". Because even though Hell may be, it holds no fear for those who follow Jesus. Jesus says, "If anyone declares for me in the presence of men, I will declare myself for him in the presence of my Father in Heaven. But the one who disowns me in the presence of men, I will disown in the presence of my Father in Heaven".

When we live the way Jesus asks; we are declaring for him. When we don't live the way Jesus asks; we are disowning Him. The decision on where we spend eternity - is ours, not His. Far more important than polls or surveys is the life we live. Far more important for us to concentrate on that. To do otherwise would be to be like the foolish man who believes that if he convinces himself, that there is no such thing as the law of gravity, he can jump from the 40th storey and not get hurt.

13th Sunday in Ordinary Time

Do we see the price of what He is asking or the privilege of what He is offering?

Our Gospel today could be read in two ways. How difficult it is to be a follower of Jesus, or how blessed we are to be His followers! How we read it decides which of the two messages we get. The words of Jesus to the disciples and to us; "anyone who doesn't take up his cross and follow me is not worthy to be My disciple",

Love is a funny thing. It can transform what would have been a 'pain' to put up with, into an opportunity to show someone how much we really care about them. Love has the power to lift us beyond our limitations, to push us beyond what we thought possible, to cause us to do things we never thought we could

How could one understand the colossal act of faith, the total trust of a young couple coming up the aisle and committing their whole life to each other, for better, for worse, for richer, for poorer, in sickness or in health, except in terms of the power of love. How could one understand the un-parallel generosity of parents, their total unselfishness to their families, except in terms of the power of love?

Those two key human experiences can really help us to understand what Jesus is asking of us in that gospel and the commitment He invites us to make to Him. He is not asking for a yes in our heads to His truths, He is asking us for a yes in our hearts to His love, like the couple at the altar on their wedding day, like the parent with his/her child, who is in difficulty, no price is too big, no pain too great, when relationship is right, it can cope with all. We see this all around us in the couples we know. Difficulties do not divide them; they bring them closer together

We see this all around us in families. Sometimes it is only when someone gets into trouble, they discover the depth of their parents' love for them, how loved and accepted they are, warts and all. Just as the relationships around us between couples and the relationship around us in families, brings us the very heart of what 'love being lived' looks like, so the words of Jesus in the gospel today, bring us straight to the heart of the relationship He wants us to have with Him. When the relationship is right, as with a couple or family, the privilege of what they share is so great that beside it, the difficulties begin to appear so small.

When Jesus invites us to take up His cross, as in today's gospel, when our relationship with Him is right, we no longer see that as a burden, we see it as part and parcel of the relationship, of being close to the one we love, of being close to the one by whom we are loved. When my relationship with Jesus begins to challenge me, do I see these challenges as difficulties or as privileges?

When relationships are right, difficulties diminish. When the challenges begin to pinch me and bring pain, do I see it as a time to go "a la carte" with Jesus, picking and choosing the nice bits and dropping the others? What would you think of a couple who took that approach in their relationship; when challenges came, each just suited themselves and put themselves first. What would that tell you about their relationship? What would you think of a family who took that approach that, when their child got into difficulty, they withdrew their love. What would it say about our relationship with Jesus, if when it begins to challenge or make demands on us, we turn into fair weather friends of His; seeing only the price of what He is asking, not the privilege of what He is offering in our relationship. The choice we make in those situations, when the pressure come on, gives us an insight into the quality of the relationship we have, or want to have, with Him

14th Sunday in Ordinary Time

It is when I'm ready to fall limply into His arms, that He can save me and bring me ashore

In the car during the week, I was listening to the story of the dramatic rescue of a child from the sea. The helpless mother of a child, swept out to sea by a treacherous rib-tide, had been screaming for help on the beach. A mother of two young children put her own life at risk and almost lost it by diving in and heading out to sea to save the little child. The conversation on the radio was between the mother of the child who had been rescued and the mother who had risked her own life to save her. Even the presenter, himself no stranger to dramatic stories, called it the most moving description of bravery, he had heard

Thank God that the little girl was rescued. Thank God there are people like woman who rescued her. But it reminded me of a similar story I had heard. It was of a young couple on their day at the beach. He got into trouble, and she realised he was not going to make it. On the beach she began to scream for help. She spotted the lifeguard's station and made straight for it. She pleaded with the lifeguard to go and save him. The lifeguard located the man in the water. He could see he was in deep trouble. But for whatever reason he did not do anything. She got more and more angry as he was not taking action. She began to scream at the lifeguard. It was his job to save people, and he was doing nothing, and her screaming gathered a crowd around them. And then suddenly the lifeguard took off for the water. He ploughed through the waves and got to him. He grabbed him from behind and made it back to shore. In moments, he had him revived and he was fine. The girl was still very angry with the lifeguard. She wanted an explanation for his delay. Those minutes were an eternity, the man was drowning, and he was doing nothing to save him. Calmly the lifeguard took her aside and explained to her. I was not wasting time, he said. I had to time it perfectly; I had to wait for the critical moment, the moment the man was helpless and realised it. Then I was able to take over. Only then was I able to rescue him. If I had jumped into the water when you wanted me to, he said, neither of us might be here now. We could both have well been drowned

In life, there are times when we are all overwhelmed, when it seems beyond human powers to help us, when we become truly desperate. Maybe it is when the medical profession can do no more or when the cross has become unbearable, we realise there's only one with the power to rescue us. We turn in desperation to God, pleading with Him for help. We cannot understand why He does not instantly react. Why He does not do something and do it now and maybe we too can get angry, very angry with Him. The Lord is waiting, - waiting, for the critical moment, for the moment when I realise its beyond me. I'm beaten and it's all over. And that's the moment the Lord is waiting for, because its only when I'm ready to fall limply into His arms, and trust totally and absolutely in Him, that he can wrap His arms round me and bring me ashore. Psalm 34:18   The Lord is close to the broken-hearted; He rescues those whose spirits are crushed.

Today He tells us. "Come to me you who are overburdened, and I will rescue you". But like the little child being swept away by the rib tide, or the man fighting the might of the sea for his life, the Lord, just like the lifeguard is waiting for that moment, until we are ready to entrust ourselves entirely into His care. That's the moment He takes over. That's the moment He can save us

15th Sunday in Ordinary Time

"Father you should have seen the place when God had it to Himself."

There is story about a parish priest out walking one evening in his old parish. And as he walked along a winding little road, he noticed things had changed. A field which he remembered from his young days as wasteland, scrub, covered in briars and bushes, had been totally transformed. Smooth as a billiard table, it was now covered in a coat of lush green grass. Leaning on the gate to admire, he said to the farmer who was still working there: "Is it not marvellous the miracles that can be produced when God and man work together in partnership?" Perhaps feeling a little cheated that the credit for all his hard work was being shared with the Divine the farmer answered: "Father you should have seen the place when God had it to Himself." The man who had invested hours and perspiration tilling that field, who had broken and prepared the ground and had set the seed, knew the time and care it had taken. He didn't doubt that God could work miracles but without his human input it would have remained a barren desert

Speaking to us in today's gospel Jesus talks about the seed that lands on paths and roadways becomes food for the birds, the seed that falls on rock with little depth of soil that dies quickly, the seed that falls into the briars chokes and the seed received by fertile ground that bears fruit. The seed of course is God's word addressed to us. We are the ground on which the seed falls and that seed contains His dream, His vision and His plan for each of us. Come to me. Live my way. It is the best way for you. It is the way to peace, happiness and fulfilment while you are here on earth. It is the road that leads home with Me in Heaven.

That is the message being transmitted by Jesus to us. That is the seed being sown, but sometimes it falls on deaf ears and is disregarded, on hard pathways and becomes food for the birds. That is the seed that fails. It is the seed that falls on rock and could not take root. But when people of faith hear and recognise God's Word, they know how Jesus is asking us to live. Sometimes the pain can appear to be too much and the price too high

It is fine to talk about forgiving others, but when it is me that is hurt, the human reaction can sometimes be;

why should I let him get away with it ? It's fine to agree certain things are very wrong or sinful, but when it is my own son or daughter, why cannot I change the rules? It is fine to laud the importance of discipline and self-control for the children, but when Jesus asks for it in my own life, why can't I make an exception and change the rules? Jesus tells us about seed that grew for a little while, but when the heat was turned up, when the words of Jesus became really challenging, when the pain began to hurt, the seed sometimes withered away

And then there was the seed that landed in the thorns. The seeds took root alright. They seemed growing pretty well. There was nothing wrong with the ground. It was not the seed that was at fault, it was what was around it that was hostile, the weeds and the thistles. Today too we receive the word in a world where there are a lot of weeds and thistles that would choke that word before it could flourish. The weeds and thistles are the values of the world that conflict with the values put before us by Jesus in the gospel. Jesus says:

Put the other person first. The world says, Take care of yourself. Jesus says: Blessed are the gentle. The world says, the arrogant get the limelight. Jesus says: Place your trust in Me. The world says: material security is everything.

God's word speaks to us a few minutes each week. The world with its conflicting sets of values, shouts Him down a few hours each day. Jesus tells us today that His dream for us, His purpose in creating us is to be with Him forever. That dream will be choked in us if we allow the weeds and thistles to smother and quench it.

Finally, today, Jesus speaks of the seed that falls on the good ground. Each of us is a gardener. Each of us has our little plot. That little plot is your heart and mine. It is here that Jesus plants His seed. Come to me. Live my way, it is the best way. Peace in your heart on Earth. Oneness with your God in Heaven.'

But as the gospel today tells us, when hearts are closed and hardened, that seed can only bounce off them and be blown away. When we refuse to hear and listen because we perceive that His demand is too high or His challenge too great, then, as in the parable, the seed dies. It has dropped on rocky ground. When we are imprisoned in or enslaved to values, that are not those being presented by Jesus in His gospel, then His Word is choked and crushed, fallen among the briars.

If on the other hand our hearts are open, then the ground is fertile, we can receive the Words of Jesus, and the miracle of transformation can begin to take place in us. It's not enough to admire those who have been transformed by the power of Jesus in their lives. There are plenty of those we can think of. We are called, not just to admire, but to imitate. One day the Lord of the harvest will call in His harvest. Like the parish priest in the story, He'll stand at the gate and survey the field

Let us hope and pray the parallel will be continued and that, like that parish priest, Jesus too will look at us, at our little plot, and marvel at the miracle of transformation. But we know that miracle can only happen if we and God have worked together in partnership.

16th Sunday in Ordinary Time

I thank you Father for hiding these things from the learned and the clever and revealing them to your little ones

The story of Darky Jim was told on the radio across America many years ago. Jim was the workman in Mt. St. Mary's Seminary in Emmetsburg. Every day Jim used to spend an hour in the seminary chapel. As Jim was unable to read and had neither a book nor a beads, the seminarians were intrigued as to how he spent the time there. One evening one of them slipped into the seat beside him. Jim, he said, will you tell me, how do you spend your time in here? What do you do when you are here? What prayers do you say?. Here was his answer; I just goes into the chapel, and I says to Jesus, Lord here is old Darky Jim. Then I keeps quiet and I listens to the Lord. And after a while I says to Him again, Lord here's old Darky Jim, just dropped in to see you. That is all

During Jim's final illness a Marist priest got an urgent sick call. It was he who later related the final chapter of Darky Jim's story. "Let me tell you how he died, he said. Just after he had received the Last Sacraments and while

Our Lord was still with Him in Holy Communion, he lifted himself up in the bed and with his hands folded and a smile on his lips, he uttered feebly but distinctly these words; Lord, here's old Darky Jim, just dropping in to see you. Then he fell back in his bed and breathed his last. He had just dropped in for a visit that would never end". Who was it that said; as a person lives, so shall they die. Most of us would envy what Darky Jim had going for him with the Lord. But does it not find a very real resonance with the words of Jesus, I thank you Father for hiding these things from the learned and the clever and revealing them to your little ones

What was the secret of Darky Jim's closeness to God? Sitting with Jesus before the Tabernacle and listening to Him. 'Just sitting with' Him and listening 'to Him', putting into practice the words of Jesus. Be still and know that I am God, I am the Lord who healeth Thee. Darky Jim had no book. He had no beads. He knew no prayers. But he had what was important, a relationship that drew him into God's presence, a relationship that kept him there, when he was there. He did his part and God did the rest.

He did it for him. He will do it for you and me too, if we allow Him.

Today's Gospel presents the stark picture of final Judgement, the separation of the weeds and the darnel from the wheat, and the good or the bad consequences for us all, depending of course on how we have lived. But if we but take a leaf from the book of Darky Jim, we need have no doubt which side we will be on.

17th Sunday in Ordinary Time

Because she had not recognised the treasure that was hers, she lived in destitution

There's a story about an Irish mother who was living in very poor conditions. Dependant on her friends and Vincent de Paul for the very necessities of life But what her friends and neighbours couldn't understand was, how her son, who had done so well for himself in the States, could allow his poor mother to live in such conditions

The parish priest was visiting her one day and she was oozing with pride, telling him about her son Bob, telling him about how well Bob had done in the States, telling his about the two bars he now owned in New York City. Tell me do you ever hear from Bob the priest enquired. Oh, Bob is so good to me, she said that never a month goes by that I do not get a letter from him. Strange thing about Bob, she said, is he loves sending me pictures. With every letter he sends a picture. I collect all his pictures; I have them all here, somewhere! Then she produced this bulging envelope and turned the contents out on the kitchen table. The parish priest could not believe his eyes. On a quick count he figured there were at least fifty pictures, fifty pictures of Benjamin Franklin! You know where you would have found the picture of Benjamin Franklin? -on every $100 dollar note!. What she thought were pictures, were $100 dollar notes. On her mantelpiece was treasure beyond her wildest dreams. Because she had not recognised the treasure that was hers, she lived in destitution.

What is true in the material world is true in the Spiritual. All of us are 'millionaires'! Each of us has a Spiritual fortune beyond our dreams. Our faith, (God's gift to us), is a treasure beyond compare. Our sacraments are God's very presence with us. Our Christian

Community, God's home among us. But if we do not recognise and appreciate the riches that are ours in the gift of our faith, we can live in spiritual poverty, though surrounded with heavenly treasures.

One homilist had a lovely interpretation of the same message. God devised a special secret treasure. He gave it to the angels to deliver it to us. But He instructed them to hide it, so that we would have to search for it and would have the joy of finding it.

We will hide it in the highest mountains, the angels said. No, God said, because if you hide it on the highest mountain, only the healthiest and fittest could climb the mountain and the weak would have no chance of finding it. We'll hide it on the furthest shores of the ocean, the angels said. No, God said, because if you do, only the rich could travel that far, and the poor would have no chance to find it. Where will we hide it then, the angels asked. Well, it must be within reach of everybody, rich or poor, healthy or weak, God said, Plant it in the very centre of their being. Hide it in their hearts

The angels did as God instructed. They planted the hidden treasure deep within each of us. They planted it in our hearts as the Lord intended. So, we each have to go and search for it and experience the joy of finding it for ourselves. No one else can do it for us

How will we know when we have found that treasure? It will be instantly recognisable. What we will find will be the image of God imprinted on our hearts. When we discover that image deep within us, then we know who we really are, 'In the image of God he made us'. Then we will know that our value is not measured in silver or in gold, but in the image we carry that is imprinted on our hearts. The purpose of our journey on this earth is to discover that treasure, each of us for ourselves. to recognise it and to take ownership of it. Only when we have discovered that image for ourselves, can we reflect and mirror it to those around us. The image that we will reflect it, are the values by which we live

18th Sunday Ordinary time

The challenge is, to recognise ourselves within the story

The story in today's Gospel is very familiar to us all, so familiar that we need hardly read it. Sure, we all already know the story so well. Conscious of that, someone decided to write a different version. The new version of the same incident in today's gospel went like this

A week or so after Jesus had performed the miracle of feeding the five thousand with the five loaves and the two fish, a rumour went around the place that He was coming back again. It is estimated that the crowd had even doubled this time. The time He was expected to arrive came and went. There was no trace of Him. An hour passed, and a second hour. People were getting tired and restless waiting. Late evening came, the people were starved with the hunger as well.

Peter was there waiting with the crowd. They asked him if he could do a miracle and feed them. Peter was powerless, and he had to admit he could not. But he knew how tired and hungry they all were at this stage. He could not just send them home. The Apostles knew that many there had come prepared, They had brought their own food, just in case! So, Peter got a brilliant idea. He organized large containers and sent them around. He invited everyone who had brought food with them to drop it into the containers as they reached them. Then he would take all the food and divide it out. Everyone would at least get something. Some would lose out a bit, wouldn't have as much as they brought, but everyone, would get enough to bring them home. The response was pitifully poor. Only a small percentage parted with their satchels. Meanwhile, most of those who had brought their own, slipped quietly over the brow of the hill and together they enjoyed what they each had brought.

Just at that moment Jesus arrived, He noticed the two separate groups, Peter did his best to explain what he had tried to do. Jesus walked over to the group with all the food around them. There was sadness in His eyes, at what He saw. They were sheepish, embarrassed searching for excuses. There is not enough to go around for everyone, someone said. Not so, Jesus said. There is always enough to satisfy everyone's need, but there will never be enough to satisfy other's greed. Your apostles were not able to multiply the loaves, they said. They were not able to change them. I did not come to change things. Jesus answered, I came to change people. An eerie silence descended on the hill. They felt so exposed Jesus did not come to change things. He came to change people. Jesus did not come to change things. He came to change hearts.

Mother Teresa tells a lovely story from her work in Calcutta. Each day, she says, we cook for nine thousand people. The day we do not cook, they do not eat.

One day a young couple came to our house in Calcutta and handed in a large sum of money. "Where did you get so much money?" I asked them. "We got married two days ago, they said. We had decided not to have a big reception or feast. Instead, we are giving you the money to feed the poor".

"Why would you do this?" Mother Teresa asked. "Because we are so blessed, in what we have received, we wanted to share with others from all our blessings

I said at the beginning that the story in today's Gospel is very familiar to us all, so familiar that we do not need to read or hear it anymore, we all know the story so well already. But the people on that hillside in Palestine also knew the story. They did not need to read it in a book or hear it for a second time. They had been present the day Jesus told it. They had seen the miracle before their eyes, but had they got the message of Jesus in their hearts? If they had, would they have just hoarded what they had and tough luck on those whose lot it was to go home hungry. The parable of Jesus is a snapshot of our world today. And each of us is in that story somewhere. The challenge is not to know the parable so well that we do not even need to hear it anymore. The challenge is to recognise ourselves within the story, and whether we have allowed message to penetrate our hearts, and whether the change it made is reflected in our lives.

19th Sunday in Ordinary Time

Jump Danny, and daddy will catch you'!

In the gospel today the disciples are caught in the teeth of a violent storm

St Matthew has brilliantly reconstructed the memory of what happened on the Sea of Galilee, and he uses that incident to help us understand, that it is sometimes through the storms in life that our faith is not just challenged but deepened.

God sometimes allows us experience disappointments and failures, crosses and tragedies, that can pit our human weakness and helplessness, against seemingly impossible odds, but these can also be moments of choice in our lives, when if we are able in our weakness to grasp for the hand of God, He takes our hand in His and brings us safely through that turbulence. On the other hand, if we lose sight of Him and His presence beside us, (like Peter did for one moment, in the story and began to sink in the sea) we too can be overwhelmed by the odds against us, paralysed by our own fears and overcome by the challenge we face.

Faith is all about trust. The deeper and the stronger our faith, the more unbreakable our trust. Jesus presents the total trust a little child has in his daddy as a model for us, of the trust we should have in Him. There is a lovely story that illustrates the faith and trust of a little child in his daddy

A family home is in flames, the smoke is billowing to the heavens. Gathered in the yard, the family are looking on helplessly, as everything they own is going up in flames. Neighbours are trying to console them, telling them that at least, they are all safe and no human life is lost. But in the panic, there has been a terrible misunderstanding. As the smoke billows heavenwards, a little voice is heard calling from an upstairs window. Daddy bursts through the grip of those restraining him, and rushes headlong towards the house that is in flames, screaming at his little son; 'Jump Danny, and daddy will catch you'. The little voice comes back; 'But I can't see you daddy'. 'But I can see you Danny', daddy desperately shouted back. "Jump Danny and daddy will catch you!'

At that moment a little body drops headlong through the billowing smoke and lands safely into daddy's outstretched arms down below. Jesus said, 'unless you become like little children......'It is often in the storms of life we face the choice, to jump or not to jump. To trust or not to trust To be like that little child, whose trust in his daddy's word is so total, who does not have to see him but just hear his voice and who knows that despite the impossible odds, if daddy says jump, then jump he will. Because of his unbreakable trust in his daddy's word, he lands safely into daddy's outstretched arms down below.

In today's gospel story, the disciples and Peter are together in the same boat. They are caught in the teeth of the same storm. They both see the same object on the water in the distance. The disciples see a ghost and are paralysed in fear. Peter sees Jesus and is empowered to walk on water

In the storms of life, we face choices. We can be paralysed by our fears or empowered by our faith. I pray that we will, when the storms of life strike us, as they inevitably will, when we are plunged into that darkness, where it seems all hope is gone, that we will all be like that little child whose trust is total and that we will be able and as confident to throw ourselves into the waiting arms of God, not because we can see them, but because we know by faith that those outstretched arms are always there and always just waiting to receive us

20th Sunday in Ordinary Time

Take a leaf out of her book, and your prayer too will be answered.

You could rename today's gospel, 'The story of the Persistent Woman'. Jesus has just entered the area of Tyre and Sidon, when He is confronted by a woman shouting; Sir, Son of David take pity on me, my daughter is tormented by a demon. Now in those times a demon could be any form of evil including psychological or physical illness. This woman is desperate in her plea for her little girl and what response does she get from Jesus? Does she get any?

She is not going to be put off by that. She is desperate for a cure for her little girl. So, she persists, by making a nuisance of herself. persists, becoming an embarrassment to the disciples. She persists to the point that they plead with Jesus, to give her whatever she wanted because she was shouting after them. Jesus responded, I was sent only to the lost sheep of the House of Israel First of all, He had seemed to ignore her. Now He seems to rebuff her, not because of anything she has done wrong, but just because of who she is, a Canaanite. It is not her fault where she was born! This woman is made of tougher stuff. She refuses to give up. She planks herself in front of Him on the ground. Lord, help me, she pleads. Just when you think it could not get any worse, it gets worse. The response of Jesus: It is not fair to take the children's food and throw it to the house dogs. Now we are all getting a little embarrassed at His treatment of her. How much more can she or any human being take? Undaunted, she comes back but this time with her 'killer punch'. But even the dogs can eat the scraps that fall from the master's table. Jesus is delighted with her response and praises her faith. Woman, he says, you have great faith. Let your wish be granted

Sometimes when a match is over and you look at it later, things can look a lot different then, than they did as you watched it the first time. Similarly, looking back at that story from the end, we can see the things that happened very differently to the first time. The moment that woman confronted Him, Jesus obviously saw the depth of that mother's faith, the depth of her conviction, the certainty she had she would get her request. He drew out His interaction with her to showcase the depth and quality of her faith and to hold it up as an example to his disciples and all around

This Canaanite woman, who would have been despised by them, was giving them a lesson on what Faith really is. Faith which is genuine persists and perseveres. A faith which is genuine stays at it and doesn't give up. Faith that is genuine knows prayer is answered.

Sometimes we can lose heart when prayer is not answered, as we want it answered, and how we want it answered, when God does not answer our prayer, in the way we think He should and by the timeline we have decided. The yardsticks by which we measure our faith are the lengths to which we go in persistence and perseverance and in the certainty that the Lord will answer our prayer. The Lord gives us today the example He gave his disciples, the Canaanite Woman. To us, He is saying: Take a leaf out of her book, and your prayer too will be answered.

21st Sunday in Ordinary Time

Is my faith, information in my head, or is my faith conviction in my heart.

When I was in the seminary, a well-known theologian wrote a book on priestly celibacy, which was immensely popular at the time and required reading for all of us students. It was on all our bookshelves. Six years later he announced that he was leaving the priesthood and getting married. The news took the Church in his home country by storm. Now it is not for me, or any of us, to judge the man, he was a priest of immense genuineness and sincerity. He met the right person, fell in love and made a decision. The rest is history. I hope, [and I hope we all hope], that they had many years of happy married and fulfilled life together.

I mention this example, today, not in judgement, but simply to explore with you for a few minutes, that the fact that have got my head around something, does not necessarily mean that I have got my heart around it. Put simply, someone could write a great book about honesty, even while they are struggling hard to live it. The fact that I can reel off the truths of my faith, doesn't necessarily guarantee that I am living them. You all know that there is a very big difference, between the priest in the parish knowing your 'name' and the priest in the parish knowing 'you', personally. We can copy all the names off the Electoral List in the Post Office, but to get to know you personally maybe I have to drink tea in your kitchen!

That could of course, even apply to our relationship with Jesus too. We could know an awful lot about him. We can get that in bibles, in books or even in films. We can have immense amount of knowledge about Jesus. Does that mean we know Jesus personally? To know a person, we have to spend time 'with' them, not just time in the library reading 'about' them. There is a' knowing' that is in the head, that can be acquired by reading and by study. But there is a knowing that is in the heart that can only be acquired by living. It was not, by what they knew but by how they lived, that the early Christians were recognised as followers of Jesus. It was by how they lived that they spread Christianity across the world. 'These Christians, see how they love each other' people said. It was a very short step from that, to saying; that is the kind of community I would like to be part of. That is the kind of community that I would like my children part of. By this shall all people know that you are my disciples, not by the books you write about me, or by the wonderful homilies you give, or the fine churches you build to honour me, but by your love for one another. In today's gospel Jesus asked Peter, who do you say that I am? It would be easy to answer that with words. It is easy to get our heads around what it means to be Christian. It can be very challenging to get our hearts around living it.

There was a story doing the rounds that when Jesus got back to heaven at the Ascension, that they were dying to find out how He had got on. Moses met him and asked Him, well Jesus did you leave everything in good hands? I did Jesus said. I left it in the hands of Mary, Martha, Peter and the disciples. But what if they fail, Moses asked? Well, I set a church, Jesus said, I gave them the Holy Spirit, I gave it Seven Sacraments; I told them to carry on my work. But what if they fail, Moses asked. Jesus answered: I have no other plan. There is no plan B

Yes, Jesus promised His church will survive forever and it will. He did not promise that it would survive in Ireland, and it may, or it may not. If a few generations fail to hand on the faith by living it, then the Church could well disappear, in Ireland Every generation in Ireland since Patrick has passed on the faith. There is no guarantee that this will always be the case. There is no guarantee the next generation will pass it on. That depends on us. The sermon they depend on is our lives, yours and mine. If that sermon is not lived by us, then they cannot see it. So, the church in Ireland could be one generation away from extinction. If we don't live the faith, it dies, not anywhere else, but where we are. That puts our responsibility to them in a nutshell! Is my faith, information in my head, or is my faith conviction in my heart ? If, someone wanted me to prove my Faith to them, would I need to go to the local church and get a Baptism Certificate, so that they would be able to read the evidence in words or would I be confident enough to just say to them; Forget the Certificate, just look at how I live. There, is the evidence

And Jesus asks each of us today, 'who do you say that I am?'. The answer He is interested in, is not the one that is recorded somewhere on a Register. It is not the one that is written on the pages of a book, but the answer that is written on the pages of our life. That also happens to be the answer to the question, will the church in Ireland be still around for your grandchildren's children

Does it not all go back to where we started? How easy it can be to get our head around something with our words, but how really challenging it is for us all to get our hearts around the same thing, by our lives.

22nd Sunday in Ordinary Time

So often your example becomes our inspiration.

Jesus tells us today, 'If anyone wants to be a follower of mine, he must be prepared to take up his cross and follow me'. When we hear about 'taking up the cross', we are inclined to identify the cross with the big ones, the tragedy, illness, accident, or the unexpected death. If we focus entirely on the big ones, we could easily overlook significant ones, like the sacrifices parents continually make, going without, so that their children will have, The real cost of what your children have received is what you parents have so generously gone without, to enable them to have.

Homes are places of huge sacrifices. A sentence from the 'Little Prince' puts this very well "There is more hidden by a garden wall, then by the Great Wall of China, and the silence of a little girl's heart, encloses more than all the sands of the Sahara". In the silence of their own hearts, behind their own garden wall, many are bravely carrying their secret crosses, caring for their sick or elderly parents, their special child and those who have lost the most special person in their lives. They certainly know what taking up their cross means.

I think of those who have been wronged by others, and who have resisted the temptation to take revenge; those who have lost their quality of life and who could so easily have become embittered. But they bravely carry on against the odds. Some of the people I have referred to, we all know about because their cross is very public. Many of them live beside us but we do not know about them, because they carry their cross behind their garden wall.

So the cross that Jesus is talking about today is not to be confined to just the big ones that hit the headlines, the sudden death, the tragic accident and the likes. We are surrounded by people who are bravely taking up their cross every day; the pain of going without, so that their children will have, the pain of the daily struggle with their own situation, the pain of forgiving when it goes against the grain, doing what is right, even when it is a lonely journey, and you may feel you are the only one making it

Maybe these are some of the crosses Jesus is talking about. 'If anyone wants to be a follower of mine, Jesus said, he must take up his cross and follow me" Maybe He is telling us that in our lives we do not have to go looking for the big ones, to follow Him. There are plenty crosses and challenges in our lives already. What we have to do is recognise them. How we handle them tells us if we are following Him. We do not have to go looking for the Cross. The Cross is usually very well able to find us.

As Jesus passed through death to Resurrection, so will we if we do our best to walk in His footsteps. Inevitably, those footsteps may lead to a Calvary, for some. So often your example becomes our inspiration. For all of us there are plenty of little crosses in the daily challenges that life throws at us, in how we cope with our own failures and mistakes, in how we cope with the challenges that others throw at us. So often, it is not the weight of the cross itself that crushes, but the condition of the shoulders on which it lands. In that there is food for thought for all of us.

23rd Sunday in Ordinary Time

Our goal is to be saints. We all have a long way to go,

I remember when Tim Dolan became a bishop, a journalist approached him with a question. Now that you are a bishop, have you reached your goal in the church? No, he said, "I have not. My goal is to be a 'saint' and I have an awful long way to go".

In those few short words, he did more than define his own mission. He defined the mission of all of us Christians, to challenge others to become saints, by becoming one myself. That mission is best achieved by example. That is why parents will always be our greatest models. They shape their children by their own example.

All of us fulfil our mission by affirming, supporting and encouraging each other. Sometimes to fulfil our mission, we have to be courageous enough to correct each other, too. To correct others well, when we are called to, is an art form that can often seem to be in rare supply. It is a good rule of thumb when we must correct anyone, to be sure that we do so with the same gentleness, that we hope the Lord will use to correct us.

One thing the gospel certainly makes clear to us is, that Jesus calls on all His disciples to love one another and when love does break down, He expects us to take the initiative in seeking forgiveness and reconciliation. We live in a world where transparency and accountability are demanded of everybody and rightly so. So, let us take that as read, and let nothing I say be interpreted otherwise. But do you sometimes get the feeling that we also live in a world where there is always someone baying for a head on a plate.

Jesus walked this same earth then as we do now. I am sure that in Palestine He had plenty experience of the dark side of human nature and of man's inhumanity to man, of crookedness, corruption and cruelty, but He still preached forgiveness and reconciliation. He insisted that His Way of love, of forgiveness and reconciliation is the only way to true happiness, for all of us, both in the few years we are around here but for our eternity as well. We know, how difficult it can be to live the way He wants us to.

We know human relationships break down and when they do, we do not always find it easy to go back and ask for forgiveness for our behaviour. That is why we have to come and hear His words again and again. Then, go back to our homes and community and continue to try again to be affirmative and nurturing of the good, gentle and sensitive towards what is the not so good, prepared to forgive those who have hurt us and ask forgiveness of those we have hurt. Trying to be saints ourselves, which is what we are called to. Hopefully, by our example we will help others to be the same and do the same. Then we are living our mission as followers of Jesus. We are fulfilling our role in His church.

If anyone asks us, as they once asked Bishop Dolan, if we have now fulfilled our goal, we too will then be able to answer truthfully. No, we have not. Our goal is to be saints. We all have a long way to go, but at least we know that we're on the right road.

24th Sunday in Ordinary Time

"I will never allow that person" he said, "determine how I act."

Shakespeare said of mercy, The quality of mercy is not strained. It droppeth as the gentle rain from Heaven on the place beneath. It is twice blessed. It blesseth him that giveth and it blesses him that takes. So it is also with forgiveness, because it blesses those who give it, and it blesses those who receive it. To be able to forgive is to be free. To be unable to forgive is to be imprisoned.

Sam was a staunch Orangeman who lived in Dublin. Proud of his tradition, he never forgot his roots. Each July he made his annual pilgrimage back North to participate in the marching season with his local lodge. Living beside him in Dublin, was Molly, who ran the corner shop. She was a staunch Nationalist, and equally proud of her tradition. Relationships were normally tranquil enough, through the year. But the nearer the marching season came each year, the stronger she felt the need to vent her prejudices, particularly when Sam was within earshot. Consistently, Sam seemed oblivious to her cutting comments, never allowing her sharp tongue to upset him. And he continued to pop in, each morning, for his bits of shopping. 'Thank You Mam' he'd just say at the check-out, and he was gone about his business

Others witnessing her hurtful comments to Sam were embarrassed. They found her derogatory remarks, to be of poor taste. One morning one of them followed Sam out of the shop and challenged him. I have seen how that woman continually throws insults at you, he said. I just wish that one day, you would stand up to her and give her back as good as you are getting. Sam thanked the man for his concern. But then His response was simple and to the point; "I will never allow that woman, he said, determine how I act."

Having heard that story, how I wished, I could be like him, but some things are far easier to admire than to imitate. How often I have regretted, I could not have been like him and just bit my tongue and kept my mouth shut. And I know any time I did succeed in taking a leaf from Sam's book, the outcome has been far better not just for me but for everyone. The times I have not succeeded in doing so, I know I was the person that regretted it most

Being a forgiving person, does not just change relationships, it changes people, and the one it changes most is me. To fail to forgive, is to let another person determine how you act. It is to give someone else power over us. It is to allow them to continue to cause us pain

To nurse grievances, is to be less attractive to be around. It tempts you to become embittered, to even become resentful towards another, to become burdened with a chip on the shoulder. Chips are so easy to pick up, but so difficult to discard. Resentment takes on a momentum all its own. it seeks out material to feed its appetite, to justify the feelings and perpetuate them. The resenter suffers far more that the resented. The un-forgiver suffers more than the unforgiven. The hater endures far more pain than the hated. Unforgiveness, is a form of self-inflicted self-destruction. It is anathema to the Lord. It is a living contradiction to what He calls us to be.

To forgive a hurt done may never be easy. But to nurture a hurt is to self-destruct. We are all going to need God's forgiveness very badly, one day.

We ask Him all the time to forgive us as we forgive each other. What will we do if He takes us at our word and applies to us the standard, we sometimes apply to each other. The Lord is not that interested in our admiring our Orange friend in Dublin, He is not even that interested in our retelling of his story. He is far more interested in our taking a leaf out of Sam's book and we ourselves ensuring, that we will never let others determine how we act

25th Sunday in Ordinary Time

They were nursing their wrongs, not because they were less blessed but because their neighbours were more blessed

There is a story told about two missionaries giving a mission in Abbeyfeale many years ago. They were staying in Leen's hotel in the Square. In those days missions were a serious business. Their day began with a 7.00am mass for those going to work. The clock went off at six one morning. One of the missionaries jumped out of bed, opened the window, stuck his head out, filled his lungs with fresh Kerry morning air and greeted the new day with the words; 'Good morning, Lord'. The racket he made woke up his colleague, who turned over in his bed in disbelief that dawn had broken and grunted grudgingly 'Good Lord, morning!' Two men of similar backgrounds, on a shared mission, but approaching the new day with very different attitudes; "Good morning, Lord "Good Lord, Morning!!"

Today's gospel seems to be about a landowner and his workers. Look a bit deeper, it is about something far more important. We could get hung up on the landowner, trying to figure out why, having made a deal with some workers for a wage for a full day, then comes along and pays the same money to other workers who had only worked for a fraction of the time. We could get hung up on the rights of the workers, trying to figure out how it could be fair or just, that people who only did an hour's work went home with the same money as the ones that did a full day. To get hung up on that, we could miss the message of Jesus. Because this is not a story about rights. It is a story about attitudes

The landowner does behave a bit unusually. But in fairness to him he does a deal with his workers. In fairness to him he hands over what they agreed to.

If he left it at that, they would have gone home very happy. But what annoys them and makes them unhappy, is not that he was not just to them, but that he was generous to others. When challenged he explains; Can I not do what I like with what is my own? Then comes the punch line. Why are you envious because I choose to be generous?

The workers had done a deal in the morning. They were happy with the deal they did. They did their day's work. They got their cheque as agreed. It was a day's work they might not have expected. It was a day's pay they may not have anticipated, when they were hanging around at the gate earlier. What ruined their journey home that evening, was not what they had in their hands, but what the others had. That morning, they were appreciating their blessings. That evening they were nursing their wrongs, not because they had lost anything, but because others had gained something, not because they were less blessed but because their neighbours were more blessed

So far, we have been looking at the story in the book. Now let us look in the mirror to see if we recognise the reflection. That parable is a mirror, a mirror that Jesus is holding up before each of us today. Unless I can recognise my reflection in that mirror, I can so easily enjoy the story but miss the message. The parable is the story of all our lives, yours and mine. The parable is the story of our community and our family

As a parent who has been up at daybreak, who has worked hard for what your family enjoy, are there not times when, being only human, you look at what you have in the evening? You look at your return for the hours you have put in. You see what others have received for what seems like less effort. You look at the struggle you have had to make. You look at the knocks you have had to take. You look at the sacrifices you have had to make. You might well look at the cross you have had to carry. Like those workers in the story, you look at God and say, God, you are not fair

How could you have given these others more than you gave me. How can they go home in the evening of life better off than I am. Generous people look at what they have and thank God for it, because they are so blessed they count their blessings and in doing so the blessings they have received are doubled

Envious people become preoccupied with what others have. Disgruntled, they lose sight of what they have themselves. In doing so their blessings are halved

The landowner in the parable speaks to us of our God; a God generous beyond measure and merit, a God people can believe in, when they meet Him in us. The disgruntled workers are what we could easily become when we allow envy take hold in our hearts. The reason we then find our blessing hard to count is because we can sometimes have decimated them by our attitude.

26th Sunday in Ordinary Time

God is the giver of life, and he alone has the right to decide when a life should end.

As you probably know from the media, today has been designated as a 'Day for Life'. Those who are sick or frail, and older people, deserve our respect. They are our brothers and sisters in Christ.

We are asked to deepen our awareness of the role that older people are called to play in society and in the Church and in so doing, to prepare our hearts for the loving welcome that we should always have for them. The Pope's message was particularly forceful, as it was written by an elderly man showing the world that everyday life is worth living. He reminded us with his own painful witness, that we can never say that a person, weakened by sickness or age, is useless or is a burden to society. We are challenged to love the life of older people, with a reminder that in scripture reaching old age is a sign of God's benevolence and long life is prized as a special divine gift.

When a decision is taken to terminate the life of a person who is sick or elderly, on the grounds that his or her life is no longer worth living, this is euthanasia. Whether it is by doing something, or by not doing anything when something should be done, be it with or without the consent of the person, euthanasia comes down to the same thing in moral terms. It is the deliberate ending of an innocent human life, and it is contrary to the law of God.

God is the giver of life, and He alone has the right to decide when a life should end. In the words of John Paul, human life is a precious gift to be loved and defended in each of its stages. The commandment 'Thou shalt not kill' always requires respecting and promoting human life, from its beginning to its natural end. It is a command that applies, even in the presence of illness and when physical weakness reduces the person's ability to be self-reliant.

Must we, in the case of terminal illness, do everything and anything possible to stay alive, despite our condition. The answer to this is clearly 'No'. There is no civil or religious law, which says that we must be kept alive at any cost. What is never permitted, however, is any act which directly and intentionally takes away an innocent human life. It is permissible to alleviate pain by administering drugs, which are foreseen may shorten life, but the intention being to ease distress, not terminate a life. The right to be able to choose to die could, in some circumstances, be perceived as a duty to die.

Once our society allows voluntary euthanasia, we will have set foot on a slippery slope, which will lead us inevitably to involuntary euthanasia. People who are dying want to know that even though there is no prospect of recovery, they will not be abandoned. It is important that the kind of care a sick person receives is not dictated by the fears of the convenience of others

We cherish the 'Evening of Life' as we pray; May He support us all day long, till the shade lengthens and the evening comes, and the busy world is hushed and the fever of life is over and our work is done. Then in His Mercy, may He give us safe lodging and a holy rest and peace at the last

27th Sunday in Ordinary Time

Let us never take all Gods gifts to us for granted

I remember my early years as a priest being in the classroom. My job was teaching religion to second year boys. As you might imagine, I often found myself very challenged. When trying to explain to them what a parable was, I found myself often searching for examples in my own experience.

As children we walked a few miles to school every day. Going and coming we passed a sweet shop. We had often to call there to pick up a few messages The woman in the shop had a soft spot for us children. And if you were lucky enough to be in the shop, when an adult was buying sweets, she had this lovely habit of passing the big jar of bull's eyes around to those waiting and we all got a free bull's eye to shorten the journey home. One evening she was busy serving people and trying to do a few things at the same time. As she passed the jar around, her attention was elsewhere. She was scanning the shelf behind her, looking for something. Next thing she felt a tug on her sweet jar and swiveled around. Poor Johnny was frozen to the floor. With paradise staring him in the face, and her back turned, he couldn't resist and went for the kill- a full fistful of bull's eyes. Unfortunately, his loaded fist jammed in the mouth of the jar. Caught in the act, he left embarrassed, and empty handed. He learned one of life's basic lessons. Try to grab the world and you risk losing the lot. The power of the parable or the little story is in its simplicity. You don't have to be a genius to get it. It hits you between the eyes. You don't have to get the message; the message gets you.

The parable is a favorite teaching method used by Jesus Today Jesus uses the Parable of the Landowner and his tenants. The landowner standing for the generous God, the great giver. The tenants, rather than appreciating their great blessing, set out to exploit the situation for their own gain. In their attempt to 'grab all, they lose all'. It is a constant challenge for us all to keep an eye on our own attitudes. To the degree that we allow ourselves become takers rather than givers, to the degree that we become self-centered rather than other centered or indeed self-centered rather than God centered, we shrink the welcome space available to Jesus in our hearts. And the more it shrinks, the less space there is for Him. The ultimate of course is when He becomes totally squeezed out, the point the tenants reached when they said, 'This is the Son let's kill Him and the inheritance will be ours'

Let us not forget the story of the little boy in the sweet shop, not appreciating the generosity of the shopkeeper, blinded by the attraction of instant personal gain, in attempting to grab all, he lost all. It is a temptation we can all sometimes face, not only in our interaction with each other, but also in our interaction with the God of generosity and blessings. If we give in to it and let that attitude of 'me first' grow, we can gradually squeeze the Lord out of our life and what He wants can become secondary to what we want.

His Father's judgement on those who did this to His Son in the parable was, I will take the vineyard from you and give it to others who will produce its fruit. Let us never take all Gods gifts to us for granted. Let us never lose sight of how blessed we are by Him. Let us always be grateful for what we have received from Him. Let us ensure we never become so self-centered that He can no longer find a space in our hearts

28th Sunday in Ordinary Time

To love someone is to allow them to be free

I remember in our younger days, in our great innocence or naivety, we used to grapple with big questions like, Is God really fair? Is God really just?

We used to debate the hypothetical case of "Johnny v Paddy." Johnny, a good living man, walked the straight and narrow, avoiding the big pitfalls. Then totally out of character he commits a 'whopper'. That night, the priest was called to a serious accident. Johnny was gone; -never got the chance to make his peace with God.

His friend Paddy played the field. He was never too worried about his wayward habits. He would not have known a Confession box if he saw one. He developed serious chest pains one evening and was rushed to hospital. The chaplain was called. Paddy made his peace with God and passed away that night.

The question we grappled with was, how could a God who allowed this to happen, be just? Need I tell you; we never solved the dilemma. But we did learn that like all humanity since time began, we will never grasp the mystery of God's ways.

In the recent Sunday gospels, Jesus is putting before us images of generosity and ingratitude; the workers in the vineyard who instead of being grateful for what they received, resented that other workers had got more, others who because of their greed lost everything and got themselves thrown out of their vineyards altogether, and the ungrateful invitees to the feast who had their invitations transferred to others.

The Father Jesus presents to us is a God who is crazy about us, showering us with blessings, lavishing us with gifts and opportunities, wanting and wishing us to accept them. Is He also pointing out that there can be consequences of ingratitude? Can we put these very gifts at risk by our lack of appreciation of them? Is Jesus telling us that in the end of the day, His Father always respects our freedom and the choices we've made to accept or reject His gifts?

To love someone is to allow them to be free. To love someone is to respect the choices they make. God's love for us is so total, so perfect, that He treats our freedom as sacred. His respect for our choice is absolute, God invites us to His Final Wedding Feast in Heaven. God blesses us with His roadmap on how to get there. God gives to us everything we need to make it safely home.

But let's never forget that God respects the choices we make. Where we spend eternity is by our choice, not His decision. That choice is not made in isolation from the rest of my life. That choice is being made today, tomorrow and each day of my life. I make the choice. God respects the choice my life has made.

The story of Johnny and Paddy is fine for discussing at the bar counter. But each of our final destinations is decided by the full book of our lives, not by the last sentence of the final chapter!

29th Sunday in Ordinary Time [Mission Sunday]

If we are one, they will believe in Him, if are divided, they will not

Priests are privileged to accompany people in life's final hours. One of the things we learn at times like that is that when people are close to death, it's not everyone they're interested in talking to. They don't wish the whole parish around the bed. The people they most want to see and be with are those who are closest to them, those who are special to them, those whom they love and are loved by. At a time like that, It is not everything they want to talk about. The closeness of death brings a clarity of vision. It separates the important from all the trivialities and there is only time for the important, when each breath is a numbered one. They are far too precious to be wasted.

Think of the way we recall, remember, hang on to, and treasure the last words and final sentences of those close to us. "It was only last week that she was saying..." "Sure, I was talking to him Tuesday and he said to me..." If the person now gone, knew the end was coming, and knowing that, remembered us or asked to be remembered to us, or sent a special message to us, that we really treasure.

Jesus Christ was fully human. His time came to die. He knew it was imminent. He had choices to make. He could have worked His greatest miracle before thousands. He could have given us the world's greatest parable. But He did not do either of those. What did he do? He gathered around Himself those who were closest to Him. He took them into a little room and spoke to them.

The words He spoke were possibly among the most powerful, the most important words He spoke in His whole life. And remember they were the words of a man about to die, a man who knew he was about to die. Into these final words He packed every ounce of His being. It was His Last Will and Testament. It was His death-bed message. These words were his dying wish. They were not just for his apostles, but they were for us

This is His dying wish and prayer for us gathered here today. 'Father, may they be one. May they be completely one'. His last wish and prayer was that we would be 'one', that we would be united, that we be fond of each other, that we would take care of each other. This is not just for our own sake, but because so many would depend on seeing it. "Father may they be completely one ...He said, 'so that the world will believe' ....it was you who sent me."

On the night before he died, Jesus staked His credibility before the world on us, specifically on how we live with each other. Splits, divisions, old sores, people not talking to one another, divisions or bitterness between us, have no place. They are a contradiction of how Jesus asks us to live and because of that, are a scandal before the world

Jesus came to save all. He gave His life for that. He told us out straight the night before He died that if we live in unity, love and friendship with each other, the world will see, be attracted and want to follow Him. If we are divided, bickering and in factions, the world will see us as fraud and steer clear of us.

Today is Mission Sunday. Missions are about bringing the message of Jesus to others. Most of us will never see Africa or South America, but we are all missionaries, here at home. Our 'mission land' is our own home, parish and community. How we live there, will determine whether others believe. We have it from the heart of Christ, that if we are one, they will believe in Him, if are divided, they will not. We have often heard it said that old divisions and old sores die hard. The luxury of retaining them comes at a heavy price. The Lord spells that out for us today. On this Mission Sunday, He does not put a tooth in it . He tells each of us, that He's staked His Credibility before the world on us, specifically, on how we live with and treat each other. Speaking of us gathered here He says of us today. Father may they be one, Father may they be completely one. May they be so completely one that the World will believe it was you who sent me.

30th Sunday in Ordinary Time

Signposts, confirm we are on the right road, or alert us, that we have strayed off it

Generally, the Pharisees do not come out well in the Gospel. Today might just be an exception. In fact, today they do all of us a great favour. They asked Jesus a big question, straight out; Which is the greatest commandment.?

And they got a crystal-clear answer for us.' Jesus said, 'You must love the Lord your God with all your heart, with all your soul, and with all your mind. This is the greatest and the first commandment. The second resembles it:

You must love your neighbour as yourself.

Those words are directly from the lips of Jesus Himself. They are worth repeating many times so that their full meaning can really sink in. To love God with all our heart, all our soul, all our mind. What would that look like in practice in our lives. Well, when I was going to school, we had a question in the Catechism. The question was; How do we show our love for God? and the answer, which we learned off by heart was; We show our love for God by keeping His Commandments. There are ten of them and all of us here know them. They are the markers laid down for us, the signposts placed along the road of life for us. Signposts confirm that we are on the right road, or alert us to the fact that we have strayed off it

During the week I visited someone who lives alone. Living alone in the heart of the country can be tough. It is tough to have lost your independence. It is tough to be dependent on others for everything. But I was really touched when this person said to me. I have the best neighbours in the whole world. Every one of them is better than the next. They would not know what to do for you. I am blessed in my neighbours

It struck me that these are the people who are living the second Commandment that Jesus named, "To love your neighbour as yourself". It struck me too, how blessed we are in our communities. And I think it is so important when we see this that we name it and celebrate it. In all these pockets around the parish we have little communities who are living the words of Jesus; –' Neighbours who would not know what to do for each other. So, we thank God today, that we live in a community, that gathers with us here, each weekend, helping us, to keep God at the centre of our lives. And we thank God today that we live in a community, that is peppered with people that model for us all "How to love our neighbour as ourselves"

31st Sunday in Ordinary Time

Earthenware jars whose function is to deliver to you a treasure.

There is a sentence in this gospel that is a bit strange. Jesus Says: "The Scribes and the Pharisees occupy the Chair of Moses. You must therefore do what they tell you and listen to what they say, but do not be guided by what they do." Jesus would seem to be saying that the Scribes and Pharisees had a licence to preach one thing to the people, but to live by different standards themselves.

"Do what they tell you, listen to what they say, but do not be guided by what they do." That advice is even more surprising coming from Jesus when we hear Him describe them as laying heavy burdens on men's shoulders but not lifting a finger to remove them themselves. He describes them as "blind guides". How then are we to understand what He says in the Gospel today; - you must listen to what they say, you must follow what they tell you, even if they are poor examples themselves.

We can look at some of the other things He says. "The Scribes and Pharisees occupy the Chair of Moses." Who was Moses? He was the messenger of God to His People. Moses was only the messenger! It was not Moses that was important, it was what he brought that was. The people clearly understood what Moses brought, the Ten Commandments, God's law for them. And when Moses clapped the Ten Commandments before them, they fell on their knees in awe. It was not in awe of Moses they were, but in awe of their God who spoke through Moses.

So, Jesus told them that these pharisees occupy the Chair of Moses. They stand in his place. They are God's messengers to you. They hand you on God's message. Take it seriously. Listen to it. Follow it. Do not be distracted by the messengers who bring it.

Wind forwards from then to today. Jesus says, 'He who hears you, hears me and he who hears me, hears not me but hears the one who sent me' For us today, our church occupies the Chair of Moses. For us, our church is the messenger of God. Jesus is saying to us; Listen to My voice in the teaching of My church. Follow its instructions on how you live. Do not allow yourself to be distracted by accidentals. Those that I send to preach the gospel to you today, are in the language of the Bible, "earthenware jars", but earthenware jars whose function is to bring you a treasure. Don't be distracted by the jars. Lots of us are battered and bruised and chipped and broken. We are not the ideal containers for treasures. But thank God, we are only messengers. We hold no brief, other than to hand on what we have received. The divine truth is guaranteed against error. The bearers are not guaranteed against faults.

Just as the Pharisees were often less than the models they might have been expected to be, so those who take their place today, are also struggling with their own weaknesses. Just as the Pharisees were reprimanded by Jesus for not practicing what they preached, so those who take their place today carry the wounds of their own failures. But Jesus is asking us today not to use the weakness of the messenger to discredit the message, the failures of the messenger to avoid the message, the shortcomings of the messenger to escape the challenge of the message. Don't use the 'look' of the jar to pass judgement of the quality of its contents.

Jesus is asking of you, that despite their personal failures, which will be obvious to you, despite their weaknesses which you may have experienced, despite their brokenness with which they struggle, "Listen to what they say". Follow the teachings they pass on to you because they are messengers of God to you. They bring you His truth, of which God is the guarantor. Please concentrate on the teaching rather than the teacher, on the message rather than the messenger, the contents rather than the earthenware jars that contain it. After all, it is not you who will be answering for the latter. Trust God to be able to take care of the messengers then. He won't be asking you any questions about them. He'll only be interested in hearing from you, about how you handled the message He sent you, through them. The Scribes and Pharisees occupy the Chair of Moses. "Do what they tell you, listen to what they say, but do not be guided, or maybe we should say misguided, by "what they do."

32nd Sunday

They have just gone on an earlier bus; we will be along in a later one

Years ago, during a holiday by a lake in the North of Italy, one evening the water was so inviting, so totally calm, I decided to swim across the lake to the other side. I had been swimming for quite a while, when the penny dropped. The far shore was still as far away as when I had started. Those of you who have experience of being on the water will know that 'distance' over water is deceptive. The awful thought crossed my mind, that I wasn't going to make it to the other side. I don't need to tell you how scary it is to be in that space, when thoughts begin to flash across your mind like; How far down is it to the bottom of this lake? How long does it take to drown? How long will it be before my friends miss me and raise the alarm?

Other pictures too began flashing across my mind, pictures of my life through a different pair of eyes, God's eyes. Let me just say, I was in no doubt that there were some things in my life that wouldn't be there, and many things that would be there, if only, I got just one more chance to put things in order!

The parable Jesus tells us in the gospel today, brought me back to that moment in my own life; the story of those who were prepared for that moment and the story of those who weren't, the ones who were ready with oil in their lamps and the ones who weren't ready, who had no oil when the bridegroom arrived. The door opened. Those who were ready entered. The door closed. Those not ready were left outside. They began pleading; Lord, Lord let us in! The Lord answered, 'Sorry I do not know you'. You knew the rules, But you played it your way!. And then comes the final word of the Lord Himself 'Stay awake, you do not know the day nor the hour'

In November we remember. We remember all those who have gone before us.

We know that where they've gone, we will one day follow. Our loved ones have just gone in the 'earlier' bus. We will be along in a later one. For those who are ready when the bus arrives, for those who have kept this moment in focus, the message in the gospel is; 'Come Inside'

This does not mean that as Christians, we go around living with a morbid shadow of impending death, any more than the driver who always fastens his seat belt, can be accused of going around with a morbid fear of accidents. God wants us to live every moment of our lives to the full. He also wants us never to lose sight of its final purpose. In life, we are standing at the bus stop.

We know that the bus has left the bus station. We know it is already on its way. When it will arrive, we know not. But when it does arrive, we need to be sure that we're not boarding the wrong bus. As Christians, we live remembering the words of St. Paul; 'For those who die in Jesus, God will bring them with Him'

As Christians we live, taking to heart the words of Jesus. Stay awake and be ready, for we know neither the day nor the hour that the Master may call us home. Prepared, with our lamps lighting, we know what happens. Unprepared, with no oil, we also know what will happen

33rd Sunday in Ordinary Time

If you like me and you love me, tell me now

Today's parable is about the talents. I wonder would you agree with me, that we can be better at recognising other people's talents than we are at acknowledging our own. The master in today's parable seemed to know what his servants were capable of, so he distributed the talents, to each according to his ability. The one who got five made five more; The one who got three made three more. The one to whom he gave one, made none. The first two delivered according to their ability. The third didn't use his talent but buried it in ground. I wonder why? 'I was afraid' he said

I think we might, not just understand him, we might even have some sympathy with him. Fear can hold us all back a lot of the time. Fear can stifle, creativity. Fear of failure can kill initiative. The tragedy of the third servant is that he gave into this fear and buried his talent in the ground

We have all received talents from the Lord. Some have received more than us, some less. Our talents are given to us to be shared. They're not given to us to be buried. As in our parable today, one of the real blocks to our sharing our talents can be fear; fear of what people may think; fear of putting our head above the parapet or being seen to be different; fear people will think we're 'getting notions' about ourselves

It is a positive sign of a healthy community, when people who take the risk of stepping forward, are appreciated, when people who show initiative are supported and when people who offer their talents to the community are welcomed. Sometimes we can be reluctant to give compliments, lest we are misunderstood as being phony or insincere. Genuine compliments, given from the heart, are so supportive and affirmative to the recipient

We are all familiar with the Irish proverb, 'Mol an óige agus tiochfaidh si'. (Praise the youth and they will blossom). I suggest that applies to the 'not so young' as well. I suggest it applies to us all!. We all need a little gee-up from each other from time to time. A little affirmation never goes astray. Indeed, we all need it and profit from it. As St Paul writes, "Encourage one another and build up each other", as indeed you are doing

The opposite is starkly described in Sheila Cassidy's Sharing the Darkness "I weep that there are so many missed opportunities for comforting, so many smiles withheld, so many hands untouched, so many kind words unspoken", and we could add; so many gifts unnamed, so many thanks unsaid, so many compliments ungiven, so many hugs withheld. Let that never be how it is between us. Let's not wait till people are gone to affirm their gifts. Wouldn't it be lovely, if we made the following words our motto between us in our homes and in our community.

'If you like me and you love me, tell me now. Do not wait till life is over and I am underneath the clover, because I cannot read my tombstone when I'm gone.' (Berton Braley; - "Do it now') Talents get buried beneath the ground, when they are denied the opportunity_to flower above the ground

Our Lord Jesus Christ, King of the Universe

The palace He wants to live in, is the human heart

Today is the Feast of 'Christ Our King'. When we think of a king we think of a crown, of a palace, of armies and conquests and of royalty and of power. The contrast could hardly be more striking between The King sits in his palace and the baby in His stable. The king sits on his throne while the fragile baby rests in a manger. The great Empires forged by weapons of war, now survive only in monuments of stone. The Kingdom He founded, He founded with the only weapon He had, love. He came, not to dominate His followers, but to serve and save them. He came to be with us, each day in this world, so that we could be with Him for eternity in the next. The palace He wants to live in, is not one made of stone, but one made of flesh, the human heart, yours and mine. If I ensure His Kingdom is in my heart now, He will ensure I will be in His Kingdom for eternity

I like the story about the Palace Clown summoned by the king. The King handed him a stick and said to him, I want you to take this stick and keep it with great care.

Don't part with it until you meet a Clown greater than yourself. Then pass on this stick to Him. Years passed. The time came and the King was coming near to his end. From the highest ranking to the humblest in the palace, they lined up around his bed to say their last farewells. At the end of the queue was the Palace Clown. To him as to all the others, the message of the king was the same. 'I am now about to embark on my final journey', he told them, 'and this is the one journey from which I shall not return'

It was the palace Clown who said to the King; 'you made so many journeys in your life, but you never set out on any without being sure you were ready, with all the preparations made for your return home. For this, the greatest journey you are now going on, what preparations have you already put in place?'. 'None', the dying king answered, 'I kept putting it off. This was one journey I hadn't planned on taking, for many years yet'. The Clown reached inside his coat and retrieved the stick, the king had given him many years before. He gently laid it on the dying king's bed. 'Master, he said I think you should have this stick, because finally, I have found a fool greater than myself'

In a world of busyness and pressures from every side, we can be so engulfed by the urgency of things that pass, that we get distracted from the important things that last. We know that the way to be always ready, is by always putting first the signposts He has given us, the only ones that ensure that we are ready for our final journey. Today we celebrate the feast of the Kingship of Christ. He would love us to celebrate it every day, by living it in our hearts.

YEAR B

2nd Sunday Ordinary Time

If God lives in me, then He also lives in Johnny next door,

In the First Reading today Samuel was in the Sanctuary of the Lord. The Lord was calling him by name, 'Samuel, Samuel'!. Samuel could hear his name being called but couldn't figure out who was calling him. The Lord was calling Samuel, by name but was having equal difficulty getting Samuel to recognise Him. When the penny dropped, Samuel immediately answered the call; 'Speak, Lord', he said, 'your servant is listening 'and from that moment Samuel's life was changed forever

God is always calling. He is always calling each of us. Normally His call to us comes through His Word, or thro events or people in our lives. Today, for instance in the second reading of our mass, God uses St Paul to convey His message to us. If we get it, it would be surprising if it didn't change us. This is the Message that God sends us through St Paul today; "Your Body is the 'Tabernacle' of The Holy Spirit". In other words, God is actually living within each of us

And if I really believe that my body is a Temple of the Holy Spirit and that God lives in me, then it follows, that if God lives in me, that He also lives in Johnny next door, in the person I work for in the person who works for me and He lives in the person across the table from me at my dinner to-day. If I really believed that, wouldn't I feel challenged?

If I really believe that God is in me and in everyone I meet, then I will be challenged to treat the people I meet, with the same respect as I would treat Him. It is the same God who is in the Eucharist I receive in church, that is present in the person beside me in the seat and in the person that serves me in the shop. Now if, like Samuel, I recognise God speaking to me in His Word today, can I now say with Samuel; Speak Lord, I'm listening, and I'm hearing your message to me.

There may be times when, with the best will in the world, we are unable to be present at mass, when we would really want and love to be there. This can cause us great pain and disappointment. Ever think, that at a time like that, when you really wanted to be with the Lord and close to Him at mass, but are unable to, you can be close to Him in the people around you? Could the Lord be whispering to you; 'If you really miss me that much, don't forget I'm still beside you and you can meet and be close to me in your home. I'm having the dinner with you today. Remember that when you're passing me the salt. I'll be meeting you when you are at work tomorrow. I'd love you to recognise me there and let me know that you do

Then He will surely know that we did hear His voice calling us by name and that we do recognise Him present in the people around us. Come to think of it, wouldn't our families and all the people we meet, see quite a bit of a change in all of us too !

3rd Sunday in Ordinary Time

Enjoy the journey don't lose sight of the destination.

In the second reading Paul talks of 'not becoming engrossed in the world, because the world as we know it is passing away'. That could sound a bit like an invitation to 'opt out'. What is the point in getting stuck in, if life as we know it is just transient and passing away. Maybe there is another way we can look at what Paul is saying,

A very well-known footballer, in an interview, was asked to describe his feelings when, on running out onto the hallowed surface of Croke Park on All Ireland Final day he was hit with that thunderous roar of eighty thousand people. Did it not cause him to freeze on the spot. Did that explosion of sound not totally intimidate him?

No, He said, I look around at those teeming thousands of people, I feel the atmosphere and excitement in the air. I savour it, I soak it in, and I say to myself: Jack, enjoy every moment of this and savour it, because one day soon you won't be here anymore. Enjoy it while you are. It obviously didn't distract him from why he was there. If it had, he wouldn't have multiple provincial and All-Ireland medals in his pocket. I think Jack's attitude and approach to sport, could help us understand St Paul's attitude and approach to life. When he talks to us in that reading today about 'not becoming engrossed in the world, because the world as we know it is passing away'

So, St Paul is not suggesting we 'opt out' but he's saying to us about life; appreciate every day, enjoy it, while we are here. Appreciate it, soak up the good that is around us. Avail of the opportunities that come our way. Enjoy it now to the full, because one day we won't be here anymore. But, while savouring and enjoying the present, don't lose track of the purpose of our being here. Enjoy the 'journey' but don't lose sight of the 'destination'.

The world as we know it will pass away for each of us. But if we have done our best while we are in it, if we have tried to live as God asks us to, then when it passes, a better place awaits us. We too will one day climb the steps to receive the Cup

Doing our best is what God wants of each of us. It is not about being perfect. Even the great saints didn't get it right all the time. Of course, we'll make mistakes, and we make lots of them, but our God is more understanding than the whole lot of us put together. He understands our making mistakes. But what He might have a problem with, might not be our mistakes, but our unwillingness to admit them and be able to say those two beautiful words, 'I am sorry'

In the first reading today, we hear about the people of Nineveh. 'God saw their effort to renounce evil'. and as soon as He saw them making the effort, everything changed for them. God does not expect the impossible of any of us, but He does expect that we do our best. When we make the effort, when we do our best, He does the rest.

So, the message I'd share with you today is, soak up, savour and enjoy and live your life to the full. But let's never allow ourselves to forget, that one day we won't be here any longer, and if we want to be among those going up the steps to accept the cup, we have to be very sure that while enjoying the Journey, we never allow ourselves to be distracted from our destination. Enjoy the journey don't lose sight of the destination.

4th Sunday in Ordinary Time

There was a consistency between what He taught and how He lived

There is an interesting statement in today's gospel. Jesus goes into the Synagogue and begins to preach. And Mark tells us that, His teaching made a deep impression on them, because unlike the Scribes, He taught with authority.

Scripture scholars have studied that phrase, 'He taught with authority' and they tell us what it really means is, that there was a consistency between what He taught and how He lived. The people could see that what he spoke with His lips, He believed in His heart and reflected in His life and that was the secret of His success as a preacher. He put into practice in his own life what He asked others to do in theirs. I think we can all understand what Mark meant. Each of us has experienced that kind of integrity in people around us

The fact that we are together at mass today is no accident. We share a set of values that are important to us. We didn't pick them up off the bushes! They were instilled into us. They were modelled for us. If we were each handed a questionnaire today and the first question for each of us to answer was; Name two people who had the deepest influence in shaping the values that are important to you today, I'm fairly sure, that when the questionnaire came back, the vast majority of us would have the same answer; our parents. Why did their values make such a deep impression on us ? The answer is obvious. They taught with authority. That authority was the example of their own lives; a consistency between what they believed and how they lived. Because the values they shared with us from their lips, they believed in their hearts, and they reflected in their lives. That was transparent to us. The formative influence of home is crucial. Parents are the best teachers. Your teaching comes with authority, -the authority of example

In the synagogue, the teaching of Jesus made a deep impression on all, because unlike the Scribes, He taught with authority. What He proposed to others, He lived Himself. In our homes, our parents made a deep impression on us, because they taught with authority. What they proposed to us; we saw them live themselves. Today, you the parents of a new generation are continuing the tradition you received. That's why you have the capacity to make such a deep impression on your family. You teach with authority. Your children see lived in your life; what you expect them to live in theirs. So, when you look around today and ask, where is this gospel happening today, you don't have to look too far away. This Gospel is happening in each of your homes, where parents are the 'Model' of values to your children.

May your values continue to make a deep impression on them, as they see the consistency between what you profess on Sunday and live on Monday, and only expect of them what we are prepared to live ourselves.

5th Sunday in Ordinary Time

The beautiful lady invited Bernadette to come closer

During this week, two feast days will be celebrated, The Feast of Our Lady of Lourdes on Tuesday the 11th and the Feast of St. Valentine on Friday 14th. Most people are very familiar with the story of Lourdes, the story of the little girl Bernadette, born in the Boly Mill in Lourdes, a little village at the foot of the Pyrenees. Separated from her family at the age of ten months, because of a domestic accident, her mother was unable to care for her. Back again in the Boly Mill to celebrate her third birthday. Separated from her family again as she began her teens. Separated this time because they had hit hard times. They had lost their mill, and they were on the street looking for shelter. They were given the use of an old gaol room. There wasn't enough food to go round, someone had to go, the oldest, Bernadette. Out to the hillside of Bartres, where she would be housekeeper and shepherdess for the Aravant family. Life was rough in Bartres. She herself tells us that she got meat twice a year, Christmas and the feast of St. John, a local feast there. No longer able to cope with it, she returned to Lourdes. Already fourteen, she hadn't yet seen the inside of a school. Back to the poverty of the Boly Mill. But back to the love of her family

On February 11th. 1858, there was no fire in the hearth in the Boly Mill. There was no food on the table. Bernadette, with her sister Toinette and friend, left the Boly Mill to go in search of bones to sell. Down by the rock of Massabielle they went, then the town dump on the banks of the Gave river. It was there on February 11th. that 'the beautiful lady' appeared to Bernadette, standing on the Grotto, inviting Bernadette to come closer. 'I didn't dare' she said. Instead, she took out her beads and began to pray the rosary. As she did the Lady fingered the beads with her. She invited her to come back each day for fifteen days. Bernadette kept her promise to the Lady on the rock, the Lady who promised that she would make her happy, not in this life but in the next. Through the period of the apparitions, she gave Bernadette many messages. The best known, probably being the invitation to come to the Miraculous Spring and wash in the waters. Since then, Lourdes has been synonymous with the sick. It has been a place of pilgrimage of prayer and of healing. Often not spectacular healings of the body, but deep inner healing of the heart and mind. Ironic that Bernadette, who brought the message of healing to so many, was herself destined to be always sick. 'My vocation is to be sick', she said.

The church has set aside February 11th, Feast of Our Lady of Lourdes, as a very special day for the sick. It would a be a nice gesture this week to visit someone in one of the many nursing homes around us here, or wherever someone you know is. Maybe Tuesday could be a special day for our sick, when we remember them. Maybe we could come to mass or visit the Blessed Sacrament. Our prayer might be; Thanks Lord for our health, be with and take good care of those we love, who are sick

St Valentine's Day

Valentine, the simple Roman priest who became the patron saint of lovers

There is another well-known feast occurring this week, one that might even get a bit more attention than Our Lady of Lourdes! that of course is the feast of St. Valentine.

There are many theories around how this feast originated. One being that in ancient Rome the lives of boys and girls were strictly separate. On February 14th there was a custom. The names of the girls were written on slips of paper and dropped into a jar. Each young man came along and drew a name from the jar. The lucky or unlucky girl became his partner for the festival of Lupercalia, which began the next day February 15th. The pairing originally was meant to be for the festival. But their ending didn't always coincide, indeed, it sometimes became the beginning of a long-term romance

During the reign of Emperor Claudius, Rome was experiencing a huge difficulty in getting young men to sign up for the army and go to war. Claudius believed that the reason they would not sign up was that men did not want to leave their wives and family. So, to solve his problem, he introduced an edict banning all planned marriages and terminating all existing engagements. Valentine was a priest in Rome at the time. He would not accept the right of the emperor, to deny Christians the Sacrament of Marriage. He secretly continued to do marriage ceremonies for Christian couples who did not want to live together, without the grace of the sacrament. Valentine was caught in the act of marrying a young couple. He was arrested for disobedience to the emperor. He was tried, convicted, thrown into jail. He was sentenced to be put to death with clubs and have his head cut off

While awaiting execution in the jail, he and the jailer's daughter became close friends and when going to his death he left a note in his cell addressed to her. He signed the note 'From your, Valentine'. On the 14th. of February 270 AD. he was executed. The day of his martyrdom, February 14th. became a day for exchanging messages of love, and Valentine became the patron saint of lovers

So when you are out Friday night having that lovely dinner, or when you are painstakingly selecting that priceless present for that someone special, spare a thought for poor Fr. Valentine, the simple Roman priest in the third century, who was clubbed to death, who had his head cut off, rather than deprive you of your Sacrament and consecration to each other in Matrimony. I'd hazard a guess that not too many of you came into mass today, thought that you would leave, believing that Valentine, the inspiration for all that happens on Valentine's Day, was in fact a simple priest. As an old man in the parish is fond of saying, every day we learn something new, is a good day! May St. Valentine bless all who share their love. May Our Lady of Lourdes take care of our sick, not just this week but always

6th Sunday in Ordinary Time (Before Ash Wednesday)

"Lord, please give me the eyes to see myself as others see me and as You see me"

This coming Wednesday is Ash Wednesday, the first day of Lent; a good time for all of us to look at and reflect on our Lives. It is a time, that we try to weed out the things that don't belong and to nurture and cultivate the good things that do, to try to become our 'Best Self', which is the person the Lord created us to become.

My favourite pre- Lenten Story Is about a 'padre' in New York, who was called out of bed one night to go on a sick call. It was bitterly cold with subzero temperatures.

So, he wrapped himself up in his warmest clothes, the heavy topcoat, the scarf, the hat and the gloves. On his way home, in the small hours of the morning, he got mugged, was dragged into an alley way and ordered to empty out everything that was in his pockets. All alone, and not a soul in sight, he didn't hesitate to do as he was ordered to. As he opened the top buttons of his coat to reach inside for his wallet, the scarf around his neck slipped off. The blinding light of the torch picked up the white of his collar. To his disbelief the voice said, 'Sorry, I didn't know you were a Padre, if I did, I wouldn't have laid a hand on you'.

Recovering his composure, the padre thought, this guy is not all bad, maybe I could reach him, and help him change his ways, So, picking up his packet of cigarettes and the lighter from the footpath, he pulled out one and lit it and offered one to his would-be robber. There was an even bigger surprise in store for him, "No thank you, padre', the replied, 'I'm off the smokes for Lent!'. I'm sure I don't have to point out the striking contradictions. Might be far better if he forgot about giving up the smokes for Lent and let people go their way in safety

We all have our blind spots, and we can often be the last to see them ourselves. Anyway, Lent is not about identifying the blind spots of others, but about discovering and doing something about some of the ones we have ourselves

Which do you think the Lord would be more pleased with; our giving up the "chips" that come in a bag, or our giving up the "chips"- we carry on our shoulders? And while I don't doubt that He loves us to spend time with Him in prayer, I wonder would He sometimes prefer if we spoke to that neighbour, we haven't spoken to in years

As I said, we all have our blind spots, including of course myself. We can be the last people to recognise our own. If we could name and tackle a couple of them this Lent, it will have been a good Lent for us and maybe even a better one, for those who benefit from the changes we've made. This Lent, beginning next Wednesday can be a time of grace for each of us and a time of change in all our lives. Before it can be either a time of grace or of change, it has to first be a time when we take a really honest look at our own lives and relationships, identifying what in my life Is causing harm to me, or pain or harm to those close to me

Our Lenten prayer might well be "Lord, during this season, please give me the eyes to see myself as others see me!' and even better, to see myself as You see me"

Amen

ASH WEDNESDAY

Jesus says; 'When you pray, not if you pray...'

Jesus, our healer, dispenses a triple prescription to help us break loose from things that bind us and offload the baggage that burdens us. Medication comes with important conditions printed on the box. The directions on the outside of the box are often as important as the medication inside. So, I invite you to open your hearts to the words of Jesus this morning. The Lord makes it clear that while others see the externals, what He sees is the Heart.

We notice too, that each section of the gospel passage begins with the words when: when you pray, when you fast, when you give alms. Jesus does not say, if you pray do it like this, or if you fast do it like this, or if you give alms do it like this. He says, when you pray and when you fast and when you are giving alms... Jesus takes it for granted, takes it as a given, that anyone who is His disciple, who is His follower or who is His friend, is doing all these already. He doesn't see them as counsels of perfection. He sees them as the tickets, without which you can't even get on the bus. If this is how Jesus sees them, that is a very good reason for our seeing them that way too; as essential medication Jesus prescribes for the journey, not emergency first aid kits we carry in case of a crash. So, let's all double down and make a real effort this Lent.

1st Sunday of Lent

For Christians, fasting was the norm rather than the exception

Some years ago, we saw Perseverance Rover land on the planet Mars, having already travelled four hundred million miles from this Earth. Science was already speculating on the prospect of someone from planet Earth one day landing on Mars too. Science pushes back the horizons of possibility, as it has been doing since the dawn of time. There is another science that enables us travel in the opposite direction, back into the story of our origins and our history, discovering from artifacts and habitations left behind in the distant past, the footprints of our ancestors on this Earth - the science of archaeology.

We can learn so much from ancient artifacts that have been discovered, as we can from the words and language our forebearers used. That was where I took a little journey recently, back into the story of our own people on this island, the people who tilled the soil and walked the ground we all walk today, the legacy they have left behind. Even the language they spoke is a little window into their inner world. The words they used with their lips spoke the values they held in their hearts, even something as simple as the days of the week. We learned them in Irish going to school, De Luain, De Mairt , De Ceadaoin and so on. While we learned them at school, few of us ever explored their origins. If we had, what would we have discovered about the mind and culture of our people? De Cead Aoin for instance, the Gaelic for Wednesday, means 'the day of the first fast'. De Deardaoin (Dara D'Aoin), the day of the second fast. De hAoine, the day of the great fast.

On Spy Wednesday Jesus was betrayed. They didn't just know this in their heads, they felt it in their hearts; they felt the need to honour the day by fasting. Thursday, (De Dara Daoin) the day of the second fast, because it was on the First Holy Thursday Jesus instituted the Eucharist at the Last Supper. They fasted on Thursday in appreciation of His gift to them. Friday, (De hAoine) the day of the great fast, because it was on Good Friday that Jesus died on the cross for us. They joined with Him in His pain and suffering to become one with Him.

The practice of fasting extends right back deep into our Gaelic roots. It is embedded in our Gaelic tongue. The words they used, and the tradition of fasting goes right back to our faith roots. The Lenten fast was for forty days, living in their own lives the forty days Jesus fasted in the desert. And fasting for them was not about giving up grapes or oranges for Lent! Fasting for our ancestors was bread and water.

Why Bread?

Jesus had used the miracle of bread to feed people.

Jesus promised the Bread of Life, which was precious to them.

Jesus broke bread and give it to His disciples in the Eucharist.

Jesus promised those who eat this bread would live forever.

Why water?

Water had flowed from the side of Christ on Calvary.

In the waters of the Jordan Jesus was Baptised.

Water is the symbol of life. Water is an instrument of purification.

For Christians, fasting was the norm rather than the exception. The purpose of fasting was not to endure hunger, for its own sake, but to totally join themselves with Jesus on His journey; Jesus, in whom they had at one and the same time total trust and total dependence. It is no secret that the total trust they had was in a God who was all around them and always beside them. Their total dependence was in a God who was always at their side. As the Gaelic would say, 'Fitte Fuaite' in their everyday lives. Their fasting united them with Him, giving them strength to cope with and adjust to everything life threw at them, in a world far tougher to survive in than the one we inhabit today.

Do we need at this moment in our history to embrace again that total trust they had in a God who is all around us and beside us and that total dependence they had in a God who is always at our side? Because if we do, there is no better time to do it than right now as this Lent begins. No better way to do it, than to take a leaf out of their book and take this Lent with some of the seriousness with which they took it. Taking Lent seriously means rising to the challenge as they did. Covid taught us how vulnerable we all are, how fragile and powerless we are on our own. Has the time come for us all to be humble enough to acknowledge it? Has the time come for all of us to return to realising our total dependence on God, as so acknowledged by our ancestors? Has the time come to take seriously their example and their practice of some genuine fasting during the season of Lent?

2nd Sunday of Lent

Lord, open our eyes that we may see ourselves as You see us

On the mountain top with Peter, James and John Jesus is transfigured before them. They must have been in shock at the difference between the Jesus with whom they climbed the mountain and the Jesus they saw on the mountain top; the contrast between Jesus, as seen through their human eyes on the way up, and Jesus, as seen through the eyes of His Father at the top.

Come to think of it, couldn't each of us say; there is the 'me', as I am seen through human eyes and the 'me' as

I am seen through God's eyes, and quite a contrast between those two also! I sometimes wonder if others, who really believe they know us well, saw us for a moment as God sees us, would they even recognise us, or like the apostles would they too be in shock. I remember one time when I was embarrassed by a bad mistake I had made. I wasn't in a good place and feeling disgusted with myself. I said to a good friend of mine, "if my late mother could see me now, she would be pretty disappointed at what she saw." My friend gave me a very good answer. "If your mother saw you now, she'd be seeing you through God's eyes. She would see you as God sees you, not as people see you. She would be seeing the totality of who you are as a person, not just the stupid mistakes you have made." Imagine if only we could all see the person in front of us as God sees them, not being blinded or blinkered to each other's faults, but seeing them in the broader canvas of all the good and the positives in each other's lives, seeing the person in front of us as God sees them.

The story of the Transfiguration reflects the stark contrast between Jesus, as seen through human eyes, and

Jesus as seen through His Father's eyes. It is a nice challenge to see ourselves as God sees us, through His eyes, and to see other people as God sees them, through His eyes. When we begin to see others as God sees them, they too become unrecognisable, from the person see through our own eyes.

Wouldn't this Lent be a good time for us all to ask the Lord to bring us too to the mountain top, asking Him to open our eyes like the apostles' eyes, to help us see each other as He sees each of us. Then, we won't be just celebrating a transfiguration, that happened on a mountain two thousand years ago. We will be celebrating a transfiguration, that's taking place in our own times and within ourselves. How we see and feel about each other in our own hearts will be reflected in how we treat each other in our relationships.

I think Jesus would be very pleased with us if we took away that message from today's Gospel, and even more pleased with us when He saw us living it. Maybe that's the message Jesus would like us to leave with today.

3rd Sunday of Lent

Knowledge informs us of what is right. Motivation empowers us to it.

Reading the commandments in the first reading today reminds me of the question I have been asked more than once. "Do they teach the commandments at school, anymore?" I get a sense there's more to that question than meets the eye, that if only the commandments were properly taught at school, they would be observed by everyone. I am not at all sure that that's the case. Knowledge informs us on how to be good. Knowledge in itself doesn't cause us to be good. Knowledge can tell us what is right. Motivation causes us to do what is right, and motivation is far more likely to come from relationship; what someone means to us, rather than from how much knowledge we have about them.

When someone is special and means a lot to us, we convey those feelings to them in how we relate to them. The phone call to a friend is not made because we have to, but because we want to. That trip home to visit our family is not made because there's a rule that says we have to, but because our family is important to us, and we need to. The visit to the hospital is not made because the patient's doctor prescribed it, but because our love for someone demands it. The extraordinary care for a sick family member is not because a daughter or son is trained in nursing skills, but because they have matured in loving skills.

As we relate to each other, so we relate to God. What He receives from us, just like what our mom or dad receive from us, is the measure of what He means to us, of how important He is in our lives. The stronger our motivation to please Him, the more influence what He wants, will have on our lives. Lent is a good time for all of us to look in the mirror, not to check if our height has changed, but to check if our heart has changed since Ash Wednesday; not to discover what we have done about our weight, but what we have done about our values. If knowledge was the highway to Heaven, those with doctorates and masters would be first in the queue at the gate. If knowing all the commandments was the way to Heaven, the devil would be the first one in the gate. He knows them all better than any of us ever will.

The key to goodness in our lives, is not the knowledge in our brains, but the motivation in our hearts. Motivation is driven by relationship, not by knowledge.

What's true of our relationships with each other is true of our relationship with God. Just as it's the strength of our relationship with each other that drives what we will do for each other, so it is the strength of our relationship with God that drives what we will do for Him. There's a saying in sport. 'If you are not improving, you are going backwards'. It's a wisdom we can all apply to our own lives during Lent. If our relationship with God is not improving during Lent, do we need to check if it is in fact going backwards. If we find that to be the case, it might have little to do with how we were taught the commandments in school, but everything to do with our relationship with God in our lives. The key to relationship is not knowledge in our heads, but the love and motivation in our hearts.

4th Sunday of Lent (Laetare)

A mother's love

Because today is Mother' Day, a day we pay tribute to the virtues and blessings of motherhood, I am conscious that some of what I am saying may not be the life experience of all mothers. To begin I want to acknowledge that there are mothers and their children, who as I speak, may well be trapped in very difficult relationships. We think of the people who were deprived of mothering because they had their children taken from them at birth. We think of people who are not mothers either by personal choice, or because they didn't find that loving relationship they wanted to share. We think of mothers in pain, who have lost their child. For some, motherhood is an accident, and not always a welcome one. For some, biological motherhood may not have been possible. We think of all who are in a difficult place today, still struggling to cope with the death of their own mother. On this Mother's Day we are remembering all of you, as we recognise the joys and blessings of mothers

I would like to begin what I have to say on Mother's Day with some lines that I particularly like, These are from a poem by Ms Moem:

Whose is the heart that bursts with pride, each time she sees your face

Whose are the eyes that dart about, to check your world is safe

Whose are the arms that wrap you up and hold you tight and close

Whose is the love that is always there, whenever you need it most

Whose are the tears that cry for you as you grow mature and free

Whose is the heart that aches so much in the space where you should be

Whose is the head that knows that you must find your path alone

Whose is the voice that welcomes you, each time you go back home

George Washington, who gave his name to America's capital city is quoted as saying this about his mother; 'All I am, I owe to my mother, I attribute all my success in life to her, everything I received, I received from her.'

I will conclude my tribute to all you mothers today by sharing with you the beautiful words of Helen Steiner Rice in her poem about mothers

A Mother's love is something that no one can explain,

It is made of deep devotion and of sacrifice and pain,

It is endless and unselfish and enduring come what may

For nothing can destroy it or take that love away.

It is patient and forgiving when all others are forsaking,

And it never fails or falters even though the heart is breaking

It believes beyond believing when the world around condemns,

And it glows with all the beauty of the rarest, brightest gems.

It is far beyond defining, it defies all explanation,

And it still remains a secret like the mysteries of creation.

A many splendored miracle man cannot understand

And another wondrous evidence of God's tender guiding hand.

Author: Helen Steiner Rice

5th Sunday of Lent;

Who will answer the little child's question; 'I want to see Jesus?'

The Gospel today begins with some Greeks coming to the Temple and saying to one of Jesus' disciples "We would like to see Jesus." A word on the background might be helpful. The Jews and Greeks at the time had something in common. They were both proud of who they were, but each for very different reasons. The Jews saw themselves as the religious elite of their era, chosen by God out of all the nations of the earth to be His people. The Greeks saw themselves as the cultural elite of their era, being seen by the world as the fathers of civilisation. At the heart of the pride of the Jewish people is their awareness of what God has done for them. At the heart of the pride of the Greeks is their awareness of what their people have done for themselves and the world.

They might be like the proverbial chalk and cheese, poles apart, but strangely they present a little microcosm of our world today, not just the big global world out there, but the world we are all part of, right here at home. There are those who see life's meaning through the eyes of faith and through the eyes of what God has done for us. They see this life as a journey, heaven as the destination and ultimate failure as not reaching that destination. There are others who see this world of ours very differently. They see this world as the destination, not the journey, and they see the ultimate goal as the success they can achieve in this world, not a reward that might await them in the next one.

As in Palestine two thousand years ago, so it is in our world today. There are many desperately searching to see Jesus, not just to be told things about Him. They can find all that information in the library or online, but they want to see Him. Where do they want to see him? Not in a picture or a beautiful painting, but in a life, in your life and in mine. And if they don't see Him or find him in us, where can they see Him or find Him? It's highly unlikely that anyone will knock at our door today and say; "We want to see Jesus", but our own little children within want and need to see Him. Their question may never be verbalised, but the question is deep in each of their hearts

As a great Saint of our church once put it; 'You made us for yourself O Lord and our hearts can never be at rest until they rest in you'. Who will answer our children's question; "We want to see Jesus?" Well, the easiest way to answer that question for them, is to answer that question for ourselves. Who showed you Jesus? Who showed me Jesus? You and I know who showed us Jesus, and we know that they didn't do it by handing us a book. They did it by loving us into our relationship with Him.

Do you remember how, as small children, we already knew who our favourite aunties and uncles were? It wasn't because we were told about it in words. It was because we sensed it in relationships, the warmth of our parent's relationship with them drew us into the warmth of our relationship with them

As with human relationship, so it is with our relationship with God. When we deeply love someone, we wear it on our sleeve. It becomes transparent to all who are close to us. When we have a real love relationship with God, it works the very same way; we reflect it in who we are. And that for all of us, parents and non-parents alike, is the best answer we can give to anyone asking the question today; Can I see Jesus?

2nd Sunday of Easter

Harbouring resentments is a contradiction to the gospel

Cardinal Joseph Bernardin, Archbishop of Chicago, was told in August 1996 that his cancer had returned and that he had only a short time left to live. He died the following November. During those last months of his life, he wrote a book called 'The Gift of Peace', reflecting on what had happened in the last three years of his life. A lawsuit had been filed against him by a young man named Stephen, accusing Cardinal Bernardin of the horrific crime of abuse. There was outrage and anger across the country towards him. News-media headlined the allegation across the States and it was covered coast to coast by the Television Networks. Then something totally unexpected happened: Stephen withdrew the accusation and acknowledged that it was false and without foundation.

Being falsely accused of being a predator or a perpetrator of abuse is a horrendous place to be. The media now became obsessed with the astronomical figures the courts would award the Cardinal for his upcoming defamation case. But there was a surprise in store for them. Instead of pursuing damages for defamation and potential ruination, Bernardin instead, invited Stephen, his accuser, to meet him. At their meeting Stephen delivered a heartfelt apology. "I want to apologise from the bottom of my soul" he said, "for the pain and embarrassment I caused you."

Bernardin presented him with a Bible, inscribed with words of forgiveness and celebrated mass with Stephan to heal both their woundedness. In the months left to him before his death, he wrote the book the Gift of Peace, in which he described his meeting with Stephen "as the most profound and unforgettable experience of reconciliation in his whole priestly life".

In today's gospel his disciples are terrified after the death of Jesus. They have now locked themselves away in a room, terrified that those who came for Jesus will now come for them and trying to get to terms also with what they themselves had done. In His hour of deepest need on the Cross, they had failed Him. Suddenly Jesus stands among them and says to them, 'Peace be with you' and breathes the Holy Spirit upon them. The risen Lord was reconciling His unfaithful and failed disciples to himself. In that moment they realised that they themselves were forgiven. And the bible says that 'their hearts were filled with joy'.

Having experienced the gift of the Lord's forgiveness, they are sent out to offer to others the gift of forgiveness that they themselves have received, 'Those whose sins you forgive, they are forgiven'. Like them, when we receive the Lord's forgiveness, we too are sent out to share the forgiveness we've received from the Lord, with anyone who has hurt us. We all have plenty opportunities to spread that forgiveness, in the daily challenges to forgive each other. To say those hard words, 'I am sorry' and to accept another's offer of apology.

In that book The Gift of Peace, which Cardinal Bernardin wrote, he said, "I was never angry with my accuser and had prayed for him daily throughout the ordeal. I had always hoped to meet with him." And his accuser Stephen had this to say, "I needed to reconcile to be at peace, I now have an inner peace and self-love I never had. Resentments and anger are only going to hurt me physically and spiritually."

The whole of the message of Jesus Christ, he said, is reconciliation. Division and chips on the shoulder, have no place among His followers. Harbouring resentments is a contradiction to the gospel. To be unforgiving of another is to be an agent of division, whether that be in the home or in the community. How can we genuinely say to the Lord in the Our Father, forgive us our trespasses as we forgive those who trespass against us, and then directly contradict what we've said to the Lord, by refusing to forgive or accept the forgiveness of our neighbour.

If you are ever tempted, to take that road of refusal to forgive, of holding a grudge, or setting out to get even and get your own back, just stop for one moment and think of Cardinal Bernardin. Which was he better off with, a million dollars to justify to everyone else that he was wronged, or the priceless gift of peace in his own heart and the priceless gift of peace that he gifted to Stephen? Which was the more relevant when shortly afterwards he went to meet his God?

Think of that moment in the Upper Room, when Jesus met face to face for the first time the very people, who had watched Him crucified in the wrong. And how He'd forgiven them their betrayal and released them, from their shame and their guilt. Just think, if we have walked in their shoes, how overwhelmed with love we'll be, when we meet our God and He sees the life of Jesus reflected before Him in ours. Don't let yourself be diverted by what others may think of you. What other see are only the externals. What the Lord sees is the heart, and there's nothing hidden from Him.

3rd Sunday of Easter

'Harbouring resentment against another, is like drinking from a poisoned chalice, and expecting the other person to die'.(Mandela)

Does it strike you as strange that for two Sundays after Easter, the gospel focuses on the fact that the Risen Jesus carries the marks of his Crucifixion? Not only does Jesus carry the wounds of His Passion, but He is showing them to people; Look at my hands and feet, he says, feel them, touch and see. Surely a God who could raise Jesus from the dead would have little difficulty in removing the marks of those wounds. If the marks are still there, and they are, then it is no accident that they are there. They have a meaning.

To understand the meaning of the wounds in the glorified body of Jesus, we must first understand their meaning in His crucified body. On Calvary these wounds crippled Him and crushed Him. They squeezed the last ounce of life out of His body. They left behind a corpse. On Easter Sunday we find the same wounds are there, but with one big difference, they have been stripped of their power. That is the meaning of the Resurrection, the stripping of the wounds of their power.

Most of us carry our own wounds. Sometimes it can be a mistake from the past, maybe even the distant past. I felt so bad about it, maybe so ashamed of myself.

Maybe it was someone that I wronged. I had always hoped and intended to correct the wrong. But somehow never got around to it and that person is no longer there to say sorry to. And over the years the guilt has just grown and grown. Now I carry around bucketfuls of it. Or I may feel I have been the victim of an injustice. I felt wronged. I let it play on me. I nursed it and the resentment began to grow. I let it grow. Now I have lots of resentment heaped up inside me. These wounds crush, cripple and destroy. It was well put by the person who once said that; harbouring resentment against another, is like drinking from a poisoned chalice myself and expecting the other person to die.

The message: Wounds destroy unless I deal with them. Wounds destroy unless stripped of their power to crush. How do I strip my wounds of their power to destroy me? Wounds can be stripped of their power to destroy, only by a power greater than the wounds, the power of love. My wounds can be stripped of their power, as the wounds of Jesus were stripped of their power, by the power of love.

At the heart of our faith is that truth, that we are loved. The truth is that each of us can make our own the following: God loves me as I am, not as I want to be, or could be or should be, or as others think I am, but as I am with all my faults and failings, as I am, in the mess that I find myself right now

And there is a second part to it. Nothing I can ever do, or have ever done, can change that. I am infinitely loved in my own brokenness. I am infinitely more loveable in my brokenness than in boastfulness. So, the risen Jesus in today's gospel, carries His wounds, but there is one big difference, they have lost their power over Him. Each of us may carry our own wounds deep within. If we believe in the Resurrection those wounds can be helpless to destroy us.

We celebrate today, what Jesus was celebrating in that gospel story. We carry the marks of woundedness in our bodies, but they are powerless now to come between us and God's infinite love.

4th Sunday of Easter (Vocation Sunday)

'Mom, but for that wedding ring on your finger, this ring could never have been on mine' Pius X

In the old days when priests were plentiful, June was the month when all the Diocesan changes were announced. When many saw the postman coming, they wondered if it was with the news that they'd be sleeping in a different bed in September. Which reminds me of a little anecdote of the local priest when he got his letter. He announced on the next weekend that he was being moved to a new parish. After mass people were coming across the yard, to tell him how much he was going to be missed. Things would never be the same in the parish again. One woman was particularly upset, there were a few tears. So, he felt he needed to reassure her. Mary, he said, I was talking to the bishop during the week, and he told me he is sending a particularly nice priest to you. I don't believe that Bishop, she said. But Mary, he said, why would you not believe your bishop, Because, she said, that's what he said the last time. And look what happened!

Thank God, despite impressions to the contrary often being given, the people and their priest, certainly in rural Ireland have by and large remained very close to each other.

Recent times have been difficult for both people and priests. Yet despite the many deeply upsetting things that have happened, a very high degree of trust persists in the local parishes.

Today is Vocations Sunday and I will begin with Tim's story. Tim was a neighbour's child back at home. Coincidentally he too was an only son. The year I was ordained, Tim did his leaving cert. The following September he signed into the Seminary. Fr. Tim ministered for years in Africa. But I haven't ever forgotten a conversation I had with Tim. It was about the way he described his mother's faith. You know, he said to me, for as long as I can remember, my mother went to Knock every year. It was always on the second Sunday in June. She would never miss it, not for anything. And then he said. She is going to miss it this year. The second

Sunday in June, she will be at my ordination. That is the date I will be ordained a priest. But I think she won't mind missing Knock for that!

Coincidence, that a day that had always been special for the two mothers meeting, that year, also became very special for their two sons. The day Tim was ordained a priest was the very day his mom always prayed at Knock. The values that led Tim to that altar that day, were the values that he'd absorbed in his home

It is not possible to talk about Vocations without referring to homes. Because the first seminary any young man goes to is his own home. His first Spiritual Directors are his own parents. They are also the best he will ever have because they both teach and inspire by their example. Without Christian homes, that is homes where Christian Faith values are lived and practiced and families pray together, without these, it is hard to see where vocations will ever come from. It is in the faith atmosphere of a good Christian home, that God's call can be heard and identified, and a young man or woman finds the strength to say yes. So, in a very real sense, in the most real sense of all, the future of the church does not depend on priests, It depends on good Christian homes. It depends on Christian parents living their faith

The message is beautifully illustrated in a story told about Pope Pius X. This happened long before he became pope. It was actually on the day he was ordained bishop. As the ceremony finished, the people queued at the altar to receive his blessing. As he moved along the altar rails there was a familiar face. As he gave his blessing, the woman reached to kiss his ring. He stooped low to whisper in her ear; Mom, but for that wedding ring on your finger, this ring could never have been on mine

In a sentence he said it all. You cannot speak about vocations, without speaking about homes. When I was growing up, there was a young man in college studying to be a priest.

He contracted a life-threatening disease. It became clear he wasn't going to make it. His bishop was prepared to ordain him before his death. He spoke about it with the family. It was his mother who simply said; 'If God wanted John to be a priest, he would have been a priest. It is what God wants that is important; not what we want'.

In her words were summed up what a vocation is. The mystery of God's choice has always baffled people. God calls whom He wills. We do not know why God calls some and does not call others. We don't always agree with His choice. Sometimes His choice can seem to create the perfect mess. But who would, on that first Good Friday evening, with their founder hanging disgraced on a cross and His followers scattered like scalded cats, who would have given this crazy sect any chance of survival. Two thousand years later over a billion people across the world commit themselves to following His Way of living. His church is the home of sinners and saints alike. Just as well because; if the church were only for the sinless, would any of us be eligible for membership. God uses human instruments to achieve His goal. They are only instruments, awkward and imperfect ones. In the view of today's world, often not fit for purpose - fallen ones and failing ones and sinners like us. Fragile human instruments in the mighty hand of God.

I will leave you with a final thought to reflect on that I picked up somewhere lately. I think it offers us all much to chew on. It goes; There is a crack in everything

God makes, and it is through the crack that the light comes in. In praying for vocations today, we pray not for perfect instruments. Jesus Himself didn't succeed in finding them. We are unlikely to.

We pray for ones with expansive cracks, so that despite their frail humanity, His light may shine all the more brightly, through their multiple and so transparent cracks.

5th Sunday of Easter

"Cut off from me you can do nothing".

The reference of Jesus in today's gospel to 'broken off branches', sparked off a few thoughts in my mind. I imagine most people, enjoying your walk in the park or the Greenway, if you stepped on or stumbled over a broken off branch, your first impulse would be to remove it, and get rid of it somewhere before someone else stumbles over it and they get hurt. Old broken branches, in the wrong place, aren't just a nuisance, they could also be a real danger to other's safety.

Jesus uses that image of the broken branches in today's gospel. The image He uses is so simple, so relatable to us all. Which of us hasn't at some time or other found one, picked it up and dumped it out of the way, before it hurt or damaged someone else.

And Jesus takes that image of the broken off branches and uses it to get us to reflect on our lives. He says, 'I am the Vine, you are the branches, as a branch cannot bear fruit by itself but must remain part of the tree or the vine, so neither can you, (bear fruit) unless you remain part of me'. Cut off from me you can do nothing.

Isn't that image, that Jesus uses, very clear and relatable to for us all? And as clear as the image he paints, is the lesson He teaches us by using it. 'I am the vine', Jesus says, 'you are the branches. Cut off from me, you can do nothing.' You could say, it's not a message that calls for a lot of elaboration, but rather a message that calls for serious application. And it's a message that only we ourselves can apply to our own lives. Obviously, a message no one else can apply to our lives for us.

Jesus is the vine; we are all the branches. What kind of branch am I? A living one because I am connected to Jesus the source of my life. Alive, because I have remained connected to the vine. Fruit bearing, because I am drawing my life from Him.

Or have I allowed myself to become disconnected from the vine and severed from the very source of life. Am I like that broken branch we've all knocked across, in our way? Could I have become a stumbling block, a danger to others? In the image Jesus uses; Am I bearing fruit or becoming firewood?

The values we choose shape the choices we make. The choices we make coalesce into our life's decision. The decision we've made with our lives, is the decision our God respects. It is not He who ultimately judges us; it is ourselves. He just acknowledges and respects the decision we've freely chosen to make.

Jesus says, 'It is to the glory of my Father that you bear much fruit.' Fruit doesn't grow on discarded branches. Grapes don't grow on thorn bushes. And Jesus says, 'Cut off from me you can do nothing. Anyone who does not remain in me, is like a branch that has been thrown away, he withers. These branches are collected, they are thrown in the fire and burned'. What a simple image Jesus uses to teach us. What a stark message, and what a clear choice He leaves us with

6th Sunday of Easter

"The others made me proud. Johnny made of me a saint". (an Irish mother)

I love the story about that mother who in her later years, was asked about how all her family were doing. Their dad had died, and she reared them on her own. Her pride was obvious as she related their stories one by one, and as they say, each of them had done better than the next. Hers was the satisfaction of a job well done. I thought you had seven in family, someone said, but you've only told us about six. Did I get that wrong, or have you left someone out? There was a pause, and then she continued. And then there's Johnny, she said. Johnny couldn't cope with books. In trouble with the friends at school. The only one of my family that was ever in trouble with the law. Johnny could never hold down a job. He never fitted in. Johnny was the black sheep, in the family, the failure. In truth, Johnny was the rake. All the others brought so much happiness. Johnny brought me pain. The others made me proud to be their mother. But Johnny made me something else. Johnny made of me a saint. Everyone there could see, that Johnny, the rake in the family, was the one who had that special place in his mother's heart. Johnny could not or would not claim that he'd merited or deserved it, in fact quite the opposite. That special love for him was a total gift from his mother's heart. Loved, not for what he did, or didn't do. But loved entirely because of who he was, his mother's son. Hers was an unconditional love for Johnny.

And having experienced that, Johnny was probably better placed than most of us, to understand the meaning of unconditional love. To grasp what it means to be loved for who I am, rather than for what I can do. The rake in the family, because of what he's experienced in his own life, can sometimes have a special insight into something that the rest of us often struggle with - that we are really loved as we are.

In God's family each of us is a "rake". We come to Him empty handed with nothing to show, except our total indebtedness to Him. But the emptier our arriving hands, the more we can receive!

In today's gospel Jesus says to His disciples: "As the Father has loved Me so I have loved you. Remain in My love." This is a love that has no ifs, buts, or maybes; a love we've neither earned, nor deserved, a love that is 100% pure gift. A love that you and I can only fully appreciate when we realise that each of us is a rake in God's family.

All we have to bring to Him is our empty outstretched hands. And the emptier we realise they are, the greater our capacity to receive what He's offering us.

I finish with a simple memory from Lourdes some years ago. It was confessions time in the pilgrimage and there were priests hearing everywhere. I went to confession to a fellow leaning against a pillar. Just as I was leaving, he called me back. "Don't you ever forget," he said, "that nothing you do, can change by one iota the depth of God's unconditional love for you." I try, in whatever situation I find myself; to remember those words, I offer them to you today, treasure them for yourselves. Don't ever forget, that nothing you do, can change by one iota the depth of God's love for you. That is the meaning of the opening sentence of our gospel: "As the Father has loved Me, so I love you. Remain in my Love.

Pentecost Sunday

"Son, if as a priest in the parish, you do your side of the work, God does His."

Today is the Feast of Pentecost, the coming of the Holy Spirit. It marks the fulfilment of the promise of Jesus, 'after I have gone, I will send you the Holy Spirit'.

Now I'm not going to try to explain who the Holy Spirit is by doing some quasi-forensic analysis of the Trinity, or I will end up like a good parish priest I knew who decided he would explain it, and having repeatedly tied himself up in knots, threw in the towel and his parting shot was; Yerra, "I can't explain it - 'tis a mystery anyway."
So, I'll take a leaf out of his book today and I won't try to explain the Holy Spirit, but I will invite you to meet the Holy Spirit and get to know him from His works, not from my words. It's well over fifty years ago now, since the day, still a seminarian, that I dropped in to see Fr Bob, who was certainly no teenager. The physical area of his

parish was huge. There were national schools he visited regularly dotted around it. He was all alone – no curate, and long before mobile phones.

In my innocence I asked him, how he could possibly manage. I mean, if someone died suddenly, if there was an accident, how could he be found? He simply said to me: – "Son, if, as a priest in the parish, you do your side of the work, God does His."

He had a clear conviction of God's presence among His people, a clear sense that God was in charge, not him; that he was just an instrument in God's hands, and that God ensured that he was where God wanted him to be, when God wanted him to be there. He was able to tell me, that in all his years as priest in the parish, he had never missed an urgent sick call.

It was a lesson and a truth I was to learn myself from personal experience as a priest. There are so many examples I could give you: I remember being away from my parish on a course one day. For no reason that I could put a finger on, I became totally uneasy, consumed with a feeling that I was supposed to be somewhere else. I racked my brain but could find no reason for the unease, but I was gripped by a compulsion that I had to go home. I left and drove back to the parish. Literally, as I put the key in door, I could hear the phone ringing inside. I ran to it in the hallway and grabbed it. A woman was frantic on the line. A man was dying in the parish, and she wanted a priest. At that moment I knew instinctively why I had been sent back and Who had sent me home.

I could tell you so many stories of such happenings. Like the day I walked out of a house I was visiting in a parish and a car on the road screeched to a halt on recognising me. Just up the road a man had dropped dead while feeding his cattle. The car driver was speeding off in search of a priest. Will someone try to tell me that, that was a coincidence, that at that instant I just happened to step out of the house?

I could tell you about driving up the street in the village I lived in, a man rushing out onto the middle of the road, frantically waving his arms in the air. A young father had just lost his life in an accident. Will someone believe that a was coincidence?

I could tell you about the day that I was sitting in a seat in a church reading my breviary, a church, not in the parish where I was based at the time. And someone came rushing through the door in search of a priest. There had been a fatal accident on the street outside. I could tell you many more stories, but there is no need.

I began by saying, I will invite you to meet the Holy Spirit and get to know him from his works, not from my words. When Jesus ascended into Heaven He sent the Holy Spirit. He promised that He would be with us all days, even to the end of the world.

His fingerprints are all over the place. His work is evident. The promise is fulfilled every day in our midst.

I have given you examples of his presence and his work. The Spirit of God, the Holy Spirit is among us and with us. For those who believe no explanation is necessary but for those who don't, no explanation is possible.

Communication Sunday

Keep your words soft and sweet, someday you may well have to swallow them!

A book written about life in the Kerry Gaeltacht, tells how the neighbours gathered in the 'rambling house' to share and discuss the news of the day. The star attraction was whoever arrived with a new story, like the fellow who came with the explanation for the drop in standards of the cured bacon in our time. 'God be with the days,' he said, 'when the bacon was salted, put in the barrel and then hung from the ceiling. The bacon has never been the same since they changed the way they cure it.' One by one they questioned him about these changes. 'Ah sure, nowadays', he said 'they put the bacon in a large container, they tow it out and drop it deep into the sea, leave it there for months and then bring it back. 'That,' he said, 'is the bacon on your table now.'

The woman of the house wasn't biting. She wanted proof. She wanted the source of this strange piece of information. The storyteller had his answer at the ready. 'Do chonachas sa phaipear e,' (I read it in the paper!) he said. That was the killer punch, the unanswerable proof. If it appeared in print, it was gospel, it couldn't be challenged. A little insight maybe, into the trust the printed word once had. Who would say today that if it appeared in print, it had to be true? The media plays a huge part in all our lives today. The good that media has done is beyond question. Good investigative journalism is the life blood of a democracy, demanding accountability and ensuring transparency, speaking truth to power and exposing scandals.

For people who are housebound, alone, or incapacitated, the radio, the television or social media may be their only continuous human contact. So, let's take that as read before we say anymore. The media, of course, has a responsibility to be fair, to be objective, to be truthful and unbiased. Equally we have our responsibility to be discerning and selective and to have a sense of balance evaluating what we receive.

If I may paraphrase Chesterton, one of the weaknesses of journalism is that it can present a picture made up entirely of exceptions. It presents a segment of the truth, but only a segment. It's news when a man fell off a scaffold in Limerick today. It's not news that no one fell off a scaffold in Cork. The number of divorces in Ireland last year is news. The number of couples who stayed together isn't news.

News is reporting on a 'segment' of life, but only a segment. If we are to believe all we see in the papers, unless we're going to lose faith in humanity, we ourselves have to ensure we keep a balance.

On this Communications Sunday, I would like to say something about 'words'. Words are instruments. Like all instruments they can be used or misused. The syringe in the doctor's hand can save life. In the executioner's hand, it can quench a life. Sadly, sometimes words too can get seriously misused; to bandy about slogans, to inflame emotions, provoke reaction, even to misrepresent truth. Labels, tags, and emotive slogans can be dangerous. I'll just take one example; we could take many. The word 'liberal' describes someone who is open and tolerant, who respects the viewpoint of those who differ, who allows others to cherish their own values. Liberal and tolerant people are a tonic to be with. Their philosophy, 'I disagree profoundly with what you say, but I will defend to the death your right to say it'. It's obviously a misuse of the word liberal to apply it to those who are in fact intolerant of other's views, when the other person's views differ from their own, dismissive and disrespectful of other people's values, when they differ from their own. So, on this Communications Sunday, it might be important to remember, that words have meaning; accurate and precise. Words are also instruments and can be used or misused. Misused, they can have sinister consequences.

In our time, we see plenty examples of both in media. We need to be vigilant, recognise and call it out, as we see it. We need to be vigilant, too, on how we use words ourselves. It would be hard to beat the old advice; Keep your words soft and sweet, because, someday in the future, you yourself may well have to swallow them!

The Most Holy Trinity

Faith is a plunge into the deep from a very high diving board

This weekend we celebrate Trinity Sunday. Belief in three persons in one, God; Father, Son and Holy Spirit, has been part of our faith from the beginning and is part of our faith today and will always be part of our faith. The response of faith is "I believe" not "I understand". I believe because God has said it, not because I can figure it out. In an age of unprecedented strides in science and technology, when we search and want reasons and explanations for everything, however vast the advances may be, there are truths the human mind can never comprehend. One of these is the mystery of God.

We are able to say, I believe. Many don't enjoy that capacity. We do, not because of knowledge we have accumulated, or that with our human brain we have worked out, but because of the gift we have received; our faith. Our faith was once a much easier gift to protect. We were surrounded with supports; the deep faith of people around us, the values they lived by, the eyes of faith through which they saw everything.

Many people today, don't seem to need God anymore, and this means very often that we have to make choices. As followers of Jesus, we must choose and constantly choose, sometimes the harder way, as others take the easier way, sometimes the painful way, as others take the painless way. In a world where pleasure, freedom, excess, and gratification are very much part of the daily dialogue, our faith vocabulary includes words like, control, moderation, sacrifice. It is not because they are more attractive. It is not because we like to be hard on ourselves. It is not because we always see a clear and compelling reason. We take the road we take, because someone asks us to and that someone is important to us, important enough for us to put His will before our own. We believe His way is the best way, even though not always the most attractive way. We know that His way is the right way, because we believe in Jesus and in what He said. That often demands painful choices. That puts heavy demands on us. That asks us to constantly make a choice, to take the option for Christ's way, not our way, to do so, not on proof available, but on His word.

We can't say in church on Sunday; we believe in the Trinity, three persons in one God, a mystery vastly beyond our powers to comprehend, and at the same time say on Monday; I don't believe in, or I don't accept, some other part of Christ's teaching, because that part challenges me or asks for a sacrifice. Faith is a plunge, a deep plunge into the unknown, from a very highly placed diving board. That diving board is 'personal certitude'. When we take that plunge, we leave the diving board behind. We can't have it both ways. We can't on one hand take the dive from the board and on the other bring the board with us under our arm, in case we want to change our minds on the way down.

Our faith demands of us that we be consistent. Consistency demands that we accept from God, both what He says about who He is, and about how I should live. As Pope Francis put it so well, "We can't have an a-la-carte Christianity, cherry picking the nice bits and ignoring the not so nice bits." We've heard the story of the railway gates left half open. When the gatekeeper was asked for an explanation, he said: 'I'm kind of half expecting a train!' We don't have that luxury in our faith. We can't be 'kind of half believing' in God. We either do or we don't. The response of faith applies equally to doctrine and to morals. That response applies both to the painless and the painful bits. Our response of faith to God is, "I believe", not because I have it all figured out, not because I always understand, but because I accept your Word and you have guaranteed your Word is Truth itself.

Corpus Christi

The Presence is the same, the recognition may sometimes be lacking.

The city of Lanciano, southwest of Rome, is famous because of its Eucharistic miracle. A miracle could be described as an extraordinary event, which is a clear sign of divine intervention. I hadn't heard of Lanciano until the late 90's. We were on a pilgrimage to shrines in Italy. Lanciano was included. Lanciano is known as the Great Eucharistic miracle.

There was a monk in Lanciano, who was plagued with doubts about Eucharist. Did the bread and wine really change into the Body and Blood of Christ? Was Jesus really present in Holy Communion? One day this monk, was celebrating mass. As he pronounced the words of consecration, the host miraculously changed into flesh and the wine in the chalice changed into blood. The monk was overcome with emotion. He called out to all the other monks to 'come and see'. "Behold the Flesh and Blood of Jesus Christ!" he declared. The archbishop ordered an investigation.

What had happened was certified as a miracle. The Sacred Host and Chalice are to this day in the Franciscan Basilica in Lanciano. Our pilgrimage visited the Basilica and had the privilege of praying before them. Eight hundred years later, what had happened, was again investigated. Eight centuries had passed since the miracle, but no sign of deterioration could be found. In 1970, Pope Paul VI permitted a series of thorough scientific studies on the precious relics, to verify their nature. This scientific study was conducted by Dr. Linoli, head physician of the hospital of Arezzo, (professor of anatomy, pathological histology, chemistry and clinical microscopy) in partnership with Dr. Bertelli, professor of human anatomy at the University of Siena. The analyses were performed in accord with scientific standards and documented.

In 1981, over a thousand years after the original miracle, and using more advanced scientific technology, yet another study was commissioned. The major findings were as following: The flesh, has the structure of the human heart wall. The blood is also of human origin with the type of AB. No traces of preservatives were found in the elements. Proteins in the clotted blood are also those found in the make-up of normal, fresh human blood. Given that these samples were centuries old, free of preservatives, they should have deteriorated. However, they had the same properties as fresh human blood and flesh.

That Sacred Host is still visible today in the monstrance in that church in Lanciano. The Precious Blood is also there in a crystal Chalice. The Basilica of Lanciano is a place of pilgrimage. But none of us need to go there to see the miracle. It is the miracle we experience each time we come to mass. That miracle takes place at the consecration, at the heart of every mass, and is present in the tabernacle of every church.

The miracle of Lanciano reflects the words of Jesus; 'I am the Bread of Life. He who eats my Flesh and drinks my Blood has life eternal and I will raise him up on the last day. For my Flesh is real food and my Blood real drink. The man who eats my Flesh and drinks my Blood remains in Me, and I in him.' Each time we come to mass, we witness a miracle, and when we receive Holy

Communion, we receive the Body and Blood of Jesus Christ.

Today, as we celebrate the Feast of Corpus Christi. May it help bring home to us, and may we always remember, that each time we receive Holy Communion, visit our church, or kneel before the tabernacle, we are in the presence of the miracle of Lanciano. We don't need to go anywhere on pilgrimage. This miracle leaves us in no doubt as to the presence of the Risen Jesus right here among us. The presence is the same, only the recognition may sometimes be lacking.

11th Sunday Ordinary Time

"We can do no great things, only small things with great love." (Mother Teresa)

Today's gospel is a parable, a story with a lesson. The story I'll tell you today, while it is certainly a story with a lesson, it is not a story I found in the bible, but hanging on the back of someone's kitchen door. It's a story about four people with unusual names. But I think you'll know all four when I introduce them. The names of the four people in the story are, Everybody, Somebody, Anybody and Nobody.

There was a very important job to be done. Everybody was asked to do it. Anybody could have done it. Everybody was sure that Somebody would do it, but Nobody did it. Somebody got very annoyed about that, because it was Everybody's job to do it. Everybody knew that Anybody could have done it, and Nobody realised that Everybody wouldn't do it. It ended up that, Everybody blamed Somebody, when Nobody did what Anybody could have done. I'll let yourselves work out the connection between that introduction and the next bit!

A young man went away to the seminary to become a priest. He took his vocation very seriously. He decided he was going to become perfect, and he laid out a timetable for himself to achieve it. He was going to pick one very important virtue, and he'd dedicate his first term to acquiring that. He knew, if he achieved that, he'd be well on his way. But at the end of his first term, he was still struggling badly. He found this was a lot tougher than he'd expected, but he had to be realistic with himself and he gave himself the first year to achieve his goal. He hadn't made it by the end of the first year. He hadn't made it by the end of the second year, but he had learned something important, he would have to cut his cloth to measure, and instead of trying to become 'perfect', maybe he should start with making a small change or two. The latest I heard is that he's still working on that! It is a bit like that with all of us and the great resolutions. We can be great at the sprint, but bad at the marathon. None of us are likely to convert the world, but there are things each of us can do to make our home a happier place this week.

The Little Flower once said that her method was, not to do "extraordinary things", but to do "ordinary things, extraordinarily well". She became a saint, so her way must have worked. That's something we could all try at home this week, not extraordinary things, but ordinary things done extraordinarily well. Mother Teresa has a lovely quote; "We can do no great things, only small things with great love."

So whatever about the job that everybody thought somebody should do, but nobody did, there is one job that nobody can do, and that nobody is asked to do, except ourselves. It is to take the first step, to each become the best person we can be in our own home; to make our home the happiest place it can be this week.

The longest journey begins with the first step. If each of us commits to taking the first step today, our homes will be better places tomorrow because of us. Just imagine, if we kept up that effort for a few weeks, how it could become a habit – become normal for us. Imagine how different our homes would be. Imagine how we would all be seeing each other's best selves. Certainly, none of our homes would need that poster hanging on the back of the kitchen door. In fact, the four characters in the story wouldn't live in our house anymore.

And isn't that really the message of today's gospel, planting that tiny little mustard seed in each of our homes and each of us having the patience to wait and watch it grow.

12th Sunday in Ordinary Time

Our Lord gives His crown of thorns to his friends.
(St. Bernadette)

One of the questions that I remember from my Catechism was: "Why does God sometimes permit the good to suffer and the wicked to prosper in life?" I can't remember the actual words of the answer, but what really interests me at the moment is not, what the answer was, but rather the fact that the question was there in the first place. People could obviously see that around them good people sometimes suffered, while a few 'not so goods' appeared to be getting away 'scot free'. They didn't think this was the way things should be. They wanted an answer, God needed to explain Himself.

Why doesn't God do what we would expect Him to do, reward the good and punish the wicked, not just in the afterlife, but right now in the present life? I'm sure all of us know good people, even some exceptionally good people, people whom we felt certainly didn't deserve it, who have been handed a huge cross that's crushing to carry; a young life, snuffed out before their eyes in one foul blow, the promise of youth destroyed by one wrong choice, dreams of happiness together forever in a shambles because someone betrayed their trust in a moment of weakness, the security of a life together annihilated by an illness, undreamed of the day they stood before the altar together. We hear a powerlessness in the words, what did we ever do to deserve this, and almost implicit in those words, a sense that we must have done something.

Why does God sometimes permit the good to suffer and the wicked to prosper in this life? Why, in the example of today's gospel, is Jesus asleep in the boat when a storm at sea engulfs His closest friends? Why is Jesus asleep, when the storms of life engulf His best friends today? St. Bernadette would say to us, "The Lord reserves His Crown of Thorns for His friends." To which another saint offered the reply, "Lord, it is no wonder you have so few friends, the way you treat the ones you have." But Jesus did not come to abolish suffering or to remove it, He came to give it meaning, a meaning that can only be grasped in faith, a faith not limited to a set of truths you can read in a book, but a faith which is trust in a Person. I think that message is well illustrated in a story. When the chips are down, it's not what I can prove that is important, but far more important is 'who do I trust'. This story is about a family whose home was engulfed in flames one night. The family, having gotten out safely were huddled together on the lawn in shock looking at the blaze, when one of them spotted movement at an upstairs window and realised that her little brother was still trapped inside. The father screamed through the smoke; "Jump Tommy! JUMP," his daddy shouted. "Jump and I'll catch you." Through the billowing black smoke came the answer "But I can't see you daddy." "But I can see you" daddy shouted back. "Jump and I'll catch you." The little boy jumped through the darkness into the unknown and landed safely in his daddy's arms.

In the gospel story today, the apostles were staring into a grave on the seabed for themselves, utterly powerless to control the situation, utterly powerless to do anything to save themselves. They threw themselves to the mercy of the Lord; "Lord save us, or we perish" and like that little boy, landed into the safety of His outstretched arms. The little boy, faced with the blazing inferno, plunged in total trust into the darkness of the unknown. He took his father's word in total trust and landed safely in his outstretched arms. When we are enveloped in pitch black darkness in our lives, reduced to utter powerlessness by a cross or tragedy beyond our control, the Father's arms are outstretched. He is calling us to jump. But we will never be grabbed by those outstretched arms, unless, like that little boy, we have the trust to jump. Unless, as Jesus has asked us to, we can become like little children and learn to surrender our own control and replace it with total trust in Him. We can't see beyond the darkness of that moment that surrounds us. But He certainly can. And isn't that, in the final analysis, what faith really is; the total trust, that even when we can't see them, that we know His outstretched arms are waiting to catch us.

13th Sunday in Ordinary Time

"She was dead," he said, "and she was brought back to life." (an experience related)

Today's gospel, the raising of Jairus daughter from the dead, reminds me of an incident that happened some years ago. There were over fifty of us in the room. We were taking part in a faith formation programme. We had all come to hear Fr Brendan. He was a great speaker and had come to 'shake us up' a bit. His opening line certainly set the cat among the pigeons; "There is nothing that Jesus Christ did, that I can't do". The crowd wasn't quite sure how to react, but one thing was sure, they didn't for one moment believe him.

Then he dropped a second clanger; "There is nothing that Jesus Christ did, that anyone in this room couldn't do". From the back of the room came a voice of protest; "Jesus Christ raised someone from the dead, I can't do that". "Oh Yes you can", Brendan said. "Oh no I can't, the protester held his ground".

The exchanges were threatening to become quite heated, but when calm was restored, Brendan recounted an experience he himself had. He was a curate at the time. He named the village and the woman in his story. In a tragedy she had lost her son, but that she blamed herself for the accident, had made the pain unbearable. She had become paranoid with guilt. She had pulled down the blinds on life. She had shut the door and locked herself away from people. No one could penetrate the barriers that she had set up. A good neighbour came and knocked on the door. There was no answer, she went away. She came back next day and knocked at the door again. There was no answer, but she knew her friend was behind that door. Many people would have given up. She refused. Every single day she came back and knocked, said who she was, and why she had come. Then one day to her surprise, she got an answer. The door stayed locked; they spoke to each other through the timber. That went on for a long time, but she kept coming back. She refused to stop believing that her friend could live. One day, the latch was lifted, and the light let it. It was only a small step, but it was progress. Back she continued to come every day. Eventually, and it had taken weeks, she got inside that house. She was the only one who did. The woman did not wish to talk. She wasn't able, at least not just yet. They drank endless cups of tea together. She kept returning every day. Eventually after many weeks there was a massive step, when for the first time that woman stepped outside her door. Today that woman has resumed normal living in the parish. "She was dead," he said, "and she was brought back to life. Brought back to life by someone who believed enough in her, to refuse to let her just vegetate and die, who gave herself totally to bringing her back to life."

"Miracles are not waiting to happen", he said, "miracles are waiting to be caused. Miracles don't happen," he said, "they are brought about." The potential to work that miracle is within each of us. When Brendan left that night, he left behind a lot of people far less comfortable than we were before he came. Until then the story in today's gospel of Jesus raising Jairus daughter from the dead, was something that had happened in a distant land over two thousand years ago. After he had gone, it was a miracle waiting to be brought about, in our parish. A miracle waiting to be caused by whoever among us was prepared to 'be Jesus' to that someone who is 'dead', just waiting for someone like that woman to love them enough and invest of their time to nurture them back to life.

14th Sunday in Ordinary Time

God can do most for us, when we recognise, that we can't do it for ourselves

In our second reading today, Saint Paul tell us that to prevent him getting too proud, the Lord has given him a 'thorn in the flesh'. He tells us that he pleaded with the Lord many times to take it away, but the Lord refused to remove it. And poor old Paul had to live with it and put up with it. Any of us, who has had a thorn stuck somewhere in us, even a small little one we pick up in our finger in the garden, knows that it doesn't let you forget for very long that it is there. Books have been written to try to answer the question; What was the 'thorn in the flesh' Paul had anyway, and the consensus would suggest, that it wasn't a physical thorn like one you pick up off a tree or briar, but rather that the expression is a figure of speech. That Paul, arguably the greatest missionary in the history of the church, had come face to face with his own personal weakness, which annoyed him, and he'd wanted so desperately to have got rid of it. No doubt feeling that as someone personally chosen by God he should be worthy of representing Him. He himself should be seen to have no weaknesses or failings. He should be perfect. That's what Paul wanted for God. But that was not what God wanted from Paul. This is really good news for each of us. We don't have to be perfect either.

Our faith is not like a Tesco or SuperValu Card, that keeps track of the points we clock up and that when we've clocked up the necessary total, the 'ticket dispenser' at the Pearly Gates will 'click' and out will pop our entrance ticket to heaven. Of course, we are all expected to, and we all want to do our very best, but when we've done whatever our best is, that doesn't earn our ticket to heaven. Even the greatest saints didn't 'earn' their ticket to heaven. Our ticket to heaven is a total gift from God. Earned and already paid for, not by us, but by the Son of God who died and rose for us. The goodness and quality of the life we do our best to live, and keep living, is the appreciation we show for that gift, and not the price tag that secures it for us.

So, like St. Paul, it's no harm that every so often we come a cropper, that we're sometimes disappointed with ourselves and that we have to live with weaknesses that we would prefer not to have. That is the thorn in the flesh for us, to keep us too, from getting too proud, from having any illusions that heaven is our due, and to keep reminding us of the truth of our faith. God can do most for us, when we recognise, that we can't do it for ourselves. What we have to do, like Paul, is face up to and take ownership of our own failings. It brings home to us that we can't do this on our own and we realise that we are being carried home by God. Our weaknesses and our failings are our little thorn in the flesh, that keeps pinching us and reminding us, over and over again, that perfection is not something I achieve in this life but is the gift that God has prepared for us in the next. Our inevitable mistakes are not there, to make us feel bad about ourselves, but rather that, like St Paul, they help us to realise every day, how much we need God's grace and God's help. Because this is one hill we can't climb on our own, we must allow ourselves to be carried in the arms of the one who is walking beside us, to ensure we reach our final home. Thank God for our shortcomings that make us humble. They protect us from the mistake of human pride, once we understand the reason we're given them. The Gospel then really becomes for us what it is meant to be, the Good News. The Good News that we never climb alone.

15th Sunday in Ordinary Time

To how many, has one's independence brought another's isolation?

Long before the advent of social media, Gallup ran a poll in the States to try to identify who were the happiest people in society. The group that topped the poll was older black women, who mainly lived in the cities. The second happiest group were older Hispanic women, many of them migrants from Central America, who were very strongly bonded into their communities. The third happiest group were older women generally. In 'the land of opportunity', the happiest groups of people were not those who had most of the material things to call their own, but rather those with the strongest sense of community, who lived for and took care of each other like extended families. It concluded that happiness is not found in what we have, but in who we have when the chips are down. In the gospel today when Jesus was sending out His first disciples, He sent them out, not on their own, but together in twos. Together He sends us out. Together He wants us to bring each other home. A famous French writer once wrote; When my time comes to meet my God, most questions He'll ask me, I think I'll be able to answer. There is just one that I am really fearful He might come up with, and that is that He might look me in the eye, then look around me, and ask me, Where are all the others?

We are not called to come to God on our own, in happy isolation. We are called to bring each other with us. In the Lord's eyes, we are each other's keeper. This is expressed beautifully in the immortal words of William Blake: I sought my God, and my God I couldn't find; I sought my soul and my soul eluded me; I sought to serve my brother in his need, and I found all three. My God, my soul, and thee."

Any of you who might be of my vintage, grew up in an Ireland that was rich in the values of community. We had the 'comhar' in the meadow and the 'meitheal' in the bog. In my earlier days as a curate in a parish, there was a tradition that every Spring Bill would assemble a 'meitheal' (a dozen or so men). Together, they would cut, save and bring home all my turf for the winter. In case you think I'm dropping a hint, I don't burn turf anymore!

But this was the tradition of the 'meitheal in action' alive and well in the community.

Writing about rural Ireland in those days, Christy Kenneally paints a vivid scene. It's the heart of the summer. The harvest is in full swing, and the pressure is on. The meadow of hay is down, and it has to get 'wyned' before sunset. There is a long evening ahead, all hands, or should I say all pikes are on deck. There's no question of finishing up at six this evening, there's too much is at stake. Then the news breaks that Paddy next door has just died. The men gather in a huddle in the middle of the field, caps in hand, bless themselves and respect the moment, a neighbour has just died. Life in his community came to a standstill. They stuck their pikes in the ground and headed home. How life in rural Ireland has become unrecognisable since then. Affluence has brought independence. The big meitheal has been replaced by the bigger machine. Progress is inevitable, but it can bring a downside too. To how many, has one's independence brought another's isolation?

It's a strange irony that the very tools God has given us, to build community, in our hands have brought about the very opposite; the fragmentation of community, and the loss of our togetherness. Our god given gifts are given to each of us for the betterment of each other and for the benefit of our community. But when we pulled off the label they came with and replaced it with a label that says; 'My gifts and talents are for my own use and my own use only', the result became the opposite to what was intended, bringing isolation, loneliness and lack of belonging in its trail. We need each other. We were made to be together. That's what it says on the tin. Happiness is in togetherness and community with each other. Isolation brings loneliness to us and is a super spreader of loneliness in our communities today.

In today's Gospel Jesus sends out His first disciples to build community. Two by two He sent out his disciples. Together he sent them out. Together He looks forward to our returning home to Him. And while we are on our journey here below, I know each and every one of us is doing our best, to follow the path the Lord has set down for us, as well as we can. And when that bus pulls in at our stop to collect us for our final journey, we can be confident, that if the Lord has a few questions for us, that we will be more than well prepared to answer them. Just, not to forget one little detail. Suppose He asks us the 'honours question'; "Where are the others?" will we be able to come up with the answer He wants to hear? On second thoughts, I think I have just made a mistake. That question is not actually, on the Honours Paper, it is on the Pass one. That's one of the essential questions, which means all of us have to be able to answer it. To be Christian is to be our brother's and sister's keeper.

16th Sunday in Ordinary Time

"When the sea is calm, I say my prayers. When the storm strikes, I concentrate on my boat" Recently I heard someone make the comment that it is very hard to find an atheist in a sinking ship! When I thought about it, it struck me that they are pretty scarce too in the ante rooms of operating theatres, aboard a plane being tossed around the sky, or even nearer home, in a good thunderstorm. I'm not for a moment saying, that people who say that they don't believe in God are only pretending. But I am suggesting that there is a sense of

God deep within each human being and maybe it sometimes takes the crisis to spring it to the surface.

In normal times we're happy to know He's on the sideline. But when our world begins to fall asunder around us, when our best plans begin to come apart at the seams, when the storm is whipping the slates off our roof, God tends to get instantly sprung from the sideline, handed the centerfield jersey and told to get in there and rescue us from the crisis. Maybe we're even tempted to offer him a little reward. We will see Him right if He doesn't let us down. Like my fellow county man, who when the plane hit turbulence in mid-Atlantic and he was sure the end was nigh, was heard praying, "Lord if you get me down out of here this one time, I promise you I won't ever again bother you!"

There's a story told about a Scottish boatman, who spent his life ferrying travellers the few hours journey from the mainland out to the Isles. Life on the ocean waves had brought him close to God. Setting off from the quay, he always blessed himself, shook a drop of holy water and said a prayer for a safe journey. One day he had a boatful of young revellers on board. They found this practice amusing and made it the butt of jokes. Unperturbed and unashamed, he did what he always did. An hour into their journey they were holding on for dear life, as a sudden wicked storm tossed them all over the sea, and everyone had been told to put on their life jackets. Apprehension became fear and turned to panic. The atmosphere quickly changed. Now it was the young revellers who were pleading with God. They got annoyed that the boatman ignored their prayer, concentrating entirely on his battle with the waves. When they challenged him, he simply answered: "When the sea is calm, I say my prayers. When the storm strikes, I concentrate on my boat."

A religion which keeps God's number beside that of the fire brigade, the ambulance and the emergency number for Shannon Doc, hoping it won't ever be needed, but under my hand, in the event of a major crisis, would be hard to recognise in the gospels. Today the gospel challenges us to answer a few questions. Is God a close friend with whom I'm in constant contact or a professional on-call, only when a crisis strikes? Is He captain of 'the ship of my life' when the sea is calm or the panic button to press only when I've lost control? Is He the straw I grasp when it's the only thing left afloat? Is my faith the most important relationship in my life, or an insurance policy I keep active in case of death? Is God, for me, my fire brigade service or my friend? The answer is to be found in the place He holds in my life, in the time He gets in my normal day, and in the priority He has in my home and in my personal life.

The answer is not found in my panic reaction when the storm is raging, and the slates are flying or when the diagnosis is frightening or when the blaze is gone out of control. The answer is found when the sea of life is calm, and I feel totally in control. Where is God in my life then? Is He left on the subs bench while the scoreboard looks good or have I Him wearing the No 9 shirt, steering the match on the pitch? Does that tell me whether He the insurance policy or the friend?

17th Sunday in Ordinary Time

"I did something about it, "God said "I put you in the apartment next door to him."

The incidents I'm going to share with you today will appear to you to be totally disconnected. I hope by the end; the connections might be obvious. Two ex-county footballers met in their local pub, one night. They were in total agreement on one thing, that the fellows wearing the parish jerseys today, wouldn't keep 'the ball kicked out' to the teams of their generation. Lamenting the lack of talent and the times they were rich in trophies, Johnny hit the nail on the head. 'Sure, they're doing nothing for the youngsters of the parish today!' His colleague, thought about it, took one more swig of his pint, eyed him across the table, and put this question to him. 'And who would the 'they', that you are referring to be Johnny? It wouldn't by any chance be yourself and myself.' He had hit the nail on the head all right. Even if it wasn't the nail that Johnny was aiming the blame at.

The man found in the block of flats had been dead for days. He had died of malnutrition and exposure. Neighbours, who lived in the same block, were appalled to discover the squalor and misery the man had lived in. Death had been a welcome release from the hell, he'd lived in. The very thought that any human being could be condemned to living in such appalling conditions, made the man who found him very angry; angry with life, angry with society, but most of all angry with God. After all, God was the one person who knew the squalor and misery in which this man lived. So he challenged God; Why hadn't God done something about it? He was a bit shocked at the answer he heard back from God. "But I did do something about it," God answered. "Whatever you did," he answered God back, "was pretty useless because it obviously had no effect. By the way, what did you do anyway?" And God answered, "I put you in the apartment next door to him."

In today's gospel, Jesus feeds five thousand people with five loaves and two fish. But well as know the story, we could miss a crucial little detail, the little boy who had the few loaves and fish. Even the Apostles had dismissed what he had to offer, as worthless. 'What is that between so many,' they asked. But little and insignificant though his contribution was, hopelessly inadequate, though it appeared to be, the little boy gave it. The Lord took his apparently insignificant contribution and used it to feed five thousand. A miracle triggered by the generosity of a little boy, who had little to give, but gave the little he had.

The message of it all: The two ex-footballers in the pub listing all the things that are wrong in their community and finding the solution; they, whoever 'they' might be, should be doing something about it. "And who might the 'they' you're talking about be, Johnny? By any chance, could you be talking about ourselves; you and me?"

A dead man's body lying undiscovered for days in the block of Flats: The man who found him, directing his anger at everyone else, even blaming God for allowing it to happen and doing nothing about it. "But I did do something about it," God answered back. "I placed you in the flat next door." And the message of today's gospel: the little boy who had so little to give, but gave it, and little though it was, it changed lives of five thousand.

We can all feel that we have so little to give or contribute. What difference could my puny contribution make? But, if we all gave the little, we have to give, just imagine the difference it could make. And by the way, let's not lose sight of the fact that this is what God gave each of us our gifts for. God's plan for our community is like a great big jigsaw, for which each of us is given a single piece. The plan is completed only when all the pieces are slotted into their place. But if the little piece entrusted to me is kept in my pocket and is not put on the table with all the others, God's plan for all those around me remains incomplete. And that gap in the middle of the jigsaw, is where the missing piece that I am holding onto should have been slotted in. The missing piece, that's still hidden in my pocket, is the gift or talent that God has entrusted to me, and for as long as I'm unwilling to share it, God's plan for my community can never be complete.

18th Sunday in Ordinary Time

If I could believe what you believe, not only would I be in that church each Sunday, but I'd crawl there on my knees, if I had to!

Sean was just seventeen when he took the boat. A connection had already fixed him up with a job in England. He would be working with the horses in the stables of a country gentleman. In the yard everyone had their own chores to get done. The bottom line was – they were done properly and dutifully. You were there till all your jobs were done. How long or how short it took was up to you. If you wanted to be off early on a summer's evening, then that was fine with the boss; you just got up and began that much earlier that morning.

On Sunday mornings Sean was up at cock crow. He had to be, to get his work done before heading off to mass. The nearest church was in the village a few miles away. The only way of getting there was on foot. It was a half hour's walk each way. Unlike home, mass over there always took at least an hour. Sean was the only one from the yard who went to mass on Sundays. He found that very strange, but he never missed a Sunday, not for the whole first two years that he was there. Then a couple of times, he was under pressure, he had let it slip. He was tired, or the weather was bad. Over time that got easier, and he didn't any longer feel as bad about it. And soon those Sunday morning walks to the village were just a memory. The change didn't go unnoticed. One evening the gentleman of the manor called Sean in. He wanted to know if there was something wrong. "Look," he said to Sean, "I noticed, when you came to the yard here first, you were up at dawn every Sunday morning. You got all your work done and then headed off to church. I could see that this was very important to you. I notice things have changed. I notice you don't do this any longer. Tell me" he said, "why was it anyway, that you used to get up so early and head off to church. I often wondered how and why you did it." "Oh! Sean said, "back home, where I came from it would be unheard of for Catholics to miss mass on Sunday morning." "Is that so?" the boss said, "tell me why it is so important for you Catholics to go to church every Sunday morning. What happens there anyway that's so important?" "Well," Sean explained, "when we Catholics go to mass on Sunday, we're gathering to meet our God. We tell Him about the mistakes we've made. We tell Him that we are really sorry, and He forgives us. Then our God comes down to us in Holy Communion. He comes inside each of us and stays with us." "Son," the boss said, "I'm not into this religion business. In fact, I'm not sure I even know whether or not there is a god. But I want you to know something, from me. If I could believe what you tell me that you believe; that the God who made this universe, the God you say you believe in, that on Sunday mornings, He would come especially to my village to meet me, I tell you something; if I could just believe what you believe, not only would I be in that church each Sunday morning, but I'd crawl the three miles there, - on my knees, if I had to.

Some of us are around long enough to remember the times Sean spoke about, when our weekend mass was part of the staple diet of practically every family in our parishes. Granted, things have changed significantly in Ireland in the intervening years. In more recent times we had the upheaval caused by Covid when our churches were closed for significant periods of time. The Sunday obligation was suspended. We all coped as best we could. Many parishes had cameras fitted in their churches and people were able to join with their parish community from the comfort of their own homes. This was very much appreciated. Thank God the Covid days are now behind us. But there is a sense that our parish communities have not returned to what they were in the pre-Covid days. I remember a parishioner sharing with me at the time; 'You know mass in my own home is so cosy and so intimate and I have got so accustomed to it, I think I'm going to find it difficult to start going back to the church again."

Would a little reflection on the words of that English country gentleman gently nudge us to do a little re-think. 'Sean, if I could believe what you believe, not only would I be in that church every Sunday morning, but I would crawl there on my knees if I had to'.

19th Sunday in Ordinary Time

Do we reject the message because of our problem with the messenger ?

Johnny hadn't darkened the door of the church in years, not since he'd had a difference with a man of the cloth. Sunday morning as the parishioners made their way to the church, they usually met Johnny making his point. He was usually heading off in the opposite direction.

It was on a summer Sunday morning and Johnny was on his usual walk. The sun was splitting the stones and Johnny had walked a long way. He was parched with the thirst. What he wouldn't give for something to wet his lips. And then he knocked across the 'spout', that piece of a chute sticking out of the side of the ditch. He cupped his hands to trap the water, splashed it on his face. He did it a second time and slugged it down. My god but was it refreshing! He felt like a new man. Over the ditch and through the fields, he went, to trace this spring all the way back, and find its source. He was brought to a sudden halt by something he'd never expected. He looked closer at his discovery. He knew it must have been a fox, too small to be a goat, but that carcase must have been there for months. The flowing spring had washed away everything. All that was left in the clear water now were the bare bones. My god, had he known what was upstream in the spring, he'd have been prepared to die of dehydration, rather than let a drop of that water pass his lips.

Some days later, sitting in his kitchen, Johnny was remembering how his heart had lifted when he'd first seen that spring and how he'd marvelled at the life-giving qualities of the water. It had transformed his body from dehydration to invigoration. So much so, that he'd been driven to find its source. Then the penny dropped, the contradiction in his life. He had rejected out of hand the life-giving Word of God. He had deprived himself of his mass and eucharist, not because he had any problem with them. His problem was with the channel through which they came, the flawed human being, the priest he'd had his differences with, the bones through which the spring was flowing.

In the Gospel today Jesus tells his own people I am the Bread of Life; I am the Bread come down from Heaven. Whoever receives this Bread will live forever. But the people couldn't take it, not from a carpenter's son. He'd be better advised to return to what he did best, the chisel and plane in Joseph's workshop up the road. Their problem was as much with the messenger as the message. Because they couldn't see beyond the human frame that stood before them. The scene is repeated in our gospel, today. The person speaking is the same; - Jesus the Son of God. The big difference is that we are the listeners that He is now addressing. He is saying to each of us right here, right now, I am the Bread of life come down from heaven. Whoever receives me will live forever. No ifs, buts or maybes about that, straight from the shoulder.

How blessed we are. We are here present, listening, and receiving his words. But in some ways, nothing has really changed. In our times too, how many have rejected the message, because of a problem they have with the messenger, a problem with the channels through which the message comes, the upstream bones? We all know that we can find plenty to criticise about our church, if criticism is the business we are in. We can find plenty excuses to reject our church, if finding such excuses to reject, is what we are about. Like the people in His own hometown, we can deprive ourselves of the message today because we have a problem with the messenger.

We can experience the lifegiving qualities of the spring, or we can reject it because of the bones through which it flows. Those bones can be the 'institution' or an individual priest. Many confuse the 'messenger' with the 'message' and equally confuse 'a good reason' with 'a good excuse'. Like the man walking the roads on Sunday mornings, we can even go out of our way to make our point. But whose is the loss, impoverishment, and deprivation? It ultimately returns to be our own.

Good to think about that in the context of today's gospel; "Anyone who eats this bread will live forever. The bread I give is my own flesh for the life of the world. Everyone who believes in me will have Eternal Life." What an injustice we do ourselves, if we reject the message, just because we have a difficulty with the messenger; if we reject the gift of the Lord Himself because we have a problem with the channel through which it flows.

The Assumption of the Blessed Virgin Mary

'Follow her footsteps, and you will arrive at the destination where she now is.'

When I went through the gates of Maynooth for the first time many years ago, I was looking at a seven-year journey up ahead of me. When you are just eighteen, seven years seems a lifetime. That seven-year journey was to bring many twists and turns, challenges and questions along the way. Am I being called or just deluded? One of the great encouragements for me along that road was my friend Luke. We were from the same area. He was three years ahead of me when I began, so he was always three rungs of the ladder ahead of me on the climb. When I was grappling with many questions and many challenges, I could lift the eyes and there, up ahead of me was Luke, and the dream for me, seemed to become more attainable. If Luke had coped with these challenges, maybe I could too.

I remember a few years ago watching an excellent programme on television on the history of hurling. One of the things that really struck me while watching it, was how the very heroes and idols of the game today, attributed the heights to which they had aspired, and the achievements they now had, to the motivation they themselves got from the idols of the game, as they themselves grew up. 'If he could do it, maybe so could I', became their dream. And they picked up a hurley and ball, headed out belting a sliotar off a wall. I don't doubt that today in Limerick, there are hundreds of little boys across the county, sliotar in hand belting it off a wall, seeing themselves as the new Cian Lynch and the next Aaron Gillane. Those who've gone before us and achieved their dreams, whether in the seminary or on the hurling pitch, inspire those who come behind them, to follow in their steps.

Today we are presented with our idol by the Lord Himself. 'Follow her footsteps,' He confidently tells us, 'and you will arrive at the destination where she is now.' That's the message of the Feast Day we celebrate this weekend; The Feast Day of Mary's Assumption into Heaven, a signpost and an inspiration for us who are still on our journey. Where she has reached, we can one day arrive. As Mary has made it safely home, so can we if we follow in her footsteps, each of us doing our very best to say yes to what God is asking of us, each day, as Mary did, what was asked of her.

One ship has rounded the headland in the final journey. We are all the 'little' boats following on behind in her slip stream. And when things are tough and challenging, as of course they will be, knowing that we are following in her slip stream, will give each of us the strength to rise to the challenges and to stay the course as Mary did. Mary's boat has rounded the final headland and made it safely home to harbour. By doggedly following in her slipstream, we too will berth beside her at our eternal port.

21st Sunday in Ordinary Time

He's not into the business of lowering the standards to keep the crowd!

There are stories going around in Palestine about a 'strange' man who is preaching a 'strange' message. Gone is the "eye for an eye and tooth for a tooth". In its place, "offer the wicked man no resistance, do good to those who hate you, pray for those who persecute you". There are stories about a paralyzed man getting up and walking. Some are even saying that 'this strange man' can walk on water and feed thousands out of a few baskets of bread. And the strangest thing of all is that huge crowds follow Him.

Today for a few minutes we join the crowds who have gathered. The scene is set. Jesus is above them on the side of a hill. Crowds stretch as far as the eye can see. He has just dropped a bombshell on them all. He has announced loud and clear to the thousands gathered; I'm going to give you my Flesh to eat and my Blood to drink. He's just gone

one step too far. A murmur of dissent is running through the crowd. What's more, the movement has begun. For some, this has made up their minds. They're turning their backs and walking away. Jesus, from where He's standing on the hillside up above, can see what's happening; the people drifting away. What does He do? What do we expect He would have done? What would we have done, if we were in His shoes? Call a few of the apostles and send them off after them. Call them back, tell them they've misunderstood me. Tell them to come back and I'll explain and make it easier to take.

But that's not how Jesus operates, then or now. In what must be a moment of intense sadness and disappointment for Him, as He sees the people drift away and head back home, how does He cope? What does He do? He turns to those beside Him, His closest friends, His chosen few, and He says to them: - Do you want to go and join them? "Do you also want to go away?" They say: - "To whom shall we go? You have the message of eternal life!"

That gospel passage has a powerful message. We, who are gathered here, are the crowd on that hillside today. The speaker hasn't changed. The message is the same. And in our time for many, the response is the same. This is intolerable language, who could accept it. Jesus Christ calls but doesn't force anyone to respond. He respects everyone's freedom of choice to say yes or to say no; to belong or turn our backs and walk away. But He makes it very clear what the conditions of belonging are. Now, as then, He asks us all to make our decision. We are either with Him or against Him.

The teaching of Jesus Christ is clear. For those who say "yes" and follow him, He makes it possible. By those who shake their heads, murmur and turn away, He, is saddened, but respects their freedom. He's not into the business of lowering the standards to keep the crowd. As we make our choice, there is one thing He asks for. He asks us to be honest, honest with ourselves and honest with our God. We don't have the choice of believing that the gospel is the voice of Christ, when it suits me, but not believing it is the voice of Christ when it challenges me. And since we can't pull the wool over the eyes of Jesus, the only eyes we may be pulling the wool over, is our own.

Jesus Christ calls, He doesn't coerce. He invites, He doesn't force or pressurise. For those who choose to say yes and follow Him, He lays down clearly a way of life that He expects us to live. Each of us has to choose. Each of us has to take responsibility for the choice we make.

The responsibility of the church He founded is to teach the message of Christ, not as some may think, to impose or enforce it. We teach as best we can. You respond as best you can. But once the message of the Gospel is put out there clearly, the responsibility for what happens to it then, does not rest with the preacher. It then rests with the hearer.

As Paul said to Timothy: 'In the presence of God and of Christ Jesus, I solemnly urge you to preach the message, to insist upon proclaiming it whether the time is right or not. The time will come when people will not listen to sound doctrine but will follow their own desires and teachers who will tell them what they are itching to hear. They will turn away from the truth and listen to legends. Endure suffering, do the work of preacher, perform your duty as a servant of God.'

22nd Sunday in Ordinary Time

Structures are in place to serve a purpose.

Anthony De Mello tells a lovely story about a small monastery. Brother Anthony had a pet cat. Every time brother Anthony went to the chapel, the cat came along with him. The cat, strutting around the sanctuary during their prayers, was driving all the other monks crazy with distraction. So, they came to an agreement that all the monks were happy with. The cat could be there provided he was tied to a ring in the sanctuary wall, but he couldn't be strutting around during the community's prayer time. The cat now became a permanent presence at the monks' prayer. Years passed by, older monks passed on. Younger monks came and took their place. During the monks' time of prayer together, brother Anthony's cat was always tied to the ring in the sanctuary. Finally, brother Anthony died, but the cat continued to join the monks at prayer, so the cat continued to be tied in the sanctuary. Finally, the cat himself died. When he did, the monks found a replacement cat, because by now no one in the monastery could remember a time when the monks had come to pray, that there wasn't a cat tied in the sanctuary during prayer time.

And so, the tradition continued for generations. When the monks came to pray, they always ensured that there was a cat tied in the sanctuary during their prayer. Years later, it is said, a learned monk researching the origins of the practice wrote a distinguished thesis on the essential need to have an Ashram cat tied in the sanctuary whenever monks gathered for monastic prayer.

De Mello's story illustrates a point very well. Structures are put in place to serve a purpose. When the purpose they served is no longer relevant, the structure is binned, not canonised for its own sake. In the first reading of our mass today, Moses is telling God's people that the commandments are important, because they have been given to them by God. The purpose of the commandments is that God's people have life and that keeping the Commandment will keep them close to Him.

In the gospel, we see Jesus come down heavy on the Pharisees. Now the Pharisees were good people. The Pharisees were good religious people. They observed the law to the letter. Problem was that that was all they did.

They observed the law to the letter but had lost sight of its purpose. The purpose of the law was to keep the people close to their God. The Pharisees had elevated the law to such a height, that instead of bringing His people close to God, they had made God unreachable for His people. Jesus came down heavy on them, not for observing the law, that was praiseworthy, but for losing sight of its purpose - that was inexcusable.

Each time we gather at the altar we remember the words of Jesus; "He who eats My flesh and drinks My Blood, lives in me and I in him." He says, "as I who am sent by the Father, myself draw life from the Father, in the same way whoever eats me, will draw life from me." Jesus is talking about the mass, and He is telling us that when we receive Holy Communion, we draw new life from Him. As we leave the church, we are bringing Him with us and within us. So, we don't come to mass, just to fulfil an obligation. The purpose of our coming to mass is to ourselves receive the life of Christ into our own hearts, so that we can then take that new life out from here, in order to spread it in our community.

The final blessing of our mass does not say to us that we can go in peace because our obligation is now fulfilled for this week. What the final blessing does say is; go in peace to love and serve the Lord in your community. Jesus does not ask us to recite creeds, but to perform deeds. Our mass is where we come to in order to get the strength we need, and from where we go back bringing that strength with us, into our community during the week.

Our observance always calls to be authenticated by our lives. Outward observance not matched by inner conviction, leaves us open to those accusations levelled at the Pharisees of canonising the obligations, for their own sake. We could become like the monks in De Mello's story, deeply protective of structures and obligations but having lost the purpose for which they were put there for in the first place. Jesus is hard on the Pharisees in the gospel today. He says, "This people honours me with their lips while their hearts are far from me. The worship they offer me is worthless." God forbid that we should ever leave ourselves open to that in our own day. The best defence against it is to apply the standards of Jesus to our lives. We come on Sunday to get the strength to live by His values on Monday. This commandment that is at the very heart of the message of Jesus: "To love the Lord our God with our whole heart and our whole soul and our own mind and, to love our neighbour as ourselves." To put it succinctly, that what we come to profess together in church on Sunday, we then authenticate by how we live with each other on Monday.

23rd Sunday Ordinary Time

"Do not try to combine faith in Jesus Christ with making distinctions between classes of people."

A woman tells this story about an experience she had when she was at mass in the States one Sunday. As she arrived at the front door of the church, there was a shabbily dressed man sitting on the footpath, holding up a cardboard placard which read; 'Please help me'. In front of him on the ground was a box with some coins in it. He was trying to catch the eye of everyone going into mass. Her first reaction was to make sure he couldn't catch her eye, so she slipped past admiring the flowers at the other side and quickened her pace to get inside the church.

Just as mass was about to begin, she looked back and spotted the man now inside the church, moving slowly forward in search of a place to sit. There was an empty seat next to her. She hoped he wouldn't spot it and sit beside her. To her relief, he found somewhere else. She noticed how others were looking at him. When it came to the Readings, the man they had all being avoiding, stood up and began to make his way towards the altar. She could feel the sense of apprehension in the church, as everyone wondered what was going to happen next. The man continued walking forward, by now he was in the sanctuary. Next thing, he turned left, walked to the ambo and began to read. Then he turned around, walked back to his seat and sat down.

The shabbily dressed man begging outside the door on their way in, whom they had given a wide berth to, making sure not to make eye contact with, whom they feared was going to sit beside them in the seat, was in 'cahoots' with the pastor. He was a 'plant'. The reading from St. James he had just read was "My brothers, do not try to combine faith in Jesus Christ with making distinctions between classes of people." Leaving the church that day, they were in no doubt about the message of the reading. It was not because of the great sermon the pastor gave, in all likelihood he gave none, other than to invite them to remember the feelings they had towards that man when they saw him begging on the footpath on their way in and when he was searching around to find a seat. The Word of God comes alive within us when we recognise our own lives in the story.

Hopefully that little story will help us to pause and think and help us never to judge the book by the cover, especially when the book is another human person. The cover, just the shabby outside that we see.

24th Sunday in Ordinary Time

There is no point in walking to preach, unless you preach as you walk.

On reading the second reading of our mass today, I was reminded of a programme I had watched some years ago. It was recalling St. Francis of Assisi in dialogue with a young monk. They had decided to go into the local town to do some preaching. On arriving in the town, they walked the streets together. As they went, Francis seemed to have a word for everyone; there was a greeting for one, a handshake for another, a blessing for a child that came along, a pat on the shoulder for others, a wish for all. As the day wore on and they continued to walk the streets, the young monk, who no doubt had prepared for this assignment, grew a little impatient with what was happening, and he said to Francis, "Didn't we come to preach? When are we going to start?" Francis looked at him caringly, and answered: "My Brother, we have been preaching since we arrived." The commentator put the message beautifully when he concluded: There is no point in walking to preach, unless you preach as you walk.

In today's reading St. James puts the same message before each of us, when he asks whether we can separate faith from life. In his own case he points to his good deeds, 'the evidence of his life' as validating the existence of his faith. He challenges us to show how we can validate our claim to have faith unless the evidence of our life authenticates it. Indeed, he might even be hinting to us that whether our faith is authentic or not, is a judgement that might be better made by those who have to live with us. As somebody once said: if for a day a camera was on me, and if in the evening time a neutral were given the job of evaluating the content, would they find enough evidence to convict me of being Christian?

The Lord begins to believe our protestations that we love Him, when those around us begin to experience that love. How true the words of Francis: we cannot walk to preach unless we preach as we walk. How penetrating the wisdom of St. Paul: "Faith without good deeds is dead."

25th Sunday in Ordinary Time

'I have no idea where I got that strength from'.

Jesus then took a little child, set him in front of them, put His arms round him and said to them, "Anyone who welcomes one of these little children in my name welcomes me, and anyone who welcomes me welcomes, not me, but the one who sent me." To whom was Jesus addressing this message? He was speaking to his nearest and dearest, to the disciples who were closest to Him. He was speaking to the twelve, among them, Peter, who would be the first Pope. He wanted to tell them something that was very important and to do it He took the image of a little child. It was an image He chose to use many times.

"Unless you become like little children, you will never enter the Kingdom of Heaven."

One of the beautiful characteristics of a little child is trust. In Ballybunion some years ago, I noticed a little toddler fascinated with the sea. Gingerly he picked his steps as he waddled in its direction, toddling along the sand, right to the verge of the water. Then as a breaking wave rolled in his direction, he turns and scampers away to beat the incoming water. Having won the race, he follows the water as it recedes back. But as he sees it turn and coming again, he scampers off to safety. Each time he wins the race. He's enjoying his little victories, but he never gets the courage to venture putting his feet into the water. The fear of the unknown drives him back to safety. Daddy, who has been carefully watching from a distance picks himself up off the sand and takes his little child by the hand. Together, they approach the water. As the wave breaks, the little child gathers himself to run for safety up the beach, but daddy presses his little hand in his. In that moment the child senses a new security. The big ocean may be thundering out there, but with his hand in daddy's hand he's safe. He now has no fear as the water laps around his feet.

For many people the ocean of life can be very turbulent. Waves that crash in our direction instil fear in our heart. We can freeze and panic as we are thrust into the unknown. But those who, at such difficult moments in life's journey, find that their hand is firmly in the grip of the hand of the Man from Galilee, discover, in that grip, a strength, a courage and a protection, that leaves them wondering from where they have got it. How often have we heard them say, 'I have no idea where I got that strength from'.

Daddy, in the story may be powerless to stop the waves. Daddy in the story is powerless to turn back the tide. But when he's held securely by his daddy's hands even the crashing waves or the oncoming tide, have lost their power to scare the life out of the little child.

That in a nutshell is what Jesus is saying to us in the gospel. The meaning of faith for us is having the total trust of that little child. It is having a certainty in our hearts that, regardless of the waves that come crashing down around us, or the waters threatening to engulf us, no harm can come on us if we make sure that our hand is always safely locked in 'Our Daddy's' hand, held firmly in the grip of the hand of the Man from Galilee.

Faith, is knowing that when the waves of life's journey are threatening to overwhelm us, His protective hand is always there for us to grasp. Jesus says: "Unless you become like little children..." Faith is discovering the meaning of that kind of trust. Take home with you today the image of that little child on the beach, and you will be taking home in your heart the message of Jesus for us in the gospel today. Taking it home will be the easy part. Becoming that little child will be the challenging bit!

26th Sunday in Ordinary Time

What children see their parents do, is formative for them.

The Brothers Grimm have a lovely fairytale. I would like to share it with you.

Once upon a time there was a little old man. His eyes blinked and his hands trembled. When he was eating, he clattered the cutlery distressingly. He missed his mouth with the spoon as often as not. He dribbled his food and messed up the table. He lived with his married son because he had nowhere else to live. His son's wife couldn't cope with what was going on. "In-laws should not live in," she said, "we are entitled to our own space." So, she and her husband took the old man, gently but firmly to the corner of the kitchen. There they sat him on a stool by himself and they gave him his food in an earthenware bowl. From then on, he ate there on his own in the corner of the kitchen. One day his hands trembled more than usual. He couldn't hold the earthenware bowl any longer. It fell on the floor and smashed into little pieces. "If you are a pig," the woman of the house said, "you can eat out of a trough." So, they made him a little wooden trough. From that day on he got his meals in the trough.

The couple had a four-year-old son of whom they were very fond. One evening after supper the father noticed the little boy working intently with little pieces of wood. He asked him what he was at. "I'm making a trough," the little boy said, smiling up at dad for approval. "I want to be able to feed you and mama out of it when I get big."

Mom and dad looked at each other intently for a few minutes. No words were exchanged. Then they went to the corner, took granda by the hand and led him back to the table. They sat him on a comfortable chair. He got his meals on a plate from that day on. No one ever again scolded him, when he clattered, or dribbled, or spilled or broke things.

What children see their parents do, is formative for them. They see their parents' way as the right way for them too. Example is crucial. For most of us, our first school of faith was our home. The first teachers of the faith we had were our own parents. They were also the best. School and parish nurtured the seeds that were sown in the home. When faith is not lived within a family, it is likely to be eroded in a single generation. Fr Chuck Gallagher, world leader of Marriage Encounter had this to say; 'I know nothing at which people work harder or for which they make more sacrifices than parenting and by and large they make a great job of it'. The words have stayed with me. I still remember, because I know them to be true. Because I have seen the evidence.

Today, we celebrate what you parents are already doing by your example. We recognise what you are doing and affirm it. We support you in the challenges that you are facing. We pray God's blessing on you in your special calling. We ask the Lord to be always with you. We ask Him to help you to bring to conclusion the wonderful work you are doing for Him. You brought your children to God. You introduced each of them personally to Him in Baptism. You gave them the name that is branded on the palm of God's hand. You taught them their first little prayers. The God they believe in is a mirror reflection of you. One day it will be their privilege to return the compliment, to lead you into God's presence. That day the Lord will have brought to conclusion what He began here so many years before. St Paul has a message for all parents; 'fan into flame the gift that God gave you. Never be ashamed of witnessing to the Lord. Keep as your pattern the sound teaching you have heard. You have been trusted to look after something sacred. Guard it with the help of the Holy Spirit who lives in you.' One day you will then hear the words: well done good and faithful servant. You have been faithful in the little things enter now into the joy of the Lord. Only then will we all realise fully the moulding power of our example.

27th Sunday in Ordinary Time

Day for Life

It was Pope John Paul, who proposed that a "Day for life" be celebrated in every country each year. This special day is to encourage us all to deepen our understanding and appreciation of the dignity and sacredness of all human life, at all its stages, from conception to natural death. This special day for Life is being celebrated nationally all across Ireland this weekend.

In his letter 'The Joy of Love' Pope Francis writes, "The gift of a new child, entrusted by the Lord to a father and a mother, begins with acceptance, continues with lifelong protection and has as its final goal in the joy of eternal life." And in a particularly touching sentence he adds; "for God allows parents to choose the name by which He himself will call their child for all eternity"

Pope John Paul II, now Saint John Paul, described the parish as a family of families. He asked that all parishes be places of welcome and support for those entrusted with the precious gift of new human life. He asked that our parish be a place where we provide support for women and men who face difficult circumstances, as well as those who have experienced abortion and seek comfort in the Lord and their community. He says, God does not withhold His forgiveness from those who seek it with a sincere heart. But, even when we confess our sins and receive absolution, we are not always ready to forgive ourselves. There are many women and men still living, years later, with the emotional and spiritual scars of the past. Our mission, in our parish, to promote a "Culture of Life", must include helping these women and men to be reconciled with themselves, with their lost child, and with the God, who has never stopped loving them.

Rachel's Vineyard is a loving, supporting, non-judgemental community, that offers welcome, care and healing to those coping with this struggle. Eimear is a girl who struggled deeply with her past. I will just share with you Eimear's words.

Words could never be enough to explain the gratitude that I felt for having the opportunity to attend a Rachel's Vineyard weekend. For the first time in years, it feels good to be me. I have a huge sense of peace and happiness with myself, and also with Jesus. I met such lovely people, who had the same experience as me and who did not judge me. When I went back to work, people told me that I looked different. I looked so at peace with myself. Rachel's Vineyard has saved my life.

We know that in the Lord each of us can find peace, regardless of our failings, because God's love has been poured into our hearts through the Holy Spirit that has been given to us. I share Eimear's words with you in the hope that it may help open the door for anyone, be it a mother, father or grandparent of new life, who is currently in a dark space, because of something in their past, that they deeply regret.

Rachel's Vineyard has a beautiful website. It is well worth a visit and is where support, love, acceptance and understanding can be availed of by anyone affected by these issues. If today helps even one person find peace with themselves and God, it will have been a fitting way to celebrate the Day for Life.

28th Sunday in Ordinary Time

Could what is true of the camel become true of us?

In our gospel today Jesus is asked an important question. All we know about the questioner is that he's a young man. He seems blessed with plenty of this world's goods. But he does have some concerns about the afterlife, because his question to Jesus is; Master, "what must I do to gain eternal life." Jesus gives him a simple, direct answer; 'keep the commandments. Unfortunately for him, he didn't seem satisfied with that. "I have kept all these, from my youth," he said. In other words, that's no big deal, sure I'm doing that already. Is that all I have to do? He was obviously expecting something more challenging, and then Jesus gave him what he wanted, a real challenge. Okay, Jesus said, if you are serious, "Go sell what you have and give to the poor. Then, come and follow me". We are told that the man went away sad for he was a man of great wealth. But even His disciples were troubled by the answer of Jesus. Does that mean a rich man can't enter Heaven, they asked? Is Jesus saying that all riches are bad? Is Jesus condemning all wealth? Like many passages in the gospel, what Jesus has said, has to be taken in its context. I think we can get that context, in the next word-picture that Jesus paints, where he talks of a camel passing through the eye of the needle.

One commentator on this story, identifies a narrow pass between two great rock faces. At the base, of this pass is a narrow opening, barely wide enough for a camel to squeeze his way through. But the camel was of course, was a beast of burden, so when he arrived at this pass, he'd be laden with cargo stacked on top of him and strapped around him. Impossible for him to get through the small opening. His handler would first have to strip everything off the camel, all the cargo, all the load strapped onto and around him. Only then, stripped naked, could the camel squeeze through. Do you know what the name of this tiny pass was? It was so narrow travellers called it The Eye of the Needle. So, to those listening to Jesus' story, His words needed no explanation.

Just as the camel couldn't pass through 'The Eye of the Needle' until stripped of all the attachments strapped on to him, Jesus was telling the rich man he couldn't enter eternal life, unless and until he could extricate himself from the load he'd gathered. If he was so 'strapped' to all his attachments, that he couldn't part with them, he'd be in deep trouble, when he arrived at the exit point from this life to the next. Jesus wasn't just talking to the rich young man in today's gospel, He is talking to us too and telling us that to enter eternal life we have to be able to let go of all the material things that served us on our journey but are now surplus to requirement

The camel is not condemned for being a beast of burden. His load does not prevent him passing through the Eye of the Needle, provided it's detachable, provided it can be 'easily shed' when necessary. But if it is so much part of him, that it can't be separated from him, or left behind, then he will find himself stuck. Jesus is telling the rich man and telling us that what's true of the camel is also true of us.

It's not what we have on the journey that's the real problem. It is what we have become so attached to and locked onto. It is what we have so set our heart on that we can't part with it, whether that is material things or other attachments like habits. Figuratively speaking, The Eye of the Needle awaits all of us. Whether or not we get through it might well depend on whether or not the load we have arrived with is detachable. Let's not forget the words of wisdom; "Naked we came from our mother's womb, naked we will return."

29th Sunday in Ordinary Time

Our synod; walking and journeying together, with the Holy Spirit.

October is a month we associate with harvest thanksgiving. While harvest celebrations have a long history in other faith traditions, they have in more recent years become very much part of our own too. But far from being something that has just sprung up in our times, 'harvest thanksgiving' goes right back to the Old Testament, when from across the Holy Land thousands descended on Jerusalem for their annual harvest festival, asking God's blessing on their crops. In fact, it was during this great harvest festival that an event took place in Jerusalem that was to transform the lives of people across the world to this day. It was during this great harvest festival in Jerusalem, that the Holy Spirit descended on the apostles in the form of tongues of fire. The apostles then finding themselves empowered by the Holy Spirit, burst out on the streets with an urgency they had never known, addressing the assembled thousands, all in their different tongues. The people at first thought that they must be drunk. But Peter told the crowd that the apostles were not drunk but were full of the Holy Spirit. That day alone, over three thousand converts were added to their number. The harvest festival in Jerusalem that day is still celebrated. For the Jews it is still the 'Feast of Harvest' asking God's blessing on the crops. For Christians today it has a different name and a very different significance - it is called the Feast of Pentecost, celebrating the coming of the Holy Spirit, which marks the birthday of our church. On the evening of that first Pentecost, Christians numbered about three thousand. Today, over a billion people across the world call themselves Christian.

A friend of mine often quotes what I believe is an old Chinese proverb, which says No family can hang a notice on the outside of its home reading; "No Problem Here"! The Church may be God's family, but no more than any other family, the church certainly cannot hang on its door a notice, "No Problem Here". Over two thousand years it has lived through many problems, differences and divisions, from the Great Schism of 1054 which split the church into the Orthodox in the East and Roman Catholic in the West, to multiple other divisions down through its history. It has had its golden ages. It has also had its darkest ages, not just in history, but as we know to all our heart break, in our own time too. Equally it has had to, over and over again, look at where it has arrived at, stop in its tracks, review how it could have arrived there, take time out, and return to its roots on that first Pentecost. It has to invoke the same Holy Spirit in study and in prayer; to bring it back to faithfulness to the mission it was given by Jesus. Jesus has guaranteed that His Holy Spirit will always be with His church to guide it, but the church can only receive that guidance, if it is listening' to the Holy Spirit. Traditionally, we tended to have the sense that the guidance of the Holy Spirit came to the church through the pope, the cardinals and the bishops and that we the people of God had only to listen to and be guided by them. In our time there is a new understanding and appreciation that God's Holy Spirit 'works where He wills'. The Holy Spirit, that each of us received in Baptism and

Confirmation, is active and speaking through the words and the lives of all His people, and that listening to the Spirit today means listening to His voice in 'all' His people.

So Pope Francis decided to convene a 'World Synod' involving all the whole people of God across the globe. The word synod means walking or journeying together. It's a spiritual time of sharing and listening in faith together. It is a time of healing, as we share our story. It is time of attentively seeking and listening to Jesus and His Holy Spirit among us, to rediscover together what God wants of us as His people at this time. So, it is important that it is not confused with some kind of political convention or parliamentary debating society. The primary purpose of this synod will be to listen to God, who speaks to us in adoration and prayer. To listen to God as He speaks to us in each other's lives and experiences, ordained and non-ordained alike.

Pope Francis launched this Worldwide Synod of all the people of God invoking the Holy Spirit who descended on the apostles on that first Pentecost, to "enkindle again in us the fire of His love", as together with Him and under His guidance, we set out to reform and reshape our church now, and for the generations to come.

30th Sunday in Ordinary Time (Mission Sunday)

We are missionaries by our witness.

Looking back now at the Covid era, we can see that it was a tough time for many. People lost their jobs, some their businesses and tragically, some lost family members. Young people lost a lot of time at school or college. We were all 'locked in' in so many ways. Some described it as a dark winter of the spirit. But it was a time too when we discovered great resilience and creativity. People could no longer go to mass, but mass came to our own homes through the webcam. People could no longer do their shopping, but the shopping arrived at their door. We learned the importance of protecting others by protecting ourselves. How often did we hear the question; Will things ever be the same again?

Pope Francis saw lessons we could learn from our experience. He talked about new ways of thinking to replace the old and he referenced that, even to our Faith.

He referenced certain ways of doing things that were effective in their time but may now be redundant to give us new life, bits of baggage we had brought from bygone days, that once served us well but may now be past their 'sell by' date. We've all seen the change in the age profile we find in church at the weekend. How many candidates are entering seminaries or religious life? But our young people haven't lost their faith. Many may not have the connection with their parish church that we had. They may not be as into 'religious practice', as we were, but they certainly haven't lost their belief in God.

The history of our church shows that it was some of the lowest times that produced some of the greatest saints that broke the mould and transformed the shape of their church for centuries to follow. People like Pope John XXIII, who over sixty years ago, at an advanced age, called the Second Vatican Council, that made the church we knew, in many ways unrecognisable. That was the man who, with the whole weight of the church on his shoulders, used to kneel down beside his bed each night and his prayer was: "Lord I'm going to bed now, this church is yours. You'd better take care of it till morning."

On this Mission Sunday, when we might feel things aren't great at home, it is good to remind ourselves, that across every corner of the globe today, rich harvests are being reaped from the seeds sown by Irish Missionaries. These rich harvests will generate the seed of a new and different church, because in the end of the day, it is God's church not ours. He, not us, is in charge of where His church flourishes or flounders. It is He, not us, that will bring around the new Spring, when He chooses. Our part is to each live our faith to the full where he has planted us, and that is how we each are the best missionaries He wants us to be. Our mission field is right here where the Lord has chosen to plant us, in our own homes, in our own parish and in our community. The most effective sermon any of us will ever give will be by how we live, and how we conduct ourselves, in our homes and communities. One of the best supports we can give to our generous missionaries is, that we be seen by them, and the people they have been sent to, living at home what they have given their lives to bring to others.

<u>31st Sunday in Ordinary Time</u>

The Cross has vertical and parallel bars.

"What are the first words that roll off your lips, when you wake up each morning and roll out of the bed?" That was the question asked by an American radio station some years ago. Randomly each morning they rang a selection of the numbers. As you would expect they got some hilarious replies. One morning the presenter rang a number; 'You are live on air', he said. 'This is your favourite radio station calling, can you tell me the very first words that rolled off your tongue, as you rolled out of bed this morning?' The voice at the other end said, 'You want to know the very first words that rolled off my lips this morning'. 'Sure,' he said, 'you're live on air, go right ahead. You may even win one of our special prizes this morning!' The voice on the line responded, 'Listen Israel, the Lord your God is one Lord and you are to love the Lord your God with your whole heart and with your whole soul and with your whole strength'. There was a moment of embarrassed silence. Then presenter cut in; 'I am sorry about that,' he said, 'we obviously have got a wrong number. We will go straight to a commercial break.'

The presenter obviously didn't realise that he had gotten the right number. The voice on the phone was that of a pious Jew, faithfully following the instruction of Moses, which was; "Let these words I urge on you today be written on your heart. Teach them to your children. Repeat them at your lying and at your rising. Fasten them on your head as a sign. Write them on the doorposts of your house and on your gates." The words the man had just spoken "Listen Israel, the Lord your God is one Lord. You must love the Lord your God with all your heart, with all your soul with all your mind and with all your strength." (That the commandment given by Moses to his people). Jesus added; "and you must love your neighbour as yourself."

All world religions have their own unique symbols. The Christian symbol is the cross with its two bars: one vertical and the other horizontal. The vertical, pointing from earth to heaven represents our call to love and serve our God. The horizontal, parallel to the earth, represents our call to love and service of each other. A healthy

Christianity is one that ensures we have the balance right. Worship and prayer are central to our lives as Christians. But real worship or prayer can never be isolated from how we treat others. Praying to God is of course very important but taking care of each other is equally so. Worship and prayer are central to our lives as Christians. But real worship or prayer, can never be isolated from how we treat each other.

I remember walking out of a graveyard one day with Pat, after an exceptionally sad funeral in the parish. Pat was a young man of no more than twenty at the time. I still remember his words. "Father," he said, "isn't it a pity, that we can't always be with each other, the way we have been for the last few days". He was describing the change that had come over the community, the way everyone was bonded together. It seemed as it everyone had lost a family member. How often have we heard the same thing here in our own community? People suffer a hard blow. You drop into their home later. What do they want to talk about? Not their 'cross' but their neighbours' goodness. How often have we heard it 'the neighbours were out of this world'.

They didn't know what to do for us, night or day it was all the same.

At times like that we get a glimpse into what it is really like, when we are truly Christian with each other. We get a glimpse of what it could and would be like, if we only, we could be always like that. But you might say, that is a special effort for a special occasion. It is not the kind of standard that we can sustain, at least not on our own. But isn't that the secret. We are not asked to do it on our own. That is why we gather together here each weekend, to ask for and get the strength from God and from each other, to try a little harder in the week ahead to live the message of Jesus for us in today's gospel. Love the Lord your God with your whole heart and your whole soul. Love your neighbour as yourself. Let us go forth from here today with that Christian symbol written, not on our forehead or on our doorposts, but engraved on our hearts. Let us remember the two bars of the cross, one vertical and the other horizontal, challenging each of us in the week ahead to giving our heart to God, when we pray to Him and our heart to your neighbour, when you serve.

If that doesn't challenge me, I'm either a saint or I have missed the point!

32nd Sunday in Ordinary Time

November is a dreary month... that's what Patsy said to me.

I remember on a November's evening some years ago, picking up a man on the road, who was thumbing a lift. Along the road we were chatting. 'November is a dreary month,' he said. 'My mother died in November; she is dead twenty years now. Herself and the father died within months of each other. I'm all alone since. November is a dreary month,' he said again, 'my mother died in November.' I was struck by the connection that was so immediate for him.

November, the month of the Holy Souls, remembering, reliving his grief, thinking of those who were gone, still missing them twenty years on. And yet they were still so present to him that day. The tradition runs deep and strong. November, Month of the Holy Souls; the gaining of indulgences, visits to the graveyard. I remember my own mother, God rest her, it meant everything to her to be brought to the graveyard in November. To have to miss those visits to the graveyard, would have been for her the ultimate act of ingratitude, like an act of betrayal of those who were gone. A statement that they were forgotten, out of sight, out of mind, and that, she couldn't live with. That strong tradition of our people is now entrusted to us. Whether or not it passes on to the next generation will be of our choosing. But one thing is sure, tradition is only passed on in being lived. Traditions like this are not learned in the catechism class. Traditions like this are like our accent, caught not taught.

November is a dreary month, one hopes so. Because to have forgotten our loved ones who have gone, would be for us to have severed our connection with our roots, and that would be very sad indeed. The words that came to mind to me these last days as I was reflecting on this theme were the words of William Shakespeare

Blow, blow thou winter wind, thou art not so unkind as man's ingratitude.

Thy tooth is not so keen, because thou art not seen, although thy breath be rude.

Blow, blow thou winter wind, thou art not so unkind, as man's ingratitude.

November is a dreary month, Patsy said to me that evening. Month of Winter wind and could be that of man's ingratitude, or November can be the very opposite for each of us. It can be the month of remembering and of cherishing, a month of so many lovely memories relived, and of stories re-shared around the family table - the month of saying 'thank you' for what they've left us.

Our church tells us that we can help our loved ones on their journey home to God, so we know, for them, that November is a special time. I like to imagine the doorkeeper in purgatory making a call to the Lord and with our loved one beside him saying to St. Peter or to Jesus, 'I think, I have someone here who'd like to talk to you.' And our loved one is, at that moment, on their way to their Eternal Home. November doesn't have to be a dreary month. It never is for our loved ones who are still cherished and remembered.

33rd Sunday in Ordinary Time

"Heaven and earth may pass, my words will not."

In the church's calendar today is the 33rd Sunday in Ordinary time. Next Sunday is the Feast of Christ the King, the last Sunday in Ordinary Time. The following Sunday will be the first Sunday of Advent, the beginning of the Church's New Year. As we come to the end of the church year, the readings point us towards the final end and focus our attention on last things; the sun will be darkened, the moon will not shed its light, the stars will fall from the sky, as the world as we know it comes to its end. More than any other generation before us we realise how fragile our world is. We are in no doubt about the capacity of a nuclear holocaust to cause unimaginable destruction. We have seen changes in climate attributable to global warming. We wonder have we begun the destruction already, or at least have we done irreparable damage. Perhaps more than previous generations, we realise the fragility of our world. We can't take the future of our planet for granted. We must ensure it ourselves, by how we treat it.

Perhaps more than any generation before us, can we take the future of our faith for granted? Are we indeed the first generation to realise, that Ireland may not necessarily be Christian in the future. It is not beyond the bounds of possibility that a thousand years from now, historians and archaeologists will be sifting through various remains, trying to piece together what Christians were, where they met to worship and how they lived with each other.

Just as we can't take the future of our planet for granted but must work and make sacrifices to ensure its future, so we cannot take the future of our faith for granted but have work and invest to ensure its future. You who gather here, you who pray in your lives, who try to pass on our faith values by living them, are the people who are saying: we're not ready to let the values die. We want our grandchildren, our parish, to have the values we treasure. Even when at times things look bleak, even when at times the future of our faith looks shaky, we have the words of Jesus to reassure us; "Heaven and Earth may pass, My words will not."

Our faith guarantees us that, even as the prophets of doom are having a field day, we know that nothing in this world, can frustrate God's plan for all of us. Jesus in today's gospel, even when referring to the final end, uses a striking image, the image of growth and fruit; the image of the fig tree, the sap in the branches, the sprouts, the new life coming forth. That seed is going to grow, that seed is going to produce fruit. That seed is the struggle, the many struggles, of all of us trying to live our faith, in difficult times, against many obstacles, in the unfavourable climate of our world; the family doing their best to rear their children well, the couple struggling to love one another when it's difficult, the burdened, coping with their cross, the family trying to live their values, in their homes and outside them. None of us gets it right all the time, we are all in the struggle together, each of us doing our best. When it's all over and the end comes, what will we find in the eternal kingdom, not I hope, palaces with golden walls and angels serenading us. What I hope we will find is our humble efforts to love each other, to rear our families, to live decent lives, taken by God and perfected for us. Heaven and earth will pass away, the sun may darken, the moon may lose its light. The stars may fall from heaven, but beyond it all, our heaven will be the

Lord's appreciation of, and the Lord's canonisation of each of our humble efforts to follow him faithfully.

Heaven will be the union of all of us with God. Each of our struggles and efforts completed and transformed, rewarded in eternal happiness with Him. So the message of the Lord to each of us as we gather is; never lose heart, God's plan is being achieved in each of us in a combination of our humble efforts and His mighty grace.

Our Lord Jesus Christ, King of the Universe

The Kingship of Christ in our lives.

Today is the feast of Christ Our King. When we think of a king we think of a crown, of a palace, of servants and soldiers, of armies and conquests and of all the trappings of power. The contrast could hardly be more striking between the powerful king in the palace and the powerless baby in a stable. The king sitting on his throne, the little baby resting in a manger.

The great empires conquered by weapons of steel are now history. The great kingdoms of His era survive only in monuments of stone. The kingdom He founded with the only weapon He had, unselfish love, lives on today in the hearts of billions of people across the globe. He came, not to dominate over us, but to serve and save us. That we might enter His life someday, He entered ours one day. So that we would be with Him one day, He came to be with us every day. The palace He wants to make His home is not one made of stone. The palace He wants to live in is one made of flesh, the human heart; your heart and mine. He is king in your heart and in mine, when we make His gospel, His way of life, the blueprint of our own. As scripture tells us; "We have here no lasting kingdom, we look forward to one that is to come". But if the kingdom of God is in my heart now, the kingdom of heaven will be my home in eternity.

I like the story about the king who summoned the palace fool. He handed him a stick and said to him; I want you to take this stick and keep it with great care. The day you meet a fool who is greater than yourself, give that fool this stick. Years passed and the palace fool guarded the stick with great care. The time came when the king knew that he had little time left to live. From the highest ranking and most important people in the palace, right down to the humblest servant, they lined up around his bed to say their farewells. Among the last to get to see the king was the palace fool. To him, as to all the others, the message of the king was the same. "I am now about to embark on my final journey," he told them, "and this is one journey from which I shall not return." It was the palace fool who said to the king, "you made many journeys in your life, but you never set out on any, without ensuring all the preparations were in place beforehand for your arrival at other side. For this great journey you are now undertaking, what preparations have you put in place." "None", the dying king answered, "I kept putting it off. This was a journey I hadn't planned on taking for many years yet." The fool reached inside his coat and retrieved the stick the king had long before given him. He handed it back to the dying king. "Master," he said, "I think you should have this, because finally, I have found a fool greater than myself."

Any of us could unintentionally find ourselves in the shoes of that king if, totally absorbed and immersed in the importance of the things that pass, we neglect the most important thing of all; being always in readiness for our final journey. We know that the only sure way of being always ready, is by living our lives within the guidelines given us by Christ our King. We all know that they are the guidelines, that lead to the only lasting kingdom; the eternal one. It is by always being prepared, that we truly make Christ King in our hearts, in our homes, in our families, in our relationships, in our work, in our community and in our world. The Kingship of Christ in our lives, we celebrate today. But we can only celebrate it today, if we live it every day.

YEAR C

2nd Sunday in Ordinary Time

There is nothing that life can throw at us, that we and Him won't be able to handle together.

So, there's a wedding in Cana in Galilee. Jesus and His friends are invited. They seem to arrive late, but that's not a problem, I believe weddings, there went on for a week. But what is a problem is that the wine has run out. The drink, that was to last for the week, has all been already consumed. I wonder what's going through the young couple's mind, as Jesus and His friends arrive to join them. Will He be upset at the stack of empty barrels, all clamped up against the wall outside. Is He going to confront the bride and groom, about the amount already consumed? Surely the time has come to call a halt and send everyone back home!

But that, that was not what the Jesus who turned up saw. What He did see was a couple, deeply embarrassed on their wedding day by something they hadn't at all foreseen. Someone had miscalculated on the wine. Now, the most special day of their lives would be remembered for all the wrong reasons; Wasn't that the wedding that they ran out of drink? What Jesus did see was a happy gathering, a young couple, celebrating their love with their friends, and the risk that it could all be ruined on them, and He couldn't resist coming to their rescue when a young couple's happiness was at stake. Just listen to what He did to rescue them! Six containers, 20 to 30 gallons capacity in each, that comes to about 120 to 180 gallons. When I was going to school there were 8 pints in a gallon. So we are up to the equivalent, of a 1,000 to 1,500 bottles of wine. That was what He ordered for them. That was His wedding present to the young couple. Just one little observation on the story. Imagine the disaster it would have turned out to be for that young couple on their wedding day, if Jesus hadn't actually been on their guest list, if He hadn't been invited and wasn't there with them. What would have happened, when their world fell apart?

What happens at any situation in any of our lives, when we have excluded Jesus from the guest list. To whom can we turn, when things begin to fall apart? There's a precious message deep at the heart of that story. Those who ensure Jesus is on the guest list in their lives, like the young couple in Cana of Galilee, will always know that they have a best friend at their side. And when He's by their side, what looks like a total disaster looming, becomes transformed by Him into a special celebration.

Reflecting on that story of the young couple from Cana in Galilee, wouldn't it be lovely, if every young couple heard that message. Wouldn't they be really blessed, if they realised the importance of having the most special guest of all, present and central to their most special celebration.

None of us knows what is ahead on life's journey, but what we do know is, that if we ensure Jesus is at our side, there is nothing that life can throw at us, that we and Him won't be able to handle together.

3rd Sunday in Ordinary Time

The Good News that brings challenges to us and dignity to others.

Jesus arrives back to His own place, Nazareth. They recognise Him immediately. Sure, isn't he the Son of their local carpenter up the road! He doesn't introduce Himself as the local carpenter's son. Instead, He tells them He's the Father's anointed one. He tells them that He has been sent by the Father, with good news for them. He's welcomed with open arms. He taught in their synagogues and was praised by all.

Pope Francis asked that this weekend, we highlight the Word of God, the preaching of which is our primary and most important ministry, and the spring and source of God's life for His people. We are called to preach the Good News of the gospel, welcome or unwelcome, in season or out of season, and to do so, in a courageous and challenging way. If we are to be faithful to that today, our message must be both challenging and life giving for everyone. Into that background, we look at what Jesus has to say to us today; "The Spirit of the Lord is upon me, because he has anointed me to bring good news to the poor, release those who are imprisoned and to set the downtrodden free."

Who are the poor in our society today? We think of those deprived of the material things of life and the challenges they must face every day. But there are also so many other forms of poverty; the poverty of those who see themselves as worthless or useless, those who believe that when God was making them, something went horribly wrong in the mix and as a result they are sentenced to live with this self-rejection, constantly struggling to find a reason to face another day.

Who are those imprisoned that Jesus is speaking of? We could think just of those locked away behind physical bars. But there are many who are enchained by their own history; a bad mistake, a serious indiscretion, a secret personal failing, an addiction they are chained or locked into that has them in a living hell, seeing no hopes of escape.

And who are the downtrodden that Jesus is referring to; those who are walked on by people who have power over them, those who find themselves in coercive, controlling relationships, those exploited, just because they are weak or vulnerable, those who have no one to stand up and fight for them. It is to these, whom we can see around us, that Jesus speaks today:

"The Spirit of the Lord has been given me. He has anointed me to bring you good news."

So, whoever you are, and wherever you find yourself today, the message of Jesus to you is:

You too are God's anointed. You are a reflection of the living God. You have a destiny to be with Him. He loves you with a love you can never even imagine. Nothing you have ever done can change that. You are not worthless or useless. God does not make junk. You are precious and priceless in His eyes right now. That is the Good News, God's word to you today. That is the Good News that Pope Francis wants us to bring you; the Good News Jesus wants you to hear, loud and clear today. It is the Good News that Jesus wants us all to proclaim from the hilltops; the Good News He wants us to bring in our own lives, to the poor, the imprisoned and the downtrodden, not just in faraway places that we hear about in the news, but right here in our own community today and every day. That's the message of the gospel. That's why we call it Good News - Good News that brings challenges to us and dignity to others.

Fourth Sunday Ordinary Time

[Presentation of the Lord]

The Holy Spirit 'rested' on him.

As a priest of our diocese, once said to me. "Did you notice that when you drop into a church, you nearly always find a few people there. They might be doing their stations, or lighting a few candles, or just quietly whispering a little prayer. Did you ever notice that most of the people you find there, have something in common. They are nearly always older people, which leads some people to conclude, that religion is on the way out. Sure, it will probably die with our generation." Then he said something that I still remember; "It takes a long time to learn to love. Our older generation are the experts. They have worn their teeth on it. They have a lifetime of practice behind them." What a lovely complement to our seniors: It takes a long time to learn to love. They have a lifetime of practice behind them.

His words came back to me as I was looking at today's gospel. The scene is in the temple, a centre point of the Jewish faith. The temple was a place of pilgrimage, thousands of people milling around there. But out of all the thousands milling around there that day, only two got their names in the gospel today. Simeon and Anna certainly qualify to be called seniors. Simeon is described as an old man, Anna, as having reached eighty-four, and they are the only two people in the temple that day, who recognised this insignificant little baby for who He was; Jesus, Son of God, the Redeemer who was promised. How could one possibly explain, how Simeon and Anna could have noticed this couple arriving with a baby, doing what probably a lot more couples were doing there? How could you explain them recognising this baby as the Son of God? The answer is in that beautiful sentence, saying of Simeon: The Holy Spirit 'rested' on him.

I walked into a house one day and there was no one to be seen. So, I hollered out at the top of my voice, "Anyone home?" Someone appeared out of nowhere, finger to their mouth saying "Sheeeeh! John is resting." 'Resting' is a very powerful word in that gospel passage. Resting conjures up an atmosphere of stillness, of quiet, of calm, absence of noise or turmoil or sound blaring, tip-toeing movement; 'Don't disturb'.

God's Holy Spirit can only rest on us if He can find, a times of quiet, of calm; times of stillness, times when turmoil is distant; and these can be rare, only there when we put them there. It is in such times the Holy Spirit can 'rest' on us. And when the Holy Spirit 'rests' on us, He does in us what he did in Simeon; He makes sure we are in the right place at the right time. He alerts us to the presence of the Lord, in people and places, we could never have expected.

That same Holy Spirit, that opened Simeon's eyes in the temple, was given to each of us in Baptism and in Confirmation and is always present deep within each of us. His voice is gentle and can only be heard in quiet moments. Only in the calm and silence, that we create, can our heart hear His gentle knock. If we want to have our ears open to hear His gentle whispering, if we want our minds tuned to the wavelength where we can pick up his messages, there has to be a space on our receiver, we allot to Him; a space where, in silence, we are alone with God; a time and place of resting in His presence a time and place of listening to, His Spirit deep within, where the only sound is that of His gentle voice within

This is not something that happens by accident in our lives, but those who choose to create it are the

Simeons and Annas of our time, the ones we find so often quietly sitting in our churches, whispering their prayers, when we drop in.

5th Sunday in Ordinary Time

What God loves most is forgiving us. The pity is that we so often refuse Him the opportunity.

Growing up on the banks of the Feale, a once rich fishing ground, I remember as a child the fishermen arriving out from town on summer evenings, armed with their rods and gear, heading for the river. I remember how much I'd have loved to join them, to learn their art of casting their flies and catching trout. But it was always near our bedtime when they came. We had to be up early next morning, for the milking and the creamery, before facing a long day in the meadow at the hay. So, it was always too late for me to join them, but I remember figuring out at that time, that the reason it was so late must have been that it was at night the fish got hungry and that it was when they were hungry that they took the bait.

In today's gospel, Peter an experienced fisherman, knew well that if they'd just fished all night and caught nothing, it was pointless throwing out their nets in the noon day sun, but he said to, Jesus 'If you say so, I'll do it'. We know what happened, the miraculous catch of fish and Peter saying to Jesus; "Go away from me, Lord, for I am a sinful man!" But Jesus isn't afraid to have a sinful disciple near him. It was, after all, to gather and welcome home sinners that He came. The message of Jesus to Peter then, is the message of Jesus to us now. We are all called, not because we're worthy, but because we are chosen.

If Peter had understood why Jesus came, what he would have said to Him was not; 'depart from me O Lord because I am a sinner', but 'please stay with me Lord, because I am a sinner and if You leave me, I'll be forever lost.' Hasn't the mistake Peter made then, been one that's often been made since? Our church has sometimes emphasised hellfire and damnation, to the detriment of being good at welcoming sinners. Many were often left, or felt left, excluded. The message perceived or coming across more like: Depart from us for you are a sinful person.

Sin and sinfulness are part of the human condition, part of all of us. St John tells us; If we say we have no sin, we
deceive ourselves, and the truth is not in us. If we say we have not sinned, we make God out to be liar and His word is not in us.

That's fairly strong language. So sin is not the problem, the problem is when we refuse to face up to our own sin, to address it, ask forgiveness, and to do our best to do something about it. Jesus accepts Peter as he is, naming and facing his own sinfulness. Jesus takes him as he is but transforms him into who He wants him to be. Jesus takes away Peter's awful fears about his own unworthiness. And Peter, having experienced the total forgiveness of Jesus, is in a powerful position to bring that forgiveness to others; to welcome them regardless of their history or their shame; to welcome them as Jesus had welcomed him. I said earlier that sin is part of all our lives, Jesus tells us: "The kingdom of heaven is like a net that was thrown into the sea and caught fish of every kind." That includes all of us, in all our different states. Just as the fisherman's net, doesn't just pick the best fish to catch, we see from the gospel that Jesus doesn't just select the perfect or the worthy to call. Indeed, thinking we're perfect or worthy can be a barrier to the Lord, while our awareness of our unworthiness opens the door to Him.

Like Peter, He can take us, whatever mess we're in, and transform us. But if we see ourselves as already perfect, what can he do for us? It was when he was flattened by his own unworthiness, that Jesus was able to make Peter unrecognisable to his former self. It is when we bring ourselves into that space, that Jesus can begin the work of transforming us too.

Let's never forget that each time we come to mass, we begin as Peter did by telling the Lord, we've sinned, and asking once again for his forgiveness. Each time we approach the altar, to receive Holy Communion, our prayer of preparation is Lord I'm not worthy to receive you. As Pope Francis says, What God loves most is forgiving us. The pity is that we so often refuse Him the opportunity.

6th Sunday in Ordinary Time

The Kingdom of God is present when we love one another.

In a small rural community recently, the lights went out, and I'm not talking about a power cut, but rather heart-breaking news for a young family. A cloud of darkness descended on the community. Somebody, in that community decided not to join the chorus cursing the darkness but choose to invite others to join in lighting a candle. That cloud of darkness was replaced with a beacon of light.

I imagine that whoever it was who initially stepped forward, could have had no idea at that point of the enormity of what they had set in motion. A community of probably less than three hundred homes raised I believe something in the region €80,000. Stunning though, these figures may seem they are just a fraction of the real story. The real story is not about figures on a page but about the extraordinary outpouring of love and empathy, of caring, compassion and commitment of that community. We know that even ten times that could not undo the pain. But just think of the impact on the family of such an outpouring of love and support. Behind those figures is a story that is even more important than the sums!

I was talking to some people from that community shortly afterwards. The one thing they all wanted to talk about was this event that had taken place. The different voices all echoed the same message. They had a real pride in what their community had done. They were in awe of the effort made, and the response received. They had a new-found appreciation of all the goodness in their community. They were able to see it and name it for what it was, an amazing outpouring of love. They had a new and a deeper appreciation of the love and generosity that was at the very heart of their community and that had overflowed, when tapped into.

This brings us to the core of today's Gospel - The Sermon on the Mount. At the very heart of the Sermon on the Mount is what Jesus describes to us as 'the Kingdom of God'. And while we will experience that Kingdom in its fullness in the next life, that we don't have to wait for then to experience it or to have it. The Kingdom of God, Jesus tells us, is here, when we are living the way Jesus wants us to live, the way He came to ask us to live with one another. The life blood of that Kingdom of God is love. 'Love one another,' Jesus says, 'as I have loved you. By this will everyone know that you are my disciples; by your love for one another.'

The Kingdom of God, that Jesus is telling us about, is 'Love in Action'. The Kingdom of God that Jesus is telling us about is 'Love converted into Action'. The Kingdom of God, that Jesus is telling us about is God's love flowing into us and flowing through us into others. Where the Kingdom of God is present, present through each of us, its presence is experienced and felt by the people around us. It's felt most of all by those who most need to feel it; by those who are vulnerable or hurting, by those who are suffering or deprived, by those who feel excluded and powerless, by those who have been dealt the worst hand of cards in life.

Where, the Kingdom of God is present today, that community is already being transformed by the goodness of people, that's flowing over and into other people's lives. The lives of those around us are being transformed, by our sensitivity to their needs. By our readiness not only to notice their hurt or their wounds, but by being the people who go to them and bind them up. The Kingdom of God is present, in our community, when you are in awe of the goodness, generosity and caring of the people around you. The Kingdom of God is present when and where, we are surrounded by evidence that those words of Jesus are being lived. Love one another as I have loved you, by this will everyone know you are my disciples, by your love for one another. That is the community, the 'Kingdom of God' that Jesus wants us, to not just look forward to in the next life but build with and for each other in this life.

7th Sunday in Ordinary Time

The challenge of the gospel is not how well we can quote it, but how well we are living it

If envy is a sin, I'm guilty, and my parish priest is responsible for my sin! Because ever since I came to the parish, I envy his gift of being able to take the three readings of mass at the weekend, and in a couple of concise sentences at his introduction to mass, is able to put his finger on the message of all three readings. It's like a chef serving up a special aperitive to whet your appetite for the upcoming meal.

All of which tells me, that my esteemed pastor, isn't the priest who once caused great annoyance to a parishioner by every Sunday morning, when he went to the pulpit to proclaim the gospel, began by summarising the gospel at length before he shared it, then went ahead and proclaimed the gospel to his congregation and then, in his homily, repeated again most of what he had already read.

This annoyed a parishioner so much that she was telling her friend she was going to go and see the priest in question, to tell him that life in Ireland had changed a lot since he was ordained and that the vast bulk of those in his congregation today had at least the benefit of second level education, many of them a lot more, and they didn't need the same thing repeated three times for them. Well, we can empathise with her feelings. The purpose of proclaiming the gospel is not to help people to commit it to memory, but to motivate and help us all to put it into practice in our lives.

I'm afraid, that not just after three readings, but even after thirty-three, many of us might still be struggling with that challenge, to live it every day. And I'm sure we will still be struggling with it to the day we draw our final breath. But when we meet the good Lord Himself, I don't think His primary interest will be how much of the bible we can quote. I figure and expect that He will be a lot more interested in how much of what He's asked of us, that we have lived. There won't be a points system based on knowledge accumulated. I suspect there will be a good review of how we did in our 'practicals', how the product lived up to the designer's intention! The challenge of the gospel is not how well we can remember or quote it, but how well have we succeeded in living it; a challenge that we face every day until the day we draw our final breath.

Take todays gospel as an example. Jesus presents us with the charter and blueprint by which He wants us to live our own lives and to live our relationships with each other. He says: Love your enemies. Do good to those that hate you. Bless those that curse you. Pray for those who treat you badly. How well are we doing with this charter? How well am I doing with it? One way to find out would be to do a little test together today. Suppose I call out a few questions. This will be different to any other exam you have ever done because you will be marking your own answers for yourself. Can I name an enemy that I have made a deliberate choice to love? If I can, have I acted on that choice? You need only to find one example! Can I think of one good act that I did for someone who has really hurt me badly? Again, just one example for each of us, including myself to come up with. Can I recall one instance in the last month where I prayed for someone who had wronged me? So, three questions for each of us to honestly answer. The score you clocked up is in the silence of your own heart. Somebody put this a bit more dramatically than I just did, when they said; if tomorrow morning I was arrested and if the charge brought against me was that of being Christian; if the standard against which I was being judged was todays gospel; if the questions put to me were the ones we have just tried to answer - would they be able to find enough evidence to convict me?

Jesus says: 'He who acknowledges me before men, I will acknowledge before my Father in Heaven." We acknowledge Jesus by living by His charter, not by memorising His quotations. Jesus says: "It's not those who say to me Lord, Lord, who will enter the Kingdom of

Heaven, but those who do the will of my Father in Heaven." The will of His Father is set out for us, in the charter Jesus gave us to live by; Love your enemies. Do good to those that hate you. Bless those that curse you. Pray for those who treat you badly.

By the way, just going back for a moment to that arrest I referred to, would the verdict the court passed down on us be: yes, guilty beyond reasonable doubt – because we know they are Christians by their lives.

8th Sunday in Ordinary Time – Sunday before Ash Wednesday

The Trocaire box – an inspiration or an annoyance?

Next Wednesday is Ash Wednesday. Hopefully most of us would like to begin Lent by coming to mass and receiving the blessed ashes. Maybe we are losing many of the values and practices that were very much part of life in the past. Some might say that much of what we have lost may have been a good riddance, but there are some things that it would be a pity to lose. Lent is one of those, because it challenges us to look again at our values and to re-commit to living them. When we were growing up, 'giving up things for Lent' was a big thing to teach us self-denial and help develop our own self-control. Perhaps, sometimes we just stored away what we had given up and feasted on our stockpile Easter Week. In more recent times Lent has been given a new lease of life. We are invited to turn our Lenten sacrifice into helping others; like for instance providing education for a little child somewhere. The introduction of the Lenten Trocaire box was instrumental in that change.

One year we ran a project for Lent in the parish. Families were invited to sponsor a child in the Third World for Lent. This was how you did it. When your family had eaten dinner, you estimated what the extra portion for this little child would have cost and there and then you put the cost of that extra plate in the Trocaire box.

Just after Easter I was bringing Holy Communion to the people on my First Friday sick call list. I called to Mrs. Danaher as I did every First Friday. She didn't seem herself and I asked her if there was something wrong. She told me she was very lonely today. I had no idea what she was talking about. Then she said "my friend is going away today. She's leaving me today". She lifted the Trocaire box, bearing the picture of the little child, off the mantelpiece and handed it to me.

Every week during Lent when she prepared her own dinner, she had put the 'price of a chop' into her Trocaire Box for the child in Africa, whose picture was on the side of the Box. That little child had become for her, a real part of her family. Today she was handing me back her Trocaire box. She felt her special friend was leaving her. It was a beautiful moment, and it was so real for her. Not alone had she gone without something for Lent, the price of the chop she put into the box each week, but she had made sure a child in need in the Third World, benefitted from her sacrifice. I just thought I would share that with you; such a beautiful example of what sponsoring a little child for Lent meant for her.

When the Trocaire box was first introduced, the intention was very clear; to keep alive in our hearts the spirit of Lent. The idea was that we would leave the Trocaire box on the table, so that each time we sat down together to enjoy our meal, it would remind us of how blessed we were with what was on our table, compared to how sad it was for those who had little on theirs. It was a little incentive not to forget it. Over time I think that this practice might have changed. I think sometimes we brought home the Trocaire pack from mass, but it wasn't always assembled and placed on the table. When the time came at Easter to return the box maybe we just reached for the wallet, took out what we thought was appropriate and dropped it into the box for returning.

Now please don't get me wrong. Whatever we give or however we give is deeply appreciated. It is equally helpful regardless of how we put it together. All I am suggesting is that there was originally an element to the Box, of an ongoing felt solidarity with the less fortunate in the Third World, which we responded to each time we dropped something in the box. It would be lovely to retain this element. You are invited to pick up one as you leave the church today. I hope this will contribute to making Lent a little more meaningful for you and your family this year.

1st Sunday of Lent

The choices we make determine the destination we arrive at

Every Christian is a traveller. Our journey begins at Baptism and ends in eternity. The journey is an adventure, because the future is always hidden from us. What we do know is; that the good Lord has made this journey before us and that He is with us now as we travel. There are moments on our journey when we make new choices. The choices we make impact, not just the quality of our travel, but also determine the destination we will reach. Lent is offered to us as a time to make those choices; a time to look at where the journey we are on is going and a time to reset our sights on the destination we want to arrive at. Let's take a little bird's eye view of what life once looked like on Sunday mornings in rural Ireland. 'The chapel was crowded long before mass time. Those who travelled the longest distance were usually the first to arrive and often arrived a half hour before mass. Some used their half hour to do the Stations of the Cross, others said their Rosary. Others prayed at statues of Our Lady, the Sacred Heart or St. Anthony. Except for the whispering of quiet prayers, there was a calm, holy silence which well-expressed the idea of sabbath rest' (From Life to Sacrament – Phillip Walshe).

We are heirs to a glorious heritage, our people's faithfulness to the mass. Its preciousness to them is immortalised in literature and in the mass-rocks that we find dotted around the country. For us Catholics, it's always been 'the mass that matters'. Would it be unreasonable for us to expect of ourselves that we would make sure, especially during Lent, never to miss our weekend mass? Maybe there are some for whom it would be possible or relatively easy to join those who attend weekday mass during Lent. I appreciate it would of course take a big effort, but nothing like the effort many of our ancestors had to make. Lent is also a time when we are invited to look again at family prayer. I know this is a big challenge in the age we are in but we have someone with great influence on our side! These are the words of Saint Pope John Paul 11, his final words spoken in Limerick; "Your homes should always remain homes of prayer. As I leave this island today, a land and a people who are so dear to my heart, may I express one wish that each home in Ireland will remain or will begin again to be a home of daily family prayer. That you would promise me this would be the greatest gift you could give me as I leave your shores."

2nd Sunday of Lent

People see the externals; the Lord sees the heart.

Today's Gospel is one that is familiar to us all. Jesus goes up the mountain with Peter, James and John. At the mountain top He is transfigured before them. Our understanding is that for a moment in time Jesus stepped outside the limitations of His human body. The curtain was rolled back on the stage and His disciples saw Jesus in the full glory of His Divinity. What was the meaning of what happened on that mountain and what message might it have for us today?

The contrast for the apostles between the Jesus with whom they climbed the mountain and the Jesus they saw at the top, between the human Jesus whom they had got to know so well down by the Sea of Galilee and the transfigured Jesus revealed to them at the mountain top, was the contrast between Jesus as seen through their human eyes, the Jesus who walked roads of Palestine, who cured the sick and preached to the people and who was well known to all, and the same Jesus, as seen through the eyes of His Father. This left the apostles sprawling on the ground on the mountain top incapable of comprehending what was going on, - with the vastness of the gap between the two.

It strikes me that this could be applied to each of our lives. Our lives too can be seen to be very different, depending on the angle from which they are viewed. There is the human angle, each of us as people see us, each of us as people know us or think they know us and each of us as we appear to all those around us. Then there is each of us as God sees us, looking as He does, not at the externals but straight into the heart. He sees the me as I really am and there can be quite a gap between the two. And the gap could just be so big, that if others who think they know me well actually saw me as God sees me, they might not even recognise me as the same person.

So maybe when we think of the story of the Transfiguration and the contrast between Jesus, seen through human eyes and Jesus seen through the Father's eyes, we might reflect that what was true of Jesus could be so true of each of us. Our lives too could look very different depending on the angle from which they are viewed. We might appear to be doing very well by human standards. We might appear to have it made in the eyes of those around us. But ultimately there is only one view that matters. Ultimately only one pair of eyes are significant, the ones that see beyond the externals to the heart. It matters little the esteem in which we are held by those around us unless we have first sorted out the esteem in which we are held by God.

3rd Sunday of Lent

Love him all the more the Rabbi said

I remember reading about a meeting between a Jewish father and his local Rabbi or spiritual leader. To understand the conversation, we would need to know the background. The Jewish people were God's chosen people. They traced their ancestry back to Abraham. They knew the words of the Psalm were about them. God was saying to them, "Before I formed you in the womb I knew you. Before you came to birth, I consecrated you. I called you by name, you are mine. I have each one of you branded in the palm of my hand." They were God's chosen people, selected from all nations of the earth and they knew it. The land they occupied was given them by their God. God had made a commitment to them "I will be your God, and you will be My people". It was unthinkable for any Jewish family that one of their members could abandon their God.

This Jewish father arrived to his Rabbi, The unthinkable had happened in his family. His son had turned his back on his heritage and on his God. He turned up at the Rabbi's door in deep distress. How was he to deal with this un-pardonable offence? The Rabbi sat him down and listened to his story. The father cringed as he detailed his shame. The Rabbi listened on. Finally, he came to the end of his story and there was silence. The father kept his eyes on the floor as he awaited the Rabbi's judgement, - the sentence that he would have to execute on his son. The Rabbi reflected on what he had heard and weighed it up. Finally, after what seemed so long, he spoke. His words were few, just a single sentence, as short as it was shocking to his father; "Love him all the more" the Rabbi said and sent him home.

That sentence sums up exactly how God treats us when we have turned our back on him, when we have betrayed our heritage, walked away. As soon as we are prepared to come to our senses, as soon as we are prepared to look in the mirror, as soon as we are ready to face the mess we are in, God is waiting for us to knock at His door. We are, at that moment the Prodigal Son facing home in fear and trepidation, swamped in his guilt, only to be overwhelmed by his father's forgiving love. "You are my Son and all I have is yours". We are the woman taken in adultery in the gospel shaking in her shoes waiting for the stones to be let fly at her. What do we hear from God when we turn to Him; "Neither do I condemn you, go and sin no more."

Why would any of us go through life, dragging a trailer load of garbage or guilt on our back? Unhitch the trailer and let it go. That is the meaning of the Sacrament of Penance, unhitching the trailer and letting it go. Accept the invitation to knock on the Rabbi's door. Accept the invitation of the Lord to knock at His door. Walk from that Confession box having heard the words of Jesus to you personally, " Neither do I condemn you, Go in peace and sin no more."

4th Sunday of Lent

Preparing for Lenten Penance Rite

I remember a letter we received from our bishop during Lent one year had one significant sentence. He said that when he was a teenager, he remembered something a priest said to them, which made a lasting impression on him. He said that when we are going to Confession, we should see it first of all as an opportunity for us to say thanks to God for all the blessings we have received, His goodness to us and His constant caring for us. We first name those blessings and thank Him for them. In doing that we become aware of times we have not used them in our own family, in our homes and in our place of work. Naming these times is our Confession. That really connects the Sacrament to our everyday life.

That message struck me again during the week. We had first Confessions in each church with all the children preparing for 1st Holy Communion. This is how the children prepare for their confession. We take a quiet few minutes together here at the altar. They close their eyes and go into their inner selves where they are all alone with God. There in that space, all alone with God, they begin to name all the goodness that is in them and all the goodness God sees in them at this moment. And they name the blessings they have received at home, at school and with their friends. They take a little time, all alone with God in their inner selves, not just to name all those blessings which are very real to them, but also to say thanks to God for them one by one. They then look at how they have not always shared all that goodness God sees in them with those around them and they name those, bring them to the Lord and that is their Confession

Recently, bringing Holy Communion to the sick, a very special and saintly lady asked for Confession. This is how she began her Confession. I want to begin now, she said, by first thanking God for all his goodness to me through my life, for all his goodness to my family and all the blessings I and my family have received. And only after she had thanked God for all His blessings, did she name where she felt she might have done better, and this was what she was asking God's forgiveness for.

So, all three instances had the same in common, coming to God and naming to Him the blessings he'd given. Coming to God in appreciation of those and to thank Him. Confession centred not so much on MY sin or MY guilt, but on the amazing goodness of God to each of us in life

At the heart of the gospel today is the overwhelming love of the father for his son. The father who cannot even wait for his son to say sorry, the father who has already forgiven him. That is the Father Jesus is introducing each of us to. A Father whose love and forgiveness is so overwhelming that as soon as He sees us coming, He has already forgiven us.

Pope Francis; 'God never tires of forgiving us. It is we who tire of asking for His forgiveness'

The greatest act of worship we could offer Him is to take Him at His word by opening our hearts in the Sacrament of Returning, to allow God who is waiting for us, embrace us

5th Sunday of Lent

Knowing a person V Knowing about a person

In the Irish language there are different words for different kinds of knowledge. For facts, figures and information the Irish word used is 'Eolas', but when we are talking about getting to know a person, we use the word 'aithne', ag cur aithne ar Eoin. 'Knowing a person' is very different to 'knowing about a person'. A writer can fill pages of the paper with facts, figures and opinions about the Irish team, but they may not know them as a brother or best friend knows them. 'Aithne' is the kind of knowing that only comes in a relationship, the way I know my father, my friend or my life's partner. So, one kind of knowing is knowing information, that is 'Eolas', we get that in books, on the internet and in newspapers. The other kind of knowing is personal, that is 'aithne'. We don't get that in books. We get it in our relationships with them. That distinction is key to understanding today's gospel

The Pharisees were encyclopaedias of Eolas about God. They knew and could quote their Bible backwards. They had the Jewish Law at their fingertips. So armed with all their Eolas about God and the Law, they take this woman found in adultery, drag her up in front of the crowd, stand her up before Jesus and move in for their kill; "Teacher, this woman was caught committing adultery.

Now in the law Moses commanded us to stone such women. What do you say?"

Were He to say, leave the woman alone, let her go free,"....So He condones adultery !

If, however, he were to say, "Stone her to death," He is in big trouble. Only the Romans had authority to pass the death sentence. What is Jesus to say or do?. Whatever He says, they will have discredited Him. So, He doesn't say anything. Instead, He bends down and with his finger writes on the dust.

To this day what we don't know for sure is what He wrote. But it is believed that what He may have written on the sand was a list of the sins of her accusers. The next sentence is revealing. They all sneak away one by one into the background. Well, is that a message for our society today! We have no scarcity of Pharisees, of judgers and condemners, who have all the Eolas, all the knowledge, and God help the unfortunate who makes a mistake.

Where is the Jesus figure in our world who focusses not on the sin but on the poor sinner, not on the fall but on the person thrown on the ground. How easily we can be drawn into the shoes of the Pharisees. Someone shouts guilty, and a chorus joins them, becoming part of judging and condemning. It can be so much easier to look outward at them, rather than inward at ourselves. If our sins were written on the ground in front of us today, how many of us would remain to condemn the woman. How many of us could bend down and pick up the first stone? How many of us would be slipping away quietly? I certainly would be slipping away quietly into the background. I certainly couldn't afford to bend down and pick up a stone. And if any of us think we would be in position to pick up the first stone, it is time to get measured for our halo! .I must be very different from the rest of humanity.

Each time we come here to mass we begin by saying, I confess that I have sinned, May almighty god have mercy on me, forgive me my sins and bring me to life everlasting. We go on and three times ask the Lord for mercy. We openly acknowledge in Lent our need to repent and change. Every time we say the Our Father we ask God to forgive us as we forgive others. At the heart of our Faith is, that each of us needs redemption. Otherwise, Calvary was a waste of valuable time. Our church is the 'field hospital for sinners' not a sanctuary for saints. The central confrontation in the Gospel story today is between the Pharisees on one side and Jesus on the other, between those who knew all about God and the one who 'knew' God, between those who had all the Eolas or information about God and the One who had Aithne ar Dia, the one who knew God personally, Jesus who knew God as His Father

The Pharisees who had all the information about God, saw not the woman, but the adultery. Jesus who knew God saw not the adultery but the woman. Which is our reaction, when someone falls and is being judged? Are we in the shoes of the Pharisees joining in the judging or are we in the shoes of Jesus who can see the act as wrong, but who doesn't judge the person and refuses to join in the condemnation.

There, is the real challenge to be Christian, to look in at ourselves, before talking out about someone else. To see our own private sins written by the finger of the Lord, rather scapegoat the person whose sins are written by others. No doubt the pharisees had all the Eolas about god but did they have the Aithne ar Dia (Did they 'know' God?) Jesus by his unwillingness to join in the judging or condemnation showed people a real relationship with God (Aithne). As the gospel says, by our fruits we are known, and by our actions we show whether we know God as Jesus did or just have lots of information about His rules and regulations (Eolas).

2nd Sunday of Easter

There's a rumour he rose from the dead and I think the parish priest believes it.

Some years ago, a priest I know did a big renovation job in the parish church. When the church reopened after the renovation, the huge Crucifix that had always hung on the wall behind the altar was gone. Well, it wasn't really gone but it was changed. The timber cross was still affixed to the wall, but the figure of the Crucified Body of Jesus had been removed from it. It was now just the bare timber cross without an image. Not everyone was enamoured of the change. The sacristan in the church was a lady and the complaints of the disgruntled parishioners were being channelled through her to the parish priest.

One morning Mary arrived into the sacristy. The Parish priest was just getting ready for mass.

Mary couldn't wait to tell him there had been another complaint. They wanted the figure of Jesus crucified put back on the cross. By this time the parish priest was getting a bit tired of it and having a hunch that Mary herself was being at least partial to all these complaints, he said to her, Mary would you do me a favour. I will Father, she said. Mary, he said, the next person who complains to you about the body of Jesus being gone off the cross, will you tell them that there is a rumour going around that He actually rose from the dead and what's more, that you have a suspicion that the Parish Priest believes it!

There is a rumour going around that He is risen. Do I really believe it?. Would people I meet every day suspect that I do? For instance, when I pray, which Jesus do I turn to, the Crucified Figure on the Cross or the Risen Jesus of Easter Morning?

When do I feel Jesus is closest to me in my life, in times of suffering or in times of joy?

Where would I expect to sense His presence, at a wedding or, at a wake?

Where am I most likely to point to His Will, in the tragic accident or, in a windfall!

Do we really believe that He is risen? Do we live as though it is true? Does it radiate from our countenance? Writing an article in a magazine, a priest in New York commented; We have to wonder whether we are the cause of the lack of faith in others and having posed the question, he then relates a story from his recent experience.

I was travelling into New York in the subway the other day, he said. Across the aisle from me sat a religious in full habit. I don't know whether it was a male or a female he was describing, but he did remark they didn't strike him as the happiest of people. The expression on the face was stern and stiff. Even when I greeted the time of day, there was no response or reply. My stop arrived and I was getting off the train. Another passenger was also getting off at the same stop. He had seen what happened on that train. Walking down the platform, he said to me, "You Christians are not a great advertisement for the Resurrection". I recall that Parish Priest's comment to the parish clerk. There is a rumour going around that He is risen. And I have a suspicion the parish priest believes it.

When I posed the question earlier, do we really believe that He rose from the dead on Easter Morning, you might have felt I was being a bit out of order. You might have felt like shouting back at me, of course we believe in the Resurrection. So maybe I need to put it in a slightly different way. Does our belief that Jesus is Risen from the dead and walks among us now, does that conviction radiate in our lives this Easter Time. Would those around us have a strong suspicion that we believe it because they see the evidence in how we live.

Jesus says to Thomas this weekend. 'You believe because you can see me. Blessed are those who have not seen and yet believe'. May those who meet us and those who greet us in the week ahead go away with a' strong suspicion' that we believe it, because they have seen the evidence in how we live.

3rd Sunday of Easter

We may be the only Jesus some people will encounter this week.

Very few people go through life without hitting a personal crisis or finding themselves in a very dark place. It could be the break-up of a relationship or parents watching a child they love with all their hearts choosing the wrong road and experiencing their helplessness to rescue them. It might be having to watch something you invested your life in building up come crashing down around you. It might be that result from the x-ray, that you dreaded, or the phone call from the hospital that you hoped you would never receive, or whatever it was that brought the curtains down on life, for you. That is where the disciples are in today's gospel story. Their hero is crucified between two thieves. Their hopes are now buried in a tomb beside him. There is nothing left to say, it is all over for them

It is Peter who breaks the awful silence; 'I am going fishing', he says. We will go with you, the others say. There is little else left for them to do now. Dawn is breaking as they head back to shore empty handed after a full night spent on the lake. There is a shadow on the shoreline, as dawn begins to break. 'Throw out the nets again', He says, the last thing these experienced fishermen wanted to hear.

But things couldn't get worse could they, so they do it. Then they have a catch so great they are unable to haul in the nets. Again, it is Peter's voice we hear, 'It is the Lord'; He says. From that moment their lives were changed forever.

If you have been stripped of everything that gave life its meaning. If you have felt the very reason for living has been taken from you. if you have been in that darkness where you can see no tomorrow, but you are still here today to tell the story, you have been where the disciples found themselves today.

Can you remember who that shadow on the shoreline was for you? Can you remember whose voice it was that then reached you? Someone who, already knowing your story, gently, caringly asked, how are you? or whispered a gentle word of encouragement or gave you a gentle lift that just about helped you survive. Just like the disciples in the boat this morning, that someone was there for you in your darkest hour. How often have you said since then, but for Bridget, I know, I never could have made it, and as the darkness lifted and you began to get your life back again, you might have said it is an answer to prayer Just another way of saying what the disciples said today; 'It is the Lord'. That person was Jesus on the shoreline for you that day. Come and have breakfast, Jesus said to them that morning. Call up for a coffee or a chat, that person might have said to you. There, your journey back began. Every day people are being 'that person on the shoreline', reaching out to someone who is in pain, opening a tiny door to let in a chink of light. A little word of encouragement, caringly conveyed, the tone of their voice, was what said it all.

All of us have been blessed with such a 'Jesus person' in our lives. Today's gospel invites to name that person and to be grateful for the blessing they were to us. But it is also inviting each of us to be for each other what that someone else has been for us in our time of darkness.

The Gospel message for us today invites us to take time to notice people who may be struggling in their darkness. Be there for them, not just passively, (sure they know I'm here if they want to call on me). Be the person who makes the call, not the person who has the time, but the one who makes the time, the time to notice and to respond to those struggling with the darkness of long nights and like the disciples are wearingly trying to reach the shore.

As someone once put it well, we may be the only Jesus some people will encounter this week. Will our presence and our words have the transforming effect that the words of Jesus had on His disciples that morning. Maybe someone will look back twenty years from now and say; 'But for You', I don't think I could have made it through that darkness. Then you will have been that 'Jesus person' in their life. And He will be saying to you; Thank you, what I have done for you, you have just done for each other.

4th Sunday of Easter

Vocation Sunday. The mystery of God's choice has always baffled people.

During my time in the Seminary, a friend, either with a good sense of humour, or feeling a need to 'warn me' of what was ahead, sent me a little cutting from a magazine. I hope, you enjoy hearing it as much as I enjoyed receiving it

If a priest preaches for ten minutes, he's long winded.

If his homily is short, it is because he didn't prepare it.

If the parish funds are low, he is a poor manager

If he tries to replenish them, he is money mad

If he owns a good car he's preoccupied with worldly goods

If he's going round in a banger, he's never on time for anything

If he visits parishioners in their homes, he is nosey

If he doesn't visit their homes, he's a snob

If he takes time in confession, he is keeping people all day!

If he doesn't take time in Confession

He has no interest in people's lives

If he starts mass on the button, his watch is fast

If he starts mass late, he has no respect for people's time

If he refurbishes the church, he's squandering the people's money

If he doesn't, he is letting the parish property run down

If he is young, he is inexperienced; If he is old, he should be retired

And when he dies, no one will ever replace him!

This reminds me of another little anecdote. A friend of mine announced at mass, he was being moved. After mass, he was out in the yard as people were leaving. They were coming over to tell him how much he would be missed. One woman was particularly upset, the tears were flowing. So, he searched for a consoling word to offer her.

'Look Mary he said, I was talking to the bishop, and he told me he is sending a lovely priest to you. I don't believe that Bishop, she said. But Mary, he said, why would you not believe your bishop. Because, she said, that's what he said when you were coming too !'

Thank God, despite impressions to the contrary often given, the people and priest in Ireland have, by and large, remained very close to each other. It is healthy when we can poke fun at each other.

We have all been through difficult times together in recent years. Yet despite all we have been through together, great trust still exists between people and their local priest.

On this, Vocation Sunday I want to say a word to parents. My message for you today is contained in a lovely story. It is a story told about Pope Pius X. It was actually on the day that he was consecrated bishop, long before he became pope. The ceremony had just finished. All the people present queued up along the altar rails to receive his blessing. Moving along the altar rails he spotted a familiar face. As he gave his blessing the woman reached to kiss his ring. He stooped low and whispered in her ear.

'Mom, but for that wedding ring on your finger, this ring could never have been on mine !

His single sentence said it all. You cannot speak about vocations, without speaking about homes. The first seminary any young man goes to is his own home. His first Spiritual Directors are his own parents. They are also the best he will ever have. They teach and inspire by their example.

Example is not just the best teacher in every home, it's the only one that works. Without Christian homes, homes where the faith is lived, and Family prayer is shared, without these it is very hard to see where vocations will come from. So Christian homes are vital to the future of your church. It is in the atmosphere of a Christian home, where Christian values are learned from being lived, that a son or daughter can hear the gentle whispering of the Lord 'Come, Follow Me'

So, in a very real sense, in the most real sense of all, the future of your church does not depend on priests. It depends on the Christian homes you create. It depends on your lived values as Christian parents. God calls whom He wills. We don't know why God calls some and does not call others.

Maybe we don't always agree with His choice. Sometimes it seems to our eyes a total mystery.

There were almost one hundred fine young men in my year starting seminary. When it came to ordination day seven years later, our figures were in the mid-thirties. By human standards most of those who had left would have made the most fantastic priests. Many of us who stayed would have envied their qualities. But God works in strange ways. He doesn't choose the most suitable to human eyes. He doesn't choose the most gifted or the most brilliant. Simply, He chooses whom He wills. And that's both the joy and the mystery of vocations.

Jesus himself choose twelve. Judas who betrayed Him and Peter, who denied He ever knew the man and a bunch of disciples who disappeared like scalded cats, when He was arrested and crucified.

The mystery of God's choice has always baffled people. Who, on that First Good Friday evening with their founder hanging disgraced on a cross and His followers scattered and dispirited, who would have given this crazy sect any chance of survival?

Yet two thousand years later over a billion people across the world commit themselves to following His Way of Living. His church is home to sinners and saints alike. Just as well, because if the church were only for the sinless, none of us would be eligible for membership.

God uses human instruments to achieve His goal. But that is all they are, just instruments, awkward and imperfect ones, fragile human instruments in the mighty hand of God. I will leave you with a thought I picked up somewhere lately. I think it has much in it to reflect on. There is a crack in everything God makes. It is through the crack that the light comes in

In praying for vocations today, we pray not for perfect instruments. Jesus did not find them, Himself.

We are unlikely to. We pray for ones with expansive cracks, so that despite their frail humanity, His light will shine through them.

5th Sunday of Easter

Love one another as I have loved you

In the world of business and indeed in our own Parish, one of the things that has to be done every year Is submit the books and accounts for audit, A qualified expert trawls through them and decides if we have honoured our stewardship. and if we haven't, we get hauled over the coals. What would happen if at the end of each year, each of us had to submit our personal lives for audit. If a qualified expert were to audit how we performed under a few headings like: Life in our family home, diligence in my place of work, honesty in my dealings and love in my relationships. One of the standards against which my record is judged being, how by living by my Christian values, I have become a better human being. Have I contributed to the betterment of life for those in my family and for those in my community.

The standard of excellence against which my performance is audited is the one that the Jesus sets down for each of us in today's gospel; "Love one another as I have loved you. By this all will know you are my disciples, by your love for one another". I am afraid my auditor would be returning the books with a list of amendments to be made, before he could sign off on the account. I could imagine him poring over my records looking for answers to a few critical questions. How much of a difference has my faith in Jesus Christ made to how I lived in the last year?

Maybe a better measurement might be how much of a difference has it made to the lives of those in my family, to the lives of those among whom I work, to the lives of those who live next door to me, to the lives of those dealt a tough hand of cards in life, to the lives of those lonely or depressed around me. How much of a difference has the fact that I believe in Jesus Christ and am committed to live His Standards and Values made to the lives of those among whom I live and beside whom I work. Hopefully it has made a bigger difference than we realise or give ourselves credit for often.

But that is much harder to quantify than figures on the auditor's page, and as every parent knows can often take years to show its results. It is a great help that we gather here each weekend to pray together, to reflect and to reaffirm our support for each other. It is good, because each weekend the Lord calls us again, challenges us and encourages us. gives us hope and strengthens our resolve. We go out from here each weekend with renewed hope and a new resolve to do a little bit better, to try a little bit harder.

How much of a difference does our presence here make to the way we live, after we have gone out from here? It is bound to make some difference and have some influence for good. But how much an influence? That is the crunch question. What we do know for sure is, that whatever influence for good we each will have, will be by our example rather than by our words.

And that brings us right back to the beginning again. The standard of excellence we are given to aspire to is "Love one another as I have loved you. By this love you have for one another everyone will know you are my disciples". The Real Church in our parish is not a building but us the people. we who believe and do our best to live by our beliefs. One of the great fallacies of our time is that people think that being Catholic is about belonging to an organisation. Being Catholic is not about belonging to an organisation. Being Catholic is about being committed to a way of living

Being honest, we are all here today because of the faith of others. We saw the values our own parents lived by. We wanted to live by those values ourselves. They taught us, not by their words, but by their example. We can only hope to teach or influence others by our example. It is the way it has been for over two thousand years. It is the way it is going to be in the years ahead.

This Parish will be a better place because we are here. This community will be a better place because of our lives. The world will be a better place because we have been around. The audit won't have to be done in this life and that audit when it comes will be done by the one who has died for us.

6th Sunday of Easter

If anyone loves me, he will keep my Word

I remember a discussion I had some years ago with someone who was making a very big decision

She explained to me at the time that her faith was very important to her, that she had brought her situation to the Lord that she had prayed a lot about it before making this decision. She said to me, "I know now I'm doing what is right for me". Now how could anyone be other than happy, to find that someone prays over, and brings to the Lord, their big decisions in their life?

So, you will probably be surprised if not disappointed when I tell you that she left me very confused at the end of her story. You see, the decision she had made was, objectively at least, in direct conflict with the teachings of her Faith, which she had emphasized to me was very important to her. She knew that for as long as she followed the road she had chosen, she was excluding herself from Holy Communion, which was a huge step for her to take

Now, let me say at the outset, that I totally accept that the Lord gave each of us free will. The Lord respects the decisions we choose to make using our free will. I would be the first to guarantee that the God I believe in, doesn't strike down or bang the door on people who turn their back on Him and walk away, no more than you could imagine a mother slamming the door on her son or daughter, just because they made a decision in life that she profoundly disagreed with. But the fact that she doesn't bang the door and lock them out, does not mean that she condones the wrong decision made.

But what confused me so much about my friend in her situation was that she seemed to be implicating the Lord in reaching her decision, kind of giving Him credit for steering her in the direction she had chosen to go and seeing Him as being on her side in this decision. This God she was describing seemed to me to be contradicting Himself, telling us one thing in His ten Commandments, but, if you consulted Him privately yourself, He seemed to be telling you the opposite!

So, in other words while God had decided what was right and what was wrong for us all, but If you engaged in private consultation with Him yourself, He could change the rules to suit the situation you found yourself in.

Now I don't know about you, but I couldn't square that God with the words of Jesus in today's gospel: —

"If anyone loves me, he will keep my Word, and my Father will love him and we will come to him and make our home in him." ...Those who do not love me do not keep my word."

His Words are straight. His Words are to the point. He calls the tune on what is right and what is wrong for each of us. We can decide whether or not we dance to His tune. But He doesn't include a clause that we can change the music if we have difficulty dancing to the tune! There is only one true God, the God who revealed Himself to us in Jesus Christ, who died for us on Calvary and rose on Easter Sunday. That God is the God of Truth not a God of contradictions. Other "gods" that are presented to us today in media and private opinions are figments of human imagination. They create comfortable, temporary passing illusions; "Illusions!", that merely postpone the pain of facing truth.

Contrast those woolly illusions with the stark clarity of the words of Jesus to us in the gospel today. He who loves me keeps my word. He who doesn't love me does not keep my word. Nothing in there about dispensations available from His commandments for those who arrange 'private consultations' with Him. What is there, is a clear yardstick that applies to all our lives. Ultimately, it is the only yardstick that is relevant, because it is also the only one that is real. All other yardsticks are figments of human imagination. If you love me, you will keep my Word.

Ascension of the Lord

Where He has gone, we will one day follow

I take it most of us here in this part of the country followed with great interest the debates in the Dail some years ago, on whether or not the days of our going to the bog were over. Some of us were listening with great interest because we had spent days in the bog in our youth, cutting, footing and saving the turf for the upcoming winter. Listening to all the debates brought back to me childhood memories of the huge reek of turf that used to stand in the haggard, the firing for the winter secured.

In September it was something to behold, carefully 'clamped' to keep out the water and thatched to protect the reek's roof from the elements.

Every day I was sent off to the reek with my bucket. When I used to look at the size of the reek and look at the few sods in my bucket, sure I knew we'd never ever get to the end of the pile. But by late Spring when I came with my bucket, all that was left was little 'ciarans' and turf dust. Sure, the reek I thought was going to last forever, was no more to be seen. It was all burnt and gone. Of course, if I had a brain in my head, I would have figured that every sod I put in the bucket each day left one sod less in the reek. Then one day all that was left in the haggard was a huge black spot where the reek had once stood. It was time to tackle up, and head back to the bog and the cycle began all over again.

In the springtime of life when we were young and seemed master of all we surveyed, our whole life lay out there before us. Like those sods in the Reek in the haggard, we felt our days were without end. And since we only used them 'one day at a time', it was hard to foresee then, that one day not light years away, we'd come to the Autumn of life and find we had only the ciarans now left behind. Like the great reek of turf in the haggard in September, soon only a patch of brown ground in a graveyard would now mark the spot on this earth where we had once stood.

But for us, there's no going 'back to the bog' then, to replenish all the days we have used up. Just as there's no longer a reek in the haggard to replace all the sods that we have burned. The big question that then will confront us, is that graveyard for us to be the end, or have we made sure we have in our pocket our Passport for the New Life now to begin? The answer to that question will easily be read in the record of the life we've just lived

As we celebrate today the Lord's Ascension into Heaven, we listen with interest to His Words. He has told us that where He has gone, we are to follow Passport in hand at the Gate. Every day of our life we are living, a Chapter to that Passport we add, a page in our book we are writing. The Book of our Life is our passport. That is the book we bring on our last journey. It is the only one recognised at the Final Check-in.

Pentecost Sunday

We are sowers of the seed; it is the Lord who takes care of the growth.

Today we celebrate the Feast of Pentecost. Jesus promised the Apostles that He would not leave them on their own; that He would send the Holy Spirit to be with them. Today we celebrate the fulfilment of His promise.

We all know the story of the First Pentecost. The disciples huddled in the upper room in fear. They had seen what happened to Jesus. They feared the same fate awaited them. There came what sounded like a powerful wind. Something appeared like tongues of fire that separated and came to rest on each one of them. They were filled with the Holy Spirit. In that moment they were totally transformed. Peter who had been so scared to even admit that he ever even knew Jesus, was now openly preaching about Him in the streets with total disregard for what might happen to him. Other disciples fanned out across the Land preaching the message of Jesus. Many of them did not just die as martyrs, they actually saw it as a privilege to have the opportunity.

The Holy Spirit that descended on the disciples on that First Pentecost is the same Holy Spirit you and I received in Baptism and Confirmation. That same Holy Spirit is within each of us, otherwise neither you nor I would be here today, because Scripture tells us no one can say Jesus is Lord unless God's spirit is in them. The Holy Spirit is within each of us. He is the light that guides us and keeps us on the right road when we are hugely tempted to take the wrong one. It is God's spirit within each of us that helps us to choose the good and the right, in preference to the attractive and the wrong.

And isn't it so encouraging for us to know, that group in the Upper Room on that First Pentecost were chosen not for what they could do for God, individually or collectively. They were chosen for what God could do through them. As God choose to depend on them then, He has chosen to depend on us now. If God's spirit is to shine in the world today, He wants it to shine, through us. If God's spirit is to change the world today, He wants to use our life to bring about that change. He wants that change to be brought about by very ordinary people like you and me, trying our best to live the values of the gospel in our hearts, to pass on the values of the gospel in our homes and reflect the values of the Gospel in our lives.

So, never ever, underestimate the power of your example within the walls of your own home. The power of the witness you give, as you live your life each day here in your own community, your example at home and your witness in your parish are the fruits of the Holy Spirit within you.

All of our lives are each day planting seeds. We may be well gone when those seeds begin to flower and bear fruit. We are just the sowers of the seeds. It is the Holy Spirit that takes care of their growth. It is He who both creates and reaps the harvest. And fifty years from now, when that Harvest is finally reaped, hopefully it will have made a difference that you and I have lived.

The Most Holy Trinity

If we really want to hear the message we will cope with the flaws of the transmitter !

In today's gospel Jesus said to His disciples.

I still have many things to tell you, but they would be too much for you now. When the spirit comes, He will lead you to the complete truth. All He tells you will be taken from what is mine.

So, it is not me who is saying that God's Spirit is with us. It is not our bishop who is saying it. It is not Pope Francis who is saying it. It is not even a great saint who is saying it. These are the words of Jesus. How important are these words to me, as important as Jesus is to me

For us gathered here, Jesus is very important. We believe Jesus is the Son of God, the Second Person of the Blessed Trinity, Saviour of the world. We believe Jesus is Our Saviour, our Redeemer and that our lives are built around Him. We entrust our newborn babies to Him in Baptism. As soon as they are able to understand, they welcome Him in Holy Communion. As they enter adulthood, they commit their lives to him in Confirmation. When a young couple, full of trust, commit their lives to each other in Matrimony they do it in His presence before the altar. Every week we gather to talk to Him about how we are doing, to ask for His help to do better next week. Going out the door of our homes, we entrust ourselves into His care by sprinkling the Holy Water on ourselves. This Jesus is the very centre of our lives. From Him we take our values. To Him we go when we draw our last breath.

This Jesus we know is the Son of God. That is what we are saying by being here. Knowing that Jesus is the Son of God, we are absolutely certain that He could not lie to us. We are absolutely certain that when He tells us something, it is the truth. What does He tell us in today's gospel? I am going back to my Father now. But I still have an awful lot to tell you, so much that you could not take it all in together now. But do not worry. When I am gone, I am not leaving you on your own. My spirit will guide you and teach you through the church. He will teach you the truth. I am guaranteeing you that and I can guarantee that, because I will be with my church.

So, when you are hearing the gospel and the teaching of your church, the voice you are hearing is my voice. The teaching you are hearing is my teaching. The church does not speak of itself or for itself. It speaks in my name and for me. What it teaches, I teach. What it puts before you, I put before you.

Jesus guarantees that the Holy spirit will always guide the church. The purpose of that guidance is not for the church alone, but for you and me. We may find the message welcome or unwelcome. We may find the message challenging or difficult. But what we cannot deny is whose voice is speaking. Jesus speaks to you and me today, as directly, as clearly and as powerfully as He spoke to His disciples on the shores of Galilee. He speaks in His Church's teaching. His message is, he who hears you hears Me. He who hears Me hears Him who sent me.

It would be great if the church were perfect. It would be even better if the voice of Jesus Christ was always coming through with clarity. That is not always the case of course. Not every Pope has been a candidate for canonisation. Not every bishop has been a paragon of virtue. Not every priest can be proud of his performance or his record.

The voice of Jesus has to come through vessels of clay. The vessels of clay can be very poor transmitters. Their own frailty often comes in the way. But the challenge to people of faith is to see beyond the human frailty of the transmitter to the message of the Master. That can be a big challenge.

I'm going to finish with a story. It makes the point that however faulty the medium, if we really want to get the message we will. This might seem hard to believe, but In the Maynooth of the sixties, we were not even allowed to have a transistor radio. I believe that in the class ahead of me there were eighteen young men who had already worn their county jersey at minor level. You can imagine the interest in the GAA the student body had. On Sundays our club teams were playing back home. Match results were pearls of great price. On Sunday night the late Sean Og O Ceallachain reeled them off on radio. But no use knowing he did it, unless you could hear them. An inventive science student put together a contraption, that you could fit in a match box, so you wouldn't get caught. You attached it to a tape-recorder, (they were allowed). By some miracle the tape recorder acted as a radio receiver. There was crackling and there was tearing. There was static and every kind of interference. But with a superhuman effort and your ear up against the recorder, you could battle all the crackle, and you get the results. They were transcribed onto little bits of paper and slipped under the doors of different rooms. The boys went to sleep happy knowing how their team had done.

The match results were so important to us. We wanted so desperately to get them. That static or interference or faulty equipment did not come in the way. Sacrifices were made and risks were taken. The message was important. The difficulty of getting it was irrelevant. Today the church is the medium for us. It is not perfect, it never was. The voice of Christ can often become garbled and difficult to hear. Those who really want to hear the message will hear it, despite the faults of the transmitter. Those who do not want to hear the message will find in the faults of the transmitter, an excuse to avoid it. For almost two thousand years Jesus has spoken through the church. For almost two thousand years those who wanted to, have heard His message. Today Jesus speaks to all of us through His church. It is as imperfect today as it ever was in history

People who have the faith hear the message and ignore the static. People who lack faith hear the static and ignore the message. The words in today's gospel are the words of Jesus not our words. He who hears you hears me. He who hears me hears Him who sent me. Jesus Christ speaks to us today through His Church. People, who are determined to hear the message, are able to make allowances for the many imperfections of the messenger. But for those, who have real difficulties with the message, the frailty of the messenger can sometimes be a significant stumbling block. Unfortunately, as we messengers know to our cost, the Lord was not into the best quality of crystal. He had a weakness for earthenware jars.

The Most Holy Body and Blood of Christ

Figs are not gathered from thorn bushes, nor are grapes picked from brambles.

One Sunday, many years ago, I left some of my belongings in the sacristy after mass. I missed them when I got home and headed back to the Church to recover them. It was bucketing rain and Maggie was just leaving the church. I knew she was walking the two miles home. So, I said to her, hop into the car and I will run you home. We were chatting in the car on our way. I couldn't resist asking Maggie a question. Maggie, I said, I have been noticing for a long time that you're always in the church nearly a half hour before mass and you're the very last person to leave the church after mass. You must have an extraordinary Faith and devotion to Our Lord. I was totally unprepared for the turn the conversation took. What I'm going to share with you, you may find incredible. But it is true, and I am witness to it first-hand. I was there

Maggie explained to me that she had a very different reason for being first into the church and last to leave it. I don't have a pair of shoes of my own that I could wear going to mass, so I wear my husband's shoes, but they are a bit too big for me. But I would be awful embarrassed if anyone saw them on me. That is why I have to be in the church long before anyone could meet me. That's why I can't leave the church till everyone else is well gone. Imagine what her Mass meant to that woman, -the lengths she was prepared to go to, rather than miss mass.

Today is the feast of Corpus Christi, the Feast of the Eucharist. It is a good day for us all, to hear Maggie's story. It speaks more powerfully than any words I could say to you about the love of the Eucharist that has been handed down to us and the place the mass has always had in the lives of our people.

Much more recently I was in a house one day. I was having a cup of coffee at the kitchen table. The little ones were all excited telling me about school and showing me their drawings and their copies. They were all in the National School at the time. Their mom seemed to feel the need to explain something to me. God, I'm so sorry father, we are never able to bring them to mass. We would love to, and I have always really wanted to, but mass time on Saturday evening clashes with Jimmy's soccer training. He really loves, and lives for his soccer, and I just couldn't have the heart to deprive him of what he looks forward to so much. Then on Sunday morning the girls have their pony riding lessons. They love their ponies and look forward so much to Sunday morning. Sure, I couldn't be so heartless as to deprive them of that. But sometimes I do feel bad, that I can't manage to bring them to mass at the weekend

Now I am not in any position to judge anyone, nor do I have any right or intention of so doing. But I just put before you the two scenarios. Poor Maggie didn't even own a pair of decent shoes to wear. Her only way of getting to mass, rain, hail or sunshine, was to put her pride in her pocket, take the risk, and foot it out the two miles in Johnny's shoes. Whatever it took to get to mass on Sunday was a challenge to be overcome, not an excuse to stay at home. No challenge would stop her. No price was too high for her to pay. The other family I mentioned were in a very different place. There were two cars outside the door and two drivers inside. They certainly did not have a problem about decent shoes to wear.

Last week I was talking to a parishioner who was very much in touch with our current situation and really concerned about the shortage of priests in the diocese. He listed off all the parishes that no longer have a resident priest. I think he must have named off about fifteen of them. He asked me what is gone wrong at all. What are we going to do? Sure, if we don't have priests, we won't be able to have mass. I could have said, but I didn't; Vocations don't grow on trees. Vocations grow in the heart of families, who are both praying and practicing their Faith. Indeed, Jesus Himself told us that figs are not gathered from thorn bushes, nor are grapes picked from brambles. The Eucharist is the foundation and pinnacle of our Faith. Without vocations in our generation, how can there be Eucharist for the next generation?

Today is the Feast of Corpus Christi, the feast of the Eucharist. I have set before you two scenarios. Geographically they are situated no more than twenty kilometres apart. But in values and priorities they reflect two totally different worlds. One speaks a set of values where vocations spring up and thrive. The other, a set of values where the seed may well fall but might find it very difficult to find root and grow. We know, and our experience confirms for us, that vocations grow in the heart of families. The first seminary any young man goes to is his own home. His first spiritual directors are his own parents. They are the best spiritual directors he will ever have, because the values they transmit are the values they live by. Thank God we still have many such homes in our community. Thank God we still have much fertile soil, for those seeds to fall on.

Where the Lord chooses to drop those seeds today, may they find in our homes, both the climate and the support conducive to their growth. May their fruit ensure Eucharist for the next generation.

13th Sunday in Ordinary Time

The devil destroys with the tongue.

It is always Good to keep the ear to the ground. You never know where you knock across someone with a little nugget of wisdom to share. Reading the second reading of today's mass reminded me of the day I was at a wedding. There was this fellow beside me at the table, who not only had his own remarkable insights into life, relationships and religion, but he was also more than willing to share them.

"Look here to me" he said, at one stage during the meal. "Our religion is very simple. There is only one thing to it. That is charity. If you have that, you have it all. If people had charity, they would respect each other. They would not "be clipping' each other. They would not be tearing strips off each other. That is my religion" he said. "And 'it is all there." He then slipped in at the end, a very gentle sting in the tail. "I cannot understand" he said, "why ye priests do not just get up there and tell that to the people.

St. Paul would have been proud of him today. St. Paul says in the second reading of our mass today:—

"The whole law is summarized in a single commandment. Love your neighbour as yourself. If you go snapping at each other and tearing each other to pieces, you will destroy the whole community." We all know how a loose tongue can be the cause of great pain and hurt to innocent victims, who are defenceless, because not being present, they have no right of reply. Serious and maybe even irreparable wrong is done, when someone else's good name is taken. I was struck by something someone said in a court case recently. If you rob someone else's money or property, you can be sent to jail for it. How much more serious a crime it is to rob their good name?

Another thing worth remembering is, if we take something that belongs to another person, be it their money, or their bicycle, or the oil from their tank, in order to be forgiven we have an obligation to make restitution and to give it back. Now you tell me, how do we restore someone's good name if we have taken it. How can that obligation to make restitution ever be fulfilled?. And Paddy said to me that evening at the wedding: –

"Our religion is very simple. There is only one thing to it, charity. If you have that, you have it all. If people have charity they will have respect for each other. They won't 'clip' each other. They won't 'do' each other. They won't gossip or take strips off each other. That's my religion and it's all there."

St Paul would not only agree with him but would be more than proud to have him on his side, because this is what St Paul tells us today in the second reading, "The whole law is summarized in a single commandment. 'Love your neighbour as yourself. If you go snapping at each other and tearing each other to pieces, you will destroy the whole community."

Careless, mischievous or malicious words are like poisoned arrows, once released, control over them is lost. They do not have a recall button. No one knows how far they will travel or the havoc they will wreak on their journey. No one to my knowledge has yet found a way to undo their damage. For once at least, both St Paul and Paddy are on the same page. If we could all stay on that page with them, there would be less pain in our world. There would be less 'felt' hurt in our communities and far fewer people suffering the pain of being wronged

Just a little rule of thumb for all of us. When someone's name comes up in conversation and you are just about to say something, run a little check for yourself. Ask yourself, if this person were within hearing range, would I say this? If you would not, then it's best not said. And the same principle applies to the ears as to the tongue, because if there were no listeners, there could be no gossipers. I will leave you today with very strong words on this. But these words are not mine. They are a quote on this subject from Pope Francis. He says

The devil destroys with the tongue, The habit of gossiping is a form of 'terrorism.' The gossiper is a terrorist who throws a grenade, to destroy.

Pope Francis concludes with a request to all of us. Please fight against division, because it is one of the weapons that the devil uses to destroy the local church and the universal church.

14th Sunday in Ordinary Time

It takes courage and conviction to swim against the tide.

I think most of us are familiar with how the court system works, even if most of us would prefer not to have personal experience of it. But one thing we all know is that if we are involved in something like a road accident, and if it must go into court to sort out who was in the right and who was in the wrong, it can be vital to have good witnesses, who are prepared to take the stand. Sometimes that can take great courage, because a witness knows, that what they say can have serious repercussions for one side or the other.

But crucial though witnesses are, they are worthless unless they have two qualities. They must be truthful, and they must be courageous. Truthful, because the purpose of the court is to dig out the truth. Courageous, because sometimes it is neither popular nor easy to tell the truth, especially when others will be affected by what you have to say, and it may even have serious repercussions for yourself.

In today's gospel story, the Lord Himself appointed seventy-two and sent them out to be His witnesses. He entrusted to them the responsibility to preach the truth and have the courage to stand over it. He told them there would be a price to pay. What He asked of his disciples then, is what He asks of us today, to accept the truth of His gospel, to live it in our lives and to be prepared to do that especially when there is a price to pay for doing it. The most effective form of witness is example. We all know that from our own experience. Most of us can trace what is in our hearts today to the influence of our homes

Example is just another 'name' for Witness. At a time when everyone in a parish went to mass and everyone shared broadly in the same set of values, there was a tide that carried us all along together. Every swimmer knows how easy it is to float with the tide, to just lie on your back in the sea, surrender control and be carried along in harmony with the flow. It is comfortable, It is unchallenging, and it is effortless. But it is quite a different thing to have to grab control and fight for your life against a current that's sucking you off to where you don't want to go.

Just as in the ocean, so in the cycle of history, the tides change. When they do, in life, as in the ocean, they separate the drifters from the swimmers. In Baptism, we give our children a Certificate that tells them who they are. But only our example will empower and enable them to become who the Lord is calling them to become. It can take a lot of courage and conviction for many young people to swim against the tide today, knowing as they do, that swimming against the tide, often won't earn them brownie points from their peers.

They have to pay a price, a price we didn't have to pay. Living their truth today can come at a heavy cost for those who really want to. For them to become good witness in their world, they need us to be even better witnesses in our world. Lived example in their homes is the best witness we can give them. To be best witnesses for them, we have to be seen to live our truth with courage and ready to do so 'best' even when it 'costs most'

Sometimes a picture is better than a thousand words. A man watches a woman plant a tree and asks; How long will it take for that tree to bear fruit. The woman answers seventy years. Are you so fit and strong, he asks, that you expect to live that long and eat its fruit. The woman answered. I found a fruitful world because my ancestors planted for me., so I will do the same for my children. The heading of that piece, by the way, is; 'The Earth is not inherited from our ancestors it is borrowed from our children'

The Faith is not just inherited from our ancestors. We have been given it in trust for our children. It is on loan to us from our children. We need to take that loan seriously. For our children to enjoy the fruits of our planting, to be what the Lord called us to be, His witnesses, is to treasure the Faith we have received, to live that Faith in truth and with courage regardless of the price it asks for, and to do so regardless of the repercussions it may have for us. May I repeat.

A man watches a woman plant a tree and asks; how long it will take for that tree to bear fruit. The woman answers seventy years. Are you so fit and strong, he asks, that you expect to live that long and eat its fruit. The woman answered. I found a fruitful world because my ancestors planted for me. So, I will do the same for my children.

May our children find the trees we've planted laden with fruit, and may they so appreciate what our example has left them, that like that woman they will want to do the same for their children.

15th Sunday in Ordinary Time

The absence of listening ears can neutralise a lethal tongue.

Of all the parables in the gospel, the story of the Good Samaritan is probably not only one of the best-known, but also the one where the message is clearest. "Go and do the same yourself" Jesus said to His hearers. We can see the battered body on the roadside. We hear how differently the passers-by reacted. We are left in no doubt how we should. One way to get to the heart of the parable's message might be to take a good look at the different people in the story, and to ask ourselves, in whose shoes do I fit?

None of us would like to be found in the shoes of the priest or Levite, who ignored the victim and passed by on the other side of the road. We might all like to see ourselves in the shoes of the Good Samaritan who showed compassion, who interrupted his journey, pulled up, and went to his aid.

I am certain none of us would see ourselves as the brute responsible for the attack and robbery. We would all hope that we would never be the poor victim attacked and left half-dead on the roadside, nor would we ever want something so brutal to happen to anyone in our community, never mind the revulsion we feel at the thought that any of us could be the perpetrator. When I was at school many years ago, the master had a saying; There are more ways of killing a dog than choking him with a pound of butter! Equally there are more ways that people get crushed and have the life drained out of them than being physically attacked and left half dead on the roadside.

Many have their lives bruised and battered by broken trust and shattered dreams and by wrongs inflicted. Their wounds may not be bleeding, but their pain is no less real even when that pain is carried silently in their hearts. We do not have to wield physical weapons to mortally wound another human being. The sharpest spear of all can be the tongue and there is nothing that cuts as deep as it, when it is plunged in with a sharpened edge.

The most precious and irreplaceable possession that anyone has Is their character and good name

And the razor like edge of a sharpened tongue can be more devastating to a person's good name than the poisoned arrow piercing their body. The tongue can do little damage without the assistance of a pair of ears. The tongue may be that of someone else. But for its lethal power to be effective it needs a pair of listening ears. We have to be so careful those ears are never ours. When they are, we are the ones supplying the instruments of execution.

Let us look at that parable again. While we all admire the Good Samaritan, who was moved to compassion, stopped and helped the victim. Would it not have been wonderful if he had arrived on the scene just that bit sooner, read the signs, realised the attack was about to happen and by his intervention prevented it. He would have ensured that there was no battered body on the roadside.

Is that not an opportunity that each of us is given, to read the signs emerging and to sense that there is a tongue just about to go on a rampage. By refusing to provide a listening ear, we can rob the would-be attacker of their potential to wreak havoc.

Granted there may be a slightly different way to interpret this parable. But it might just be by far the most effective weapon, to protect each other, pre-empt the damage and render poisoned tongues powerless. Each time we succeed in doing it, we make sure that there is one less battered body dumped on the margin of life's roadside

16th Sunday in Ordinary Time

Jesus of Bethany, the real Jesus of the gospel, truly human just like us.

The winding goat-track road was just the same

Children picking flowers, hoping to make a sale

Multi-coloured goats grazing at either side

A little group of pilgrims huddle on the hillside

A gospel reading........... a few moments quiet

The 'goat-track' path is just the same

Wonder Lord, as you travelled here

Were there children selling flowers ?

Over the hill and down into the valley we go

Jerusalem sinking out of view behind us

Jerusalem of the thronging crowds

City of swirling dust and strong smells

Behind us a great door closed it out

Before us a new one opens up

Soon we'll be in Bethany

'Jesus loved Martha and Mary and their brother Lazarus'

The gospel is so direct, so unashamed of truth

So forthright, we might even say so 'daring'

In Bethany Jesus was at home

Here He could be Himself

If He ever needed an hour 'off duty' or 'off guard'

It must surely be here He stole it

Jesus needed Bethany
That makes Him so human, so real
So relatable to, so liveable with, so loveable
Sitting in that church and He was there
Not just in the tabernacle behind a golden door
I spotted Him somewhere else
Across the floor,
By the kitchen table, buried in a chair,
Wearied limbs snatching a needed break

Was it Martha made the tea, or was it Mary?
Today it was so welcome, He didn't seem to mind
We didn't crowd them out
There was space for all of us

It was peace, perfect peace
And presence, total presence

No need here to impress

No need here to prove oneself, just to be

Bethany, where Jesus shared

Not just news, events or things

But His very self,

Bethany where He had the freedom to unfold

'Who do people say that I am ?'

His need was not for answers

But hearts with whom to share

Bethany, where Jesus loved

Bethany where He allowed Himself BE loved

Where He dared accept human acceptance given

The need for human company, the need to share His story

The peeling off those layers of human onion

The occasional escaped tear

The need to love, the risk of allowing Himself be loved

The experienced human need for affirmation and support

That goodness, the value the blessing

The very sacredness of human love

Through which we are called unashamedly

To support, to accept, to affirm on another

Jesus, I never doubted that you were human

Only problem is

I never had to handle it as such close range before

Peel off those layers of onion

Our insides are just the same!

There were many beautiful moments on our pilgrimage

Many touching stories in the Holy Land

But if for one moment I lost my bearings

And slid from the shackles of the body

To savour a tiny minuscule of Heaven

That moment was in Bethany

Thank you, Mary or was it Martha, who made the tea

Thank you for sharing with us our Mutual Friend

Bethany,
Where I learned more about myself, than about a place
Bethany, where I felt so close to my Most Special friend

In Bethany I met a special friend, so truly human just like me, my brother in the flesh, with that same deep need for human friendship, that is at the core of who we are.

Jesus of Bethany, the real Jesus of the gospel, truly human just like us. Jesus, so fully human, the same Jesus who is our God. To meet Him in Bethany and in life's treasured friendships is to realise, as we have never realised before, how fully understood by Him we really are.

17th Sunday in Ordinary Time

Forgive us our trespasses as we forgive those who trespass against us.

I have a priest friend who has strong convictions about prayer; He says, 'You should be very sure before you pray for something that you actually want God to give it to you, or sometimes we might get an awful shock, if God answered the prayer we made'.

For instance, every time we say the Our Father, we pray; forgive us as we forgive others. What would we do if God took us at our word and did just that, only forgave us to the degree that we forgive each other? We would be in deep, deep trouble. My friend's words of advice deserve careful reflection. We need to be very sure before we pray for something, that we do actually want what we pray for to happen, or we could get a horrible shock if God answered our prayer.

One day Jesus' disciples asked Him to teach them how to pray and He did. He gave them the Our Father. The Our Father includes the phrase; 'Forgive us, as we forgive others'. When we say this to God, each time we pray the Our Father, do we mean Him to take us seriously?

A story is told about a small town in America that had been 'dry'. No one in the town sold alcohol. A local businessman spotted the opportunity, and he decided to open a tavern. A group of Christians from the local church were alarmed. They organised an all-night Vigil of Prayer outside the tavern. They stormed Heaven asking God to intervene, to protect their community from the evils of alcohol. It just so happened that shortly afterwards, lightning struck the tavern, and it burned to the ground. The owner of the bar sued the church-group, claiming that the prayers of the congregation were responsible. Their day in court came. The Church Group had an eminent lawyer to defend them. He argued convincingly in court that they could not be held responsible. The publican's case was that the prayers of the Christians worked. The Christians defence was that they did not! The presiding judge, after his initial review of the case, stated; "no matter how this case comes out, one thing is clear to me, the tavern owner believes in prayer and the Christians do not." Now a question for us all. Which side am I on?

Am I among the ones that believe God will hear and answer my prayer, or am I one of the bunch that believes He will not?

At mass today we will all pray to God in the Our Father; 'Forgive us our trespasses as we forgive those who trespass against us. We are asking Him to model the forgiveness He will give us on the forgiveness that we give to others! Suppose He does exactly what we are asking Him to do! Then we had better get off the starting blocks pretty fast and forgive those we need to forgive. Do I need to pick up the phone and make that call today? Do I need to knock at someone's door to extend my hand of friendship, because today I am saying to God. Lord forgive me my offence against you, as I forgive those who have offended me. I am saying to Him, Lord heal the hurt I have suffered, to the same degree that I have healed the hurts I have caused. For our prayer to be sincere, we must show the same forgiveness to others as we expect the Lord to show to us. That is what we are asking Him to do!

Once Jesus was in a certain place praying. When He had finished one of His disciples said to Him, Lord teach us to pray just as John taught his disciples. Jesus said, say this when you pray, say to God;

Forgive us our sins as we ourselves forgive those who have sinned against us. We are asking Jesus that when He goes to forgive us, to check the forgiveness that He sees us give to others and then to apply that standard to how He forgives us!. When we pray the Our Father at mass today, indeed, every time we pray the Our Father, we need to keep this in mind and address it

18th Sunday in Ordinary Time

Isn't it amazing how you exaggerate when you are in a holt!

Two Irish priests were heading to the States to work in parishes for the Summer. In mid-Atlantic the plane hit serious turbulence and began to be tossed around in the sky. Sensing the panic breaking out on board someone asked the priests if they would ever do something, say a prayer, give a blessing, to help restore calm and give a bit of reassurance.

Fr Jimmy, though he was as petrified as the rest took the microphone and led them all in prayer. They were in

God's hands he reassured them, and they would be safe. He finished his prayer by giving them all General Absolution. Then as things got even worse, he leaned over to his colleague and whispered; 'Any chance, you would hear my confession. So, they went to Confession to each other. After what seemed an eternity, though it had been only minutes, the captain's voice announced, that the danger was past. They were out of the turbulence. They were all safe. They would be on the ground in Kennedy airport at 3.30pm USA time. The relief that flowed through the plane was palpable. People could be heard chatting to each other again, as they shared the pictures that had flashed across their minds.

The two priests sat in stunned silence beside each other, staring straight ahead, as if they were still seeing a ghost before them! Not a word or even a glance was being exchanged between them. Finally, Fr. Jim, realising their silence was not going un-noticed, began to feel more and more embarrassed, until finally he plucked up the courage, leaned over to his colleague and said, Fr Johnny "Isn't it amazing the way you exaggerate things when you are in a holt!" Exaggerate, when you are in a holt, or tell the truth when it is the only choice you have got? In turbulence at thirty thousand feet, you are sailing fairly close to God!

If each time we were going to confession, we were in Fr. Jim's shoes that day and we really believed, that this confession was the last one we were ever going to have a chance to make before standing nakedly before our god, would there be a difference in the Confession we would make? Would what we poured out then really be an exaggeration, or, when the chips are down, would it be just me seeing myself, as I really am, standing in my transparency before my God. Well, the truth is that this will be the reality for each of us some day. None of us knows which confession will be our last. One way to make a really good confession always, is to prepare for each as if it were going to be our last. If we always adopted this perspective, what frankness and honesty we would show before our God!

It is so important but so difficult at times, to hold the balance, to enjoy the blessings God has given us, but to do so without forgetting that each and every one of them is God's Gift to us. That is why to-day's gospel is such a powerfully challenging message. To the person who became so absorbed and wrapped up in what he had accumulated and gathered round himself, that he had lost sight of life's purpose and the journey's end, God said, you fool, this very night your life shall be required of you, and whose will it all be then?

This life of ours, is but a journey, a journey to be enjoyed certainly, but a journey just the same. Enjoy the journey to the full. The Lord sure wants us to. But let our enjoyment never be at the price of losing sight of the purpose of the journey and what awaits us at our journey's end. None of us is in a hurry for the journey to finish, but none of us knows, when for us, it will. Being prepared is never a burden, particularly when we can so easily be, if we simply want to.

19th Sunday in Ordinary Time

For people who believe things will be so much better in the next life, it is amazing how few of us seem to be in a hurry to get there!

We're all going to die. We all know that already. You don't need me to tell you. But it is one thing to know it, it is a different thing to face up to it. There are moments when that truth hits us. It might be a near miss on the road, or if you were on a plane when it hits an air pocket and momentarily seems to be dropping out of the sky. I will never forget the day on holidays, when I decided to swim across a lake, only to realise halfway across I might not make it to the other shore. I will not share with you from the altar the pictures that flashed across my mind, realising; I'm going to die, and I'm going to die now. It can also come home to us in far less dramatic ways. I remember something that hit me as I was coming out of the graveyard the day of my father's funeral. He was the last surviving member of his family, as had my mother been of her's. My parents' generation was now gone. Mine was next. The next time the tide came in, it would be creeping up my ankles. That took time to sink in but sink in it did.

So, we all agree on one thing. we know that we are going to die. I am not sure any of us spend too much time thinking about it. Maybe that is the way in needs to be, no point in being morbid. But would it be very foolish to not be prepared when it came, because it is inevitable for all of us. Some are taken by total surprise. Have I any reason to think I will be the one to get advance notice. In the gospel Jesus tells us to 'Be like people waiting for the master's return, ready to open the door when He comes and knocks. Blessed are we, if He finds us awake when he comes'. Someone who did not believe in an afterlife once said of us; 'For a crowd of people, who believe things are going to be so much better in the next life, is it not amazing how few of you seem to be in a hurry to get there!'. If he knew us a bit better, he might have said; It is amazing how many of us, when our time comes, would use any opportunity available to postpone our departure for just a little bit longer.

Let us not be too hard on ourselves. The Lord understands us. Facing His own death terrified Him so much, that He sweated blood in Gethsemane and He said, 'Father if it be possible let this cup pass from me'. But when there was no escape, He was able to say. 'Father into your hands I commend my Spirit'. The finality of death is pretty shattering for families. The pain it brings cannot be put into words. But what never ceases to amaze me is how a devastated family, get such strength and consolation from being able to say 'But, he had a beautiful death!'. When they use that phrase 'He had a beautiful death', they are not talking about the surroundings in which he died, but about the attitude with which he faced it. It had little to do with what he had left behind, but everything to do with what he'd taken with him. It had little to do with what he had in life. It had lot to do with what he had become, in death. It had little to do with his preparedness to say his last goodbye. It had everything to do with being ready for who he was going to meet. At that moment two things had taken on huge importance, his personal faith and how he had lived. These were a great blessing to him, when he had to leave everything else behind. The best preparation for the next life is a life well lived in this one.

Since death is inevitable and none of us know when or how it will knock on our door, would we not be very foolish if it were to find us unprepared? 'You too must stand ready because the Son of Man is coming at an hour you do not expect'. The former Archbishop of Tuam, Joe Cassidy once began a homily on death with this sentence; Last Friday morning, my phone rang, I'm sorry to be bringing you this news, the voice said. But a good friend of yours died this morning. I got an awful shock he said.

This friend and I were the same age, born on the same street. We spent a lot of time together growing up. I knew, at our age, that he had years yet to live!

Sadly, someone is getting that phone call every day. How often is their reaction just the same; it can't be true. Someday, that phone call will be about me. What matters then is not the shock my best friends get on receiving the call. Far more important for me, whether or not I was prepared when the call came. Priest or no priest, none of us will be able to arrange a postponement. Be always ready; you know not the day nor the hour

20th Sunday in Ordinary Time

God's law takes precedence over culture and convention.

Knowing what we know about our history, and what our ancestors endured to keep the faith alive in our country, we might be very surprised to hear someone make this statement today; 'In our day it's a lot tougher and more demanding to live our faith, than it was fifty years ago'. If you are not inclined to believe him, ask a parent today who wants to pass on faith values and good moral standards to their family. 'Mom, get real', they are told; 'this is the twenty first century'. Is it more challenging being a parent today than it was fifty years ago?

Ask a young person who refuses to go along with the prevailing culture, who has standards and is determined to live by them, who refuses to tag along with the crowd. Ask him what he has to cope with on Social Media? Is it more challenging to be a good young person now than it was fifty years ago?

Ask a young man who is thinking about becoming a priest today? After he had spent three years in university, Jim arrived home in the summer to announce he'd changed his mind. He was not going back to Medical School in September. Instead, he was going to the Seminary to study for the priesthood. In disbelief, his father left the room almost taking the door with him off the hinges. His last words would forever ring in Jim's ears; 'Priests are parasites', he said, I don't want my son among them. 'Now', his mother said; 'Look what you have just done to our family'.

'Are you gay', his brother asked. His sister chirped in 'You never did like girls, did you'. Ask Jim is it more challenging today than it was fifty years ago, for a young man to tell his family he would like to study for the priesthood. Maybe there is something to that statement after all. In our day it is tougher and more demanding to live our faith than it was fifty years ago. We live in a society where conventional wisdom runs counter to Faith Values. We live in a society where the opinion shapers of the day are often openly hostile to the values we cherish and believe in. We live in a culture that says it is okay for us to have moral convictions about right and wrong, as long as we keep them to ourselves. Morality is a private matter

Culture is like a lake, when the water becomes polluted, the fish die. What happens fish in a polluted lake happens people in a society losing its moral values. In the first reading of our mass Jeremiah the prophet speaks out. He is the mouthpiece of God calling on His people to wake up. As God's voice, he might expect to be listened to. Because he refused to say what people wanted to hear, because he refused to peddle the pleasing and the popular and because he spoke the truth courageously, he was mocked. Because he stood for what God said was right, he was treated with contempt.

Those, who in our times choose to speak the truth, to uphold values that are sacred, can expect like Jeremiah to be ridiculed and laughed at. Parents who want to be responsible <u>know</u> the struggle.

Married couples who put their sacrament first are old fashioned. Young people who embrace moral values, will suffer for sticking to them. Idealists are presumed to be idiots or warped. Those determined to live their values in the eye of the storm can expect little support in the culture or convention of our day. Parents, married couples, families and young people living their values can expect in our world to be a minority; to be regarded as a curiosity, sometimes even be the object of ridicule.

In our past, those who refused to surrender to culture or convention gave the supreme witness to the truth of our faith. In our time, those who refuse to surrender to culture or convention can expect to suffer a different kind of martyrdom, irrelevance, cold shouldering, ridicule and isolation. Jesus was not put to death for helping widows or healing cripples. He was put to death for telling the truth and living by it. Living by that truth will always exact a hefty price. This price, often even within our own family or community. Jesus says in the gospel today; "Do you suppose I have come to bring peace on earth. No , I tell you but rather division. From now on a household of five will be divided, three against two and two against three, a father will be divided against his son and a son against his father, a mother against her daughter and a daughter against her mother, a mother-in-law against her daughter-in-law and a daughter-in-law against her mother-in-law."

The law of God will always take precedence over culture and convention. The Law of God does not change with the movement of the seasons. What is right is right. What is wrong is wrong. Those who follow God's law, and those who do not, take different roads. The times may change, but God's law never does. That is the message of our scripture for us today.

August 15 Assumption

Following Mary's boat, we will berth beside her at our eternal port.

The Feast of the Assumption of Mary that we celebrate is our assurance that where Mary has gone, we will one day follow. What has happened to Mary will happen to us. Mary today, the rest of us tomorrow. What God wants to achieve in each of us, He first achieves in one. Mary's assumption is a model of how all the baptised will one day share in the Resurrection. Mary is our sign and sure hope of what lies in store for all of us. God shows us in Mary what He wants for all of us. Mary has made it safely home, so can we. If we are faithful as she was faithful. One ship has rounded the headland in the final journey. We are all the little ones following on behind.

As we gather around the altar this evening, we all have our own preoccupations. August is the traditional time for Leaving Cert results, I am sure there are many thinking about them. We pray in our mass for all our students. We pray for all their families at this time.

But we pray most of all that we all will follow our model and guide, Mary, whose feast we celebrate., that all of us, young and old alike, will make it safely home as Mary has, that as she has rounded the final headland and made it safely home, that we, by following in her slipstream, will berth beside her at the eternal port.

21st Sunday in Ordinary Time

Sir, will only a few be saved?

Today's gospel is not the easiest to preach on and I will tell you why. The message is so obvious, so direct, so clear cut that there is little left to be explained. Jesus is asked a question; 'Sir, will there only be a few saved?" One gets a sense that the real question being asked is: "Sir, will there only be a few of us saved?" Which would suggest that he might be taking it as read that he and his friends will be okay, but wondering, apart from them, will there be many others along with them! In fairness we could understand where he is coming from. The odds are that he himself is of the Jewish Faith, which makes him a member of a very select religious group. As one of God's chosen people, his ticket is already booked, his destiny is guaranteed. He is already safe. He is just wondering about all the others gathered on the platform, about how many others will be stepping aboard. Will the train be full or will there be plenty of room?

I doubt very much if he was impressed by the answer. Save yourself the bother of worrying about the others, just make sure you get on that train yourself. Obviously, he is a bit thrown by this answer. But I already have my ticket, I am part of God's chosen group. I have practiced all my religious observances. I ate and drank in your presence. You taught in our streets. Then, as if to make sure there is no room for his complacency, a picture flashes across his mind. In that picture, he sees a great door slam shut. He hears the lock snap into position. In disbelief he watches the train roll out of the station, and he sees himself left behind on the platform surrounded by all the people who've missed the train.

Yes, Jesus did teach in his street. Yes, he did hear what Jesus preached. But did he just hear it and maybe even tell others about it. Or did he hear it, apply it to himself, and live by it. The gospel is never just the story of two thousand years ago. That gospel is always a little snapshot of our life today. We are in that gospel story today. That questioner represents us. The answer a sure antidote to any complacency, like thinking we are okay, we have our entrance ticket, our Baptism Certificate. We belong to our faith family, the family of God. We have heard His teaching. We go to mass and receive the Sacraments.

In the words of the Gospel today, we can even say to him, we have eaten and drank in your presence. But the message of the gospel for us today might well be, little use that membership card you hold unless it is stamped. It is only stamped when you have lived it, in your life. Little use having heard Him teach in our streets, unless we have allowed His words to change us. What point having recognised Him in the Eucharist at the altar, if we have not recognized Him in our brothers and sisters and welcomed His message into our homes and community. "Strive to enter by the narrow gate" Jesus says to us today, "because many will try to enter and not succeed".

It is a fair bet, that those who will succeed will have taken the commandments of God and the teachings of their church to their hearts, will have had the faith, the humility, and the generosity to the Lord, will have stamped their ticket by living His values. These are the people who do not just hear the teaching, but who make sure they practice it in their lives, the people who don't just hold a ticket in their hands but have ensured the ticked that they hold is stamped. It is only stamped when it is validated by our lives; "Strive to enter through the narrow door, Jesus tells us, for many, I tell you, will try to enter and will not be able". If we are prepared to follow His Way and live by the road map He has provided, we can be very sure that when that train pulls into the station to pick us up, there will not be a problem about the validation of our ticket.

22nd Sunday in Ordinary Time

We are all equally precious in God's eyes

Somewhere recently I knocked across a very interesting story. I tell it from memory. On a flight from Johannesburg to London a middle-aged, well-off executive type passenger was seated next to what she saw as an undesirable. She was not impressed and complained to the hostess; You have sat me next to this guy, she said, you cannot expect me to sit next to him for my whole journey. I want my seat changed. The stewardess explained that the flight was very full. She said that when everyone was settled in, she would go and check. If there was a free seat anywhere, she would do a switch. A few minutes later the stewardess arrived back. Madam, she said, unfortunately, economy is full. The only seat available is in First Class. I need to explain to you that this upgrade is most unusual. But as you are so upset at your seating arrangement, we are prepared to make a special exception for you. Turning to the person, whom this Lady had objected to sitting beside, and who had been so hurt by her derogatory remarks, the stewardess said to the man; Excuse me Sir, if you would like to gather up your things, I have your seat ready in first class at the front for you." As the man picked up his things and headed up the plane, the passengers who had heard the earlier exchange, broke into spontaneous applause for the stewardess. [This story of the "obnoxious passenger" has been in circulation in various forms over the years. I hope this doesn't lessen your enjoyment of it]

In Jesus time, as we hear in the gospel today, it was places at table that showed the pecking order. People got upset if their place did not reflect their status. It would seem that today, it is who they might have to sit beside on a plane, that gets their blood pressure climbing. As one Irish wit put it; some people spend their lives trying to get to the top rung of the ladder and when they arrive there, they discover that the ladder is up against the wrong wall!. What they expected on their climb, and what they found at the top, were very different

In life's journey, we may achieve being better off than others. That does not make us better than them. Our value is not determined by what we have, but by who we are as persons. Our real value is where we stand in the eyes of God, not where we stand in the eyes of others. Every human being is equally precious in God's eyes, the person with the most of this world's goods and the person with the least of this world's goods, the person with the greatest influence and the person with none, the person enrobed in riches, and the person clad in rags. All are equally precious in God's eyes. Every one of us is equal in dignity before God. As an Asian Proverb puts it; "Do not boast or be snobbish, you are not so inferior that you have to compensate by looking down on someone else".

The first reading has words of wisdom for us. The greater you are, the more you should behave humbly and then you will find favour with the Lord. Jesus set the standard for us to be His followers by washing His disciples' feet at the Last Supper. He said: As you have seen me do for you, you now go and do for each other. The first reading puts it this way. It is those who behave humbly, who find favour with the Lord. Let us not be like that passenger on the plane looking down on or seeing another as inferior to ourselves. I think when we meet the Lord, we will find that He operates from the same handbook as that stewardess on the flight from South Africa!!

And to return to our Irish wit; If we do want to climb to the top rung of the ladder, it is vital to ensure even before I put my foot on the first step, that the ladder I am climbing is up against the right wall. Otherwise, there may be massive disappointment and a huge anti-climax when I reach the top !

23rd Sunday in Ordinary Time

He who puts his hand to the plough and turns back is not worthy of the Kingdom of God.

In today's Gospel Jesus says, 'Anyone who does not carry his cross and come after me cannot be my disciple." These words sound very challenging. I wonder did He mean what he said. Maybe there is another explanation for them. It is important that it is an explanation of them that we are searching for, not an escape from them. He is saying that if I really want to be His disciple that there can be no place in my life for the things that go against His vision, His plan for me. I have to be ready to take up the challenges that this presents in life. He says, "He who puts his hand to the plough and turns back is not worthy of the Kingdom of God." So, we can each ask ourselves today, am I a real disciple. How do I know I am one? What are the marks of discipleship? He made sure there would be no room for doubt, no room for confusion among those who sincerely want to follow Him.

There is only one faith. There is only one baptism, one Lord Jesus Christ, and one authentic teaching authority, His church. There is only one Way, the way set out in the Ten

Commandments. There is just one package on offer from Him: To love the Lord my God with my whole heart and soul and mind and to love my neighbour as myself. There is one choice for us, to accept the package, or to reject it. It does the Lord a dis-service to misrepresent Him as a softie who cannot say no, to make of Him a Lord of compromise, someone who will take anything from us rather than turn us away. What has happened to the powerful images of Judgment Day, the graphic image of the separation of the sheep and the goats, the images of the foolish brides not ready and got locked out, the fate of the man who did not use his God given talents?

We say, but we do not think Jesus would mind this. We think Jesus would understand that. We think Jesus would allow the other thing. We do not have to think or to second-guess, or surmise, or work out what Jesus would understand or allow us to do. He has told us. Jesus has set down clearly His standards for discipleship. His disciples are those who follow Him accept His standards on His terms. Those who follow Him do their best to live by them. There is of course room for failure, we all fail. Every saint has a past and every sinner has a future. So, there is of course room for failure, but I am less sure about room for dissent, which is quite different.

Let us take an example to contrast failure and dissent. Everyone who steps out in Croke Park on All Ireland final day will fail in some aspect of his game, fail to pick up the ball, or fail to slot it over the bar. That is the reality of life and sport. There is no place on the pitch for anyone who does not accept that the ball has to be picked up, or that to score you have to put it over the bar or into the net. Similarly, with being a disciple of Jesus. It is He who makes the rules, He is Lord. We choose whether to play by them or not. Effectively we choose whether our place in on the pitch or up on the stand looking on. There is plenty of room on the stand for those who reject the rules. There is no place on the pitch for those who do not accept the rules

Is that not a parallel we can apply to our own lives. Many people seem to think today that Christianity can be reduced to a kind of a 'mix and match' religion, where everyone is free to choose their own version, 'Sure whatever you're having yourself;' attitude. The Jesus they believe in is one who says, you can pretty well make up the rules as you go along The Jesus who says; Sure, if you think it is alright, then it is alright for you. That Jesus is a fiction, a figment of someone's imagination. That Jesus is certainly not the Jesus who is speaking to us in the gospel of today's mass. The real Jesus, the only Jesus who exists, is the one who says to us in the gospel; If you follow me, then my writ will run in your life. My writ will govern how you treat each person you deal with. My writ will guide the values that you live by. My writ will be the deciding factor in the values you hand on to your children by your lived example. You will seek not to avoid my words but to understand them, so that you can better embrace them not escape them. To those who have said yes to Jesus in their lives, everything that comes from His hand is a Blessing to be accepted. Everything that comes from His lips is a guideline to be lived. Nothing on this earth will be more important to us than Him, and one day nothing in heaven will be more important to Him, than us

It can only be to people, who look at life through those eyes that the words of Jesus in today's gospel can make sense. His words always make sense to those looking for ways to embrace them. His words seldom make sense to those looking for ways to escape them.

Harvest Celebration

Sometimes it is nice to have a good news story to share.

Here is a little synopsis of how one parish celebrated the Harvest Festival in their parish in October. It so happened that during the Spring parishes were preoccupied with the whole issue of losing their priests and wondering what if will happen when we no longer have a resident priest. They realised that so much depended on themselves. A number of parishioners came together and decided to avail of some training in ministry so that they could make their contribution to the future of the faith community in their parish. One of the first goals they set for themselves was to take up the theme of Harvest for the month of October. They decided to have not one but two harvest masses in their parish. The first would be to give thanks for their faith heritage and the second to give thanks for the Harvest. For their first weekend they invited every family in the parish to reflect a little on what they had received from the generations that went before them, who worshipped in their church and to whom they owed everything they had including their presence together now. They would remember them and give thanks for them in a novel, but really challenging, way. They invited every family to participate and ensured no one was left out. Together, they said, we want to recognise and give thanks.

This is how each family was invited to participate. Find a small plant, or flower and put it in a little pot. Find an old boot, shoe or even cut-down wellington. Put the pot into it, put your family name on it. At end of September, you will be invited to bring it to the church. We will be there to receive it. We will place all these in the church for the first weekend in October. They gathered on the first weekend in October, surrounded by all the symbols brought. Together they gave thanks for all those represented by the symbols. They celebrated and appreciated the wonderful heritage of faith they had passed on by their lives, and by their example. Now, in their honour they stopped to recognise them, to acknowledge them and give thanks for all that they owed them. Most families ensured that their family ancestors and their faith heritage was included. The symbols were left in the church for the Month of October and then many families took them and placed them on their family graves for the month of November.

The following weekend every family was invited to bring something to represent fruits of the earth and again there was huge participation, and all the foodstuffs received were passed on to organisations helping the homeless. It was a memorable Harvest Celebration and so meaningful for all who participated. I include this as it may just be something a parish would like to take up

25th Sunday in Ordinary Time

"The father said you wouldn't have known the difference, but my kids would".

In the final sentence of the gospel Jesus says: 'You cannot be slave both of God and of money'

Only a couple of weeks ago, reflecting on honesty as the price of following Jesus, I posed the familiar question to you; To sign the form or not to sign the form, when to sign will put money in your pocket, money you need, but money you are not entitled to. To sign the form or not to sign it, to be fair-weather follower, or all-weather follower, of Jesus Christ. The way we handle those decisions and choices gives us a good indication of whether our faith is a flag of convenience, which we are happy to fly when there is no price to be paid, or whether it is a rock of conviction on which we build our lives, knowing that there will be times when we will have to make hard choices, choices that will cost us.

I knocked across a lovely story recently. A father had his two little boys on holidays during the summer. The two little boys loved crazy golf. You know the one where you have to putt the ball through all these crazy shapes and obstacles. The incident I tell you about happened the first day they went to the course. They came to the entrance and the father asked, how much? 'Six euro for adults' the gateman said and kids under eight play free. By the way what age are our two little champions? Eight and six the father replied. 'Looks like I owe you €12.00'. The gate man looked at him in amazement. 'Tell me something sir, he asked, have you just won the Lotto or something? Not that I am aware of, the father said, but why do you ask? Well, you could have just told me that the boys were seven and five. You could have saved yourself €6.00, I wasn't going to know the difference. That's right, the father said, you wouldn't have known the difference, but my kids would. What price the message I give them for life? What cost to their future the € 6.00 I save?

Simple moments of choice speak to our children and tell them what our values are. The simple moments of decision influence our children on what their values will be. And Jesus said, the man who can be trusted in little things, can be trusted in great, the man who is dishonest in little things, will be dishonest in great. You could have saved yourself €6, the gateman said, I wouldn't have known the difference. No, the father said, but my children would.!

26th Sunday in Ordinary Time

"To ignore our freedom to choose, would be to take away our dignity"

A priest friend of mine once remarked to me that one of the real gifts Jesus had, was being able to say the hardest of things, but that He was able to say them with great love. The gospel of today's mass puts before us such a difficult truth. A truth needs to be clearly proclaimed but proclaimed with kindness. Although we do know, that even when Jesus Himself was preaching, some people got very upset by what He said, and some responded. 'This is intolerable language; we will walk no more with Him'. Though I am sure He was deeply saddened to see them go, Jesus respected the choice they made to walk away. As He respected people's choices then, so He respects people's choices today even when deeply saddened by them.

The dilemma Jesus faced then is one many parents can face today. They want the very best for their children, putting before them the right way to live. They do everything in their power to protect them from harm. They point the pain that can follow a wrong choice in life, the consequences of mistakes now made and the regrets that can follow down the road. Having done all that is humanly possible to guide them, they then respect their right to make their own decisions, even when they believe them not to be the right ones, because to impose their own will on them is to take away their freedom. To take away someone's freedom is to take away their dignity

The gospel story that Jesus puts before us today is about taking responsibility for the choices we make and living with the consequences of those choices. The man in the gospel story who, indulged his appetites while ignoring the needs of his poor neighbour, is depicted beyond the grave consumed by regrets, pleading for mercy, mercy in the form of Lazarus, even dipping the tip of his finger in water to cool my tongue or sending Lazarus back to earth to save my brothers from coming to this place of torment. It is too late now, there is no way back for him. He had his freedom; he had made His choice.

Regarding his brothers, whom he saw heading for the same fate; 'They have Moses and the prophets, let them listen to them. If they will not listen to Moses or the prophets, neither will they, even if someone should return from the dead.' The message is for us. We have Moses and the prophets. Moses represents the ten commandments God has given us, the prophets, the teaching voice of Jesus we all have today. If we choose to ignore the commandments of God and the guidance of Jesus for us on our journey now, could we too risk making the same mistake that man did? Is Jesus telling us that if we make choices that exclude Him, we make Him helpless to undo those choices for us. Is He telling us that He respects the choices we make in life. He respects them even when He is deeply saddened by them. He respects them even when the choices we have made break His heart.

He will of course continue to love us unconditionally. He will not impose on us His Way, because to do that would be to take away our freedom and to take away our freedom would be to take away our dignity. That He will not do. He asks us to freely choose Him in the choices we make each day.

He respects the choices we make for Him and supports us in them. But He cannot make our choices for us, no more than a parent can for their adult son or daughter. He never closes the door, regardless of the mistakes we may make. He always respects our freedom and the choices we make.

In conclusion can I just say this. For a generation whose mantra in life is that our freedom of choice must always be respected by others, would it not be an amazing contradiction and inconsistency on our part, if we were to expect that the Lord would be the one who would ignore the choices we had made in life and over-rule them as we drew our final breath

No. To ignore our freedom to choose would be to take away our dignity. That is not something we can expect, even of the Lord. We are all familiar with the old phrase. As a man lives so shall he die. That certainly seems to be the message of the man in today's gospel, who obviously, if only he had another chance, would live very differently. But too late for him then to realise it

27th Sunday in Ordinary Time

Our listening ear can be what makes all the difference.

Today we celebrate 'Day for Life'. We look at and remind ourselves of the sacredness of all human lives. Scripture says; 'Before I formed you in the womb, I knew you. Before you came to birth, I consecrated you. I have called you by name, you are mine.' God has each of us branded in the palm of His hand, lest He ever forget us. To believe in God, is to believe that all human life is precious and priceless in His sight. Human life is precious to God, so it must be precious to each of us

It is hard for us to realise that someone in our community, maybe even in our own family or extended family, may have found it difficult to get up this morning, not because they had a late-night or because they over worked yesterday, but because they find it hard to find a worthwhile reason to face the day.

A great weight is pressing down on them in the form of feelings of isolation and aloneness, feelings of worthlessness and uselessness, feelings that cause a great darkness to descend on them.

And when we find ourselves in that space, which thank God most of us may never have had to experience, that sense of hopelessness can overwhelm us. It can make it so difficult to do the single most important thing, to talk to someone we really trust about what's happening to us. Trusting someone enough to talk to them, can help me overcome those negative feelings that tell me that the best favour I can do family and friends alike, is to place myself beyond their reach also. It is a very frightening place for anyone to find themselves in and it is fraught with the temptation to make wrong decisions. There is a sentence from The Little Prince that has stayed with me and is worth remembering; There is more hidden by a garden wall, than by the great wall of China and the silence of a little girl's heart can enclose more than all the sands of the Sahara. This darkness is no time for silence or secrecy of the heart, particularly in the times we are living in. Who knows the secret suffering, the fears, the uncertainties, the heartfelt worries being carried by someone who might be very close to us, a workmate, a family member, or a neighbour. What devastation to self, to family and to community, were someone to convince themselves that there was no way forward from this awful darkness. This of course is never true. There is always a way forward. It may be very difficult to see it, but there is always a way. There is always a solution to be found. There are always real friends who will accept me as I am and where I find myself, who will embrace me in my brokenness, who will feel more than privileged to be confided in. So, on this weekend we celebrate and cherish life. Together we thank god for what we have received. The morning, I find that I no longer want to get up because the burden to face another day is more than I can face, that is the day I have to trust family or a good friend to share with. The harder it is to face sharing the burden that is on me, the more important it is that I go and share it with a friend. Any of us could be called on at any time to be that friend. Our listening ear can be what makes all the difference. That listening ear is the greatest gift we bring; the greatest instrument we possess to bring the help that is needed

Today as we celebrate a 'Day of Life', we thank God for the life and opportunities we each enjoy. Tomorrow we may be called on to respect life in a very different way, by being the friend who has the time to listen and cares enough to notice and attend to someone else's pain. Please God they will feel cherished if they turn to us for help. Please God they will be saved, because they had the courage to trust and were blessed to find in one of us that listening ear they needed.

28th Sunday in Ordinary Time

Thank you, Lord, for the wonder of our being and the miracle of your presence within us.

Jesus told his friends to pray continually and not to lose heart. Losing heart is something we can all relate to, losing heart, from the child who fails to get on the school team to the student who repeats and fails to get the points. Parents can be tempted to lose heart, when after all they have done, they feel let down by a son or daughter. Spouses can be tempted to lose heart, when the dreams and hopes of their wedding morning seem to have evaporated and the struggle to keep going is draining all their energy. People who struggle with an addiction are tempted to lose heart when the mountain seems too high to scale and despite their best efforts they are sliding back down again. A family member fighting for their health gets good news and hopes soar, only to be deflated by doubts and fears again. That temptation to lose heart can haunt us all at one time or other. Two things strike me about the words of Jesus to us today. He knows how tempting it can be for us to lose heart. It is a pain he wants to save us from, because to lose heart, pulls us down and can make us miserable. So,

He offers us a recipe to avoid losing heart. At first sight a strange recipe, 'Pray continually'. A strange recipe, because to pray continually might sound like Jesus wanting us to be on our knees all day. To understand what Jesus is asking of us maybe we need to look, not just at the action of praying, but at the purpose of praying, not just what we are doing when we pray, but why we are doing it. I suggest that the purpose of prayer is to connect with and hold contact with God. Of course we can do that on our knees. Of course, we can do that using the well-established prayers we have learned, but we can also do it in other ways.

Some people can be drawn into communion with nature and from the beauty they experience around them move into a communion with God, its creator. A parent holding a newborn baby can marvel at the mystery of life, moving into thanksgiving to God, the source of that life. The presence of God is reflected in nature all around us and in the new life we touch. That mystery is also deep within each of us and to be in touch with that mystery, is to be in touch with God.

A few years ago, someone introduced me to a lovely prayer. A prayer that is not so much the words we say as the awareness we feel. A very simple prayer, just a two liner. 'I thank you Lord for the wonder of my being and the miracle of your presence within me.' The 'wonder' of my being; God says of each of us; Before I formed you in the womb, I knew you. One of the Psalms has beautiful phrases. 'You saw me before I was born, You knit me together in my mother's womb. I thank You for the wonder of my being'. Each of us is God's handiwork, His original work of art. There is only one, there are no copies. God does not repeat. When He created each of us, He threw away the mould, never to be used again, never to be repeated. Living in the awareness of that, is living in the awareness of the wonder of my being. Living in the awareness and the presence of the God who created me, that surely is prayer.

I think it is fair to say that none of us has any difficulty praying when we are looking for something, but prayer of thanksgiving is also very important. Jesus says in the gospel today; Were there not all ten made clean, where are the other nine. It seems no one has come back to give praise to God except this foreigner. Jesus asks us to pray continually. We do, when we live in this awareness of God. I thank you Lord for the wonder of my being and the miracle of your presence within me. What better protection against the temptation to lose heart. The recipe is not mine. It is the Lord's gift to you today

29th Sunday in Ordinary Time

Prayer is refusing to give up

Today's gospel is all about perseverance. The widow at the heart of the story knew what she wanted, had her heart set on getting it, and she certainly was not taking no for an answer. The odds could not be more stacked against her. On one side the judge, with the establishment behind him. On the other, a poor widow standing alone and powerless. In that gospel story, Jesus is telling us perseverance works. If we keep coming back to God. He will respond to us. That is the secret of prayer and perseverance.

I heard two stories which I will relate to you. I believe them to be true, but I am no historian, so you might like to check them out yourself. Don't just take my word for it.

Over a century and a half ago, a young man with little formal schooling ran for office in the state of Illinois. As might have been expected he got nowhere. Next, he had a go at business but failed in that too, spending years paying off the debts of his partner. He had a nervous breakdown. He ran for Congress and lost. He applied for a job in the Service. He didn't get it. But he refused to give up or throw in the towel. He had a passion for politics. He ran for the vice-presidency and lost. Two years later he was defeated for senator. Finally, he ran for office once more and was elected. They tell me that, that man was Abraham Lincoln, the sixteenth president of the United States.

Another man who became hugely famous as a politician, took three years to get through eighth grade in school because he could not pass of all things; English! Years later he was to give the commencement address at Oxford University. His now famous speech consisted of three words; "Never give up!". They tell me that famous politician was Winston Churchill. Remember his words; never give up. Those three words 'never give up' also sum up the message of Jesus to us today. When you come to God looking for something, be like that widow in the gospel today. Don't give up. Keep coming back to Him and He will 'see after' you. The more you keep coming back to God, the more you open up your life, sharing it with Him, the better He is getting to know you and the better you are getting to know Him.

Prayer has as many forms as there are people who pray. There is no special way to pray. There is no magic formula. The key is to keep 'coming back'. The key is to keep banging the door. You could say that prayer is 'bothering god' with our concerns, bothering God with our presence, bothering God by keeping banging at His door. When we do, we discover God isn't bothered at all. In fact, He has been waiting for us all along. The more we talk to Him the more He sees things our way. The more we talk to Him the more we see things His way. As we learn to see things through God's eyes, we become amazed to see how He has responded. God is not bothered by our badgering Him. God is delighted; it brings us to talk to Him.

Pope Francis has a gorgeous way of putting this. He says, come and spend time before the tabernacle. Someone said to him, but when I do I fall asleep. Francis says fine;

when you fall asleep, you fall asleep before Him. God is looking at you. Just be there and let Him look at you. He is looking at you, even if you fall asleep! Think of the widow, she never gave up. Think of Abraham Lincoln, he never gave up. Think of Churchill; never give up. Think of Jesus today. He says prayer is refusing to give up.

30th Sunday in Ordinary Time; Mission Sunday

We are all missionaries.

Many of us today probably had the experience in our school days of one of our teachers giving us a bunch of mission magazines to deliver to our neighbours. You probably remember some of their titles still, Africa, The Far East, The Messenger, Outlook and The Word. The magazines gave us glimpses into cultures we knew little about. They brought us to places we would never hope to travel to. They introduced us to people, races and tribes who without Irish missionaries would never have heard of Christ. Sadly, many of these magazines are no longer published. There isn't the same market for them nowadays. All the more, the need to ensure our missionaries are not forgotten. So, every year Catholics across the world unite on one weekend to remember and to re commit to supporting our missionaries and to remind us that forty percent of the Church across the world is missionary. Thousands of parishes are too young or too poor to support themselves. Pope Francis has his own official charity to support these churches. And what is collected across the world this weekend, goes into this official charity to support these missions.

Why should we support the mission collection on Mission Sunday. Well Pope Francis keeps telling us that we are all called to continue the mission of Jesus. During his life on earth Jesus was particularly concerned with those who were on the margins or excluded; the poor, the blind, the lepers, the persecuted and the people who had no voice in His time. He saw suffering people and was moved with compassion. That led him to act to heal them. Then He sent His disciples out to continue that work and we are those disciples today, with the same Mission. All of us here are called to be part of that work today, that same mission. Each of us is invited, not just to support our missionaries materially, but to be Missionaries in our own lives here at home with each other by living that beautiful prays of St Francis of Assisi:

'Lord, make me an instrument of your peace. Where there is hatred, let me sow love. Where there is injury, pardon. Where there is doubt, faith. Where there is despair, hope. Where there is darkness, light. Where there is sadness, joy. It is in doing our very best to live those words in our own lives, in our homes and in our parish together, that we become the people Jesus is calling us to be, His missionaries of peace and love to each other, right here where He has placed us beside each other.

31st Sunday in Ordinary Time

Jesus accepts me as I am.

The Romans were a foreign power in Palestine. To feed and fund their armies they imposed taxes on the people. How to get the taxes collected was the problem. They created 'tax districts'. They set a mandatory figure for each tax district. They farmed out the collection of the money to a local. Once he delivered the agreed sum to the Romans there were no further questions. The suspicion among the people was that the agent lined his own pockets. Zacchaeus was a tax collector for the Romans. He was seen by his own people as the agent of a foreign power. Because he was wealthy, he was believed to be cheating his people. As a tax collector for the Romans he was despised by his own people. Zacchaeus was based in Jericho. Today the City of Jericho is thronged with people because Jesus of Nazareth has come to the town. His reputation preceded Him, and everyone wants to see Him. Like everyone else, Zacheus was dying to get a look at him. But because he was a short butty little fellow, swamped in the crowds he hadn't a hope. He ran ahead and climbed up a tree to have a grandstand view. As Jesus passed by, He spotted him. Come down he said, I'm going to your house for my supper! The rest is history. His life was turned upside down and inside out. Half of his possessions, he committed to give to the poor and what he had taken from people he would give back four times over. Jesus said to him, "Today salvation has come to this house"

The story of Zacchaeus has a powerful message for all of us. God saw him in his mess. God called him in his mess. God accepted him in his mess. God ate with him in his mess. God changed him out of his mess! He didn't have to be good to be spotted by and loved by Jesus. He didn't have to deserve it, to be called by Jesus. The opposite was the case, he was despised. He didn't even have to change to be accepted by Jesus. Once he said 'Yes' to Jesus, in that instant, he was changed.

We all make a mess of things at times. We can feel embarrassed, ashamed or maybe even despised. We might feel useless or worthless or seen as a failure in life. But nothing we can do or have done, lessens our value in God's eyes. His message to us is always the same, regardless of the mess we are in. Today I would like to come to your house. Will you welcome me? If we say yes, He changes everything for us.

I will leave you with an image of a stained-glass window in a New York church. The centrepiece of the image is a great door. Outside that door stands the figure of Jesus, knocking. But the door has no handle on His side. He can only enter if the person on the inside opens. That is what Zaccheus did in today's gospel story. He opened the door when invited. When he accepted the invitation of Jesus and left Jesus into his life, His life was changed forever. That is what each of us is invited to do in the Gospel today; to open the door from our side and allow Jesus to enter. To hear what Jesus is saying to each of us; I want to come to your house tonight. The latch is on your side. I can't come in unless you let me.

32nd Sunday in Ordinary Time

November reflection

I have good news for you today. It is about the Resurrection. It is good news especially at this time of the year when we are remembering our loved ones who are gone and when we are visiting our graveyards. Graveyards are challenging places. Graveyards prompt us to think and ask questions. Is this it? Is this all there is to life - a nice plot and a headstone.? Does it all finish here or is there more, is there a life afterwards?

In today's gospel this question is put to Jesus. The Sadducees say there is no resurrection. Just suppose for a moment they are right, what are the implications for all of us ? Firstly, for our loved ones whose remains are in the graveyard, is that all there is?. Secondly for ourselves if there is no resurrection, are we not the most foolish of people to be believing in it. Life is meaningless; work, suffer and die. Make sure you leave the price of a headstone. End of story.

On the other hand, if there is a resurrection, if there is another life, what are the implications?

The first one obviously is, that death will not be the end. There will be a life after. We will pass through the gateway of death into life beyond. If that is the case, well there will be some things we will bring with us and there will be some things we will not be able to bring. The good we do will come with us, because the good we do makes us better people. So, we bring the good with us. We know that the bonds of love and friendship forged in this life do not dissolve with death, so we bring those with us. There will be an awful lot we will leave behind. Naked we came into this world and naked we will leave it. The person moves on. The trappings are discarded, no baggage allowed. As an Irish saying puts it 'there are no pockets in the shroud'.

Somebody I met leaving a graveyard during the week, remarked to me how good it made him feel to find so many people there, visiting their loved ones' graves. Our visits to the graveyard during November confront us with reality. This is either the end of the road for all of us or it is not. There is an afterlife or there isn't. There isn't a grey area in between. If there is an afterlife, we would be sensible to be preparing for it. Since we leave the baggage behind at the departure gates and since we cannot even bring hand luggage on board with us, we would be sensible to be preparing what we can carry on. The only luggage allowed on board is what we carry in our hearts so that is where we need to do the preparing. If there is a resurrection, we need to correct the language that we use. If there is a resurrection, it doesn't make much sense talking about the 'living' and the 'dead'. It is the 'living' in this world and the 'living' in the next world. Our God tells us in the gospel that He is not the God of the dead but of the living. Our loved ones are not dead. They are alive

The Good News of our gospel today is that the graveyard is not the end, just a temporary halting site. Our god is not the god of the dead, but of the living. There are no dead, just the living in this world and the living in the next. As we face the struggles of life each day, the first implication of the resurrection is that we do not face them on our own. The Risen Lord is with us. Finally, since we do believe in the resurrection, we must live by that belief; this means living, knowing that there is no 'carry on' baggage. We will carry with us from here only what we carry in our hearts.

Let's live in joy, because we know what awaits us, Resurrection.

Let's live in trust, because we know who walks beside us, The Risen Jesus. Let's live in confidence, because we know where we're off to, Life with God for ever. Let's live in readiness, because all we can take with us, is what we carry in our hearts. That is the 'Good News', – the Great News of today's Gospel.

32nd Sunday in Ordinary Time

If we believe in the afterlife, it will be obvious from how we live our present life. !

Across the Kedron Valley from Jerusalem on the Mount of Olives, there is a little shrine. Inside it, the guide points you to a small area on the floor. Carefully he focuses your attention on a flag stone. Meticulously he traces out the outline of a human foot. Expectantly he looks up at you from his crouched position to see if you have got his message. When you nod that you have, his face lights up. He has one more believer of his story. He tells you that you are now standing on the spot from which Jesus ascended into heaven. The outline of the foot he has just traced on stone, he explains, is the footprint of our saviour, Jesus Christ. Ever since Ascension Day, Christians have come here to remember that event for nearly two thousand years. They have welded the memory to this spot. The footprint pointed out by the guide, is the final confirmation of his story, the argument to silence every sceptic.

As we wound our way back down that hillside, I'm not sure I was convinced of the footprint on the stone. But neither could I say I was unconvinced. It didn't really matter whether it was authentic or not. What mattered was that the stone was a monument to two thousand years of unbroken belief in the hearts of Christians. The footprint they point you towards is on a flagstone. But far more important than the imprint on the floor is the imprint of those events on human hearts, the faith we share that Jesus Christ died and rose again and that it will be the same for those who die in Jesus; God will bring them with Him. Death is not the end, but the gateway to a new beginning. The graveyard is not the end of the road, but the launching pad to the great beyond.

One day I was by a graveside, I extended the hand of sympathy. It was firmly grasped. The old man said to me: "Father, our faith is a marvellous consolation at this time." What gave those words their powerful impact was the moving sincerity in the voice that spoke them, not from an ambo in a church, but from a heart in a graveyard. That man never saw the stone on the Mount of Olives. He has never traced the footprint and most likely he never will. But he doesn't need to. He has that imprint where it matters, in his heart.

"We believe in the Communion of Saints, the Resurrection of the Body and Life Everlasting". Do we believe in our bones, what we say with our lips? People hear what we profess, from our words. Do people see what we believe, from our lives? The Lord Himself tells us that; "it is not those who say Lord, Lord, who will enter the Kingdom of Heaven but those who do the will of the Father in Heaven"

One day I heard a priest share his vision of death; "You know" he said, "I think God has a great sense of humour." "He won't sit in judgment of us at all. He will sit with us, slip in a video of our lives and let it all play before us. He will sit there and watch it with us. By the end we will have judged ourselves." He depressed me a bit. I would prefer it the other way. But just in case he is right, it would be sensible for all of us to ensure that He only gets on that film the things we would be comfortable reviewing in His presence, which simply confirms for us that if we do really believe in the afterlife, it will be very obvious from how we live the present one.

33rd Sunday in Ordinary Time

Our loved ones who have died.

Jesus was a great storyteller. His stories always had a message. Much of the detail of the story might be forgotten. The message was remembered. There are so many of His stories in the gospels, the Prodigal Son, the Pharisee and the Publican etc. They all have one thing in common. Their message is transparent. The Prodigal Son: our God is a God of open forgiving arms, awaiting our return. He is so crazy about each of us, that nothing we can ever do will succeed in changing how he feels about us.

The parable of the Pharisee and the Publican; our God takes us as we are. We do not have to earn, deserve or merit His love. We can come to him, poor and broken. The stories of Jesus are so effective in conveying His message, because Jesus is a master at using images. An image is more powerful than a thousand words.

We are moving through November, a month we are all very specially remembering those who are gone. In our hearts we know they are still alive. In our faith we know they are with God. But we have no words to describe them now. We can only reach towards it in images. Images always fall short. But at least they point us in the right direction. Let me share with you an image. It is in essence a children's story. But peel off the packaging and the message is for us all. A few months had passed when Timmy became aware that he had a companion. They began to communicate. The time had not yet come for the twins to be born. So, Tommy and his little brother would be sharing their tiny home for some time yet. Timmy noticed that strange cord. Mammy must love them very much; she was sharing her own life with them. Little fingernails began to grow, and several other changes happen in their bodies. Wondering why all these changes were taking place, Timmy said to his little brother; 'I think we must be getting ready to leave here, but I don't want to. I feel so secure and safe where I am, I want to stay here forever'. 'We cannot stay here forever', Timmy's little brother said;' mammy is dying to see our faces'. 'I don't want to leave here Timmy said, how am I to know that if I leave here there is a life out there. Have you ever seen anyone who was born. Has anyone ever come back to tell us. Maybe this whole thing about having a mother is just something we have invented as a prop because we are frightened of the unknown'. After some time, they were born. When it felt safe to do so, they opened their eyes. They looked into their mother's face. 'Weren't we two right fools to doubt, they said. How could we ever even have imagined something as beautiful and wonderful as this is'

Our loved ones, whom we remember these days, have been reborn. They have passed through death to life. They have entered the birth channel to a new world. They have opened their eyes again and looked into the face of God. They have experienced the beautiful and the wonderful. They too must have wondered how they could have ever doubted. This new birth they have experienced we call by another name, resurrection. True, no one has come back to tell us. True, none of us has met any of them since they left us. Like the twins, we have a multiplicity of the signs around us, and we have a choice to trust.

Our Lord Jesus Christ, King of the Universe

The family I want to tell you about today lived in the days when a good harvest meant money to spend on what was wanted. A bad one meant it to wait for another year. For the family I'll be telling you about, wheat was the cash crop. A bad harvest spelt disaster and possible ruin for the family. The family depended totally on the harvest. The wheat crop depended totally on the weather. The wrong kind of weather could destroy the harvest. When the wheat was rejected at the mill, it was only fit for cattle to eat. At the end of harvest came the annual journey to the mill. The wheat was stacked onto the cart. On top was Jonathan, the man of the house. Sitting on top with him were his three little girls. As they wound their way towards the mill, each taking turns at holding the reins, the little girls chatted together. The father was unusually quiet. He was preoccupied. There had been a lot of complaints about the weather this year. A few farmers had already had their grain turned down. It had never happened to him. One could never be certain. The consequences flashed across and played on his mind; the unpaid bills that awaiting the sale of the wheat and the long winter ahead. The manager of the mill met them at the gate. He recognized the father. He remembered each of the children's names. He enquired for their mother's health. He complained about the hard times, the poor quality of this year's crop and how much of it he had been forced to reject. The children didn't miss a single word. They knew how much was at stake, the test and verdict. "Well William", the manager said at last "Dump it out. Unload the wheat. No need to sample yours." The girls could hardly contain their joy. The dreaded moment had passed. They bounced down off the load. Their father hadn't moved. They overheard him say to the manager; "No John, I think you had better sample this. It has not been a good summer." The miller looked surprised. "Alright" he said. They opened different sacks. The sample tins were filled and taken to the office. It seemed hours. Then, through the door, they saw their father emerge. He didn't say a thing. He didn't have to; it was written on his face. He just climbed onto the wagon, wheeled the horse around and headed homewards with his load.

In front of the little shop he pulled up, took a few shillings from his pocket, asked the little girl to get something for her mother and an ice cream for themselves. Emily, the youngest one, broke the silence. She was crying. Turning to her father she blurted out; "Why didn't you unload it when he asked you? Why haven't you got the money for the wheat? Why did you ask that it be tested?" We bought the ice cream and got that something for our mother. Eventually we arrived back home. It was one of the girls who years later recalled the story. That was all there was that day, she said, but I remembered."

We regard preaching as being the job of the priest. But a sermon in shoes is more powerful than a sermon in words. Example is that sermon in shoes. Emily remembered. So will your Emily. What will she remember twenty or thirty years from now; a family on their knees at night thanking God for another day, never seeing her Mom or Dad skip their weekend Mass, the place of sacraments in their lives, their total honesty - even when it came at a price? There is only one kind of sermon that's compelling, the one you give by the way you live. Seeing a sermon is always more powerful than hearing one.

APPENDIX ONE

For this season, I have taken a different approach, to the one I have taken for the others. I have just gathered here some ideas that, I found helpful myself over the years. My hope is that you may find something here, that strikes a chord or is of some help.

The three little devils job interview

Lewis tells a lovely story about three student devils who were in training for their mission on Earth, when out of the blue a vacancy arose. All three applied. In the interview for the job, there was only one question. How are you going to deceive these Christians and make sure they don't get to heaven?

The first apprentice was sure he had the right answer. "I will convince those Christians, that God does not exist," he said. You'd be wasting your time the examiner told him. Christians know God exists. You are not going to persuade them otherwise.

The second apprentice thought he had a much better answer. "I will tell the Christians that God exists", he said, "but I'll convince them that hell is a load of rubbish". You are wasting your time, the boss said. Christians know well that hell exists. Some of them have already experienced hell in their lives

The last apprentice knew the job was now his, if he came up with a better answer. "I will tell them", he said, "that God exists. They are right to believe it.

I will tell them Hell exists. They are right to believe that too. But I'll get them to believe that that's all way in the future. They don't have to be thinking about those things now. They have plenty of time to prepare later". He got the job. "Pack your things the chief devil said and be on your way. You are the one that will bring them here to me in great numbers."

Most of us know that we should always be ready and prepared. We intend to be, but we know we've plenty of time yet. If we are postponing putting things right with God till later, remember why it was the third little devil who got the job. He obviously knows us much better than the other two. The first fellow wouldn't have convinced us that there was no God. The second wouldn't have convinced us that there was no Hell. But the third little fellow is 'reaping havoc', as we say. He's convincing us there's no need to prepare just yet. It is obvious why he got the job. His message is the opposite to the words of Jesus. "Be always ready Jesus says, because you know neither the day nor the hour".

There are just a few weeks left now to Christmas. Jesus in the gospel is telling us to be always ready. That cute little devil is telling us there's no hurry, you have plenty of time yet to be thinking about preparing. Whose advise am I taking, that of Jesus or that of the little devil? When am I going to decide whose advice to follow? The little devil is hoping we will take his, because He knows tomorrow will never come!

I shared that story with someone lately. He said, "I think that little devil has taken up residence with me. He slipped in some time back and He's never left. He is obviously feeling very much at home". This weekend we ask ourselves the question, has he lodged in my place too? Sure, I'll know by whose advice I'm following

Have we been taken in by that little devil, whose telling us; 'Of course, we should be prepared to meet our God, but not yet. We have plenty time for things like that. Ignore him, and let's all take the advice of Jesus. Be always ready Jesus says, because you know neither the day nor the hour

The God who comes to us at Christmas

Preparation is coming near its end. Christmas is upon us. The birth of Jesus is not only the central event of world history, it is at the very heart of the life of our parish. It is a very special time in the life of every family, a precious moment in each of our lives. At the heart of Christmas is for each of us the infant in the crib; the God who becomes one of us, so that He can speak to us in a language we can understand. He doesn't announce Himself to us with peals of thunder or lightning flashes, to bring us to our knees and shock us into realisation. He chooses to reach us through a vulnerable defenseless little infant, arms outstretched pleading with us to pick Him up. The imagery around Christmas speaks to us of

A God who crushes not — but embraces us.

A God who forces not — but coaxes us.

A god who pressures not — but appeals to us.

A God who compels not— but invites us

A God who is not mad with us – but is 'mad about us'

Our God doesn't impose Himself on us. He pays us the complement of leaving us in charge. He has unlocked the door, but the privilege of opening it, He leaves us. He does the waiting and allows us to decide when He can enter. He humbles Himself, but does not humiliate us

The birthday of Jesus is a time when millions across the Globe make contact again and exchange greetings and gifts with each other. Wouldn't it be sad if the only one we excluded from the gift giving was the person whose birthday we are celebrating? The only gift He asks for is ourselves, a little manger in your heart and in mine, a place of welcome where He can be at home, a welcome we can all prepare by cutting with the past and leaving it behind; making a new beginning, a fresh restart; a yes to the invitation He is offering us all, to come home to Him

It matters not the roads we've strayed on. At this time, all the signposts point to home. It matters not the mess we've made of things; at this time an amnesty awaits us all. It matters not how long, or why, we've been a wanderer. Our Father is not preoccupied with our history, He just wants to welcome all His Family home for His Son's Birthday celebration, this Christmas

Christmas is for everyone, a time of homecoming. Let us allow ourselves to be carried with the wave. The experience of making a good confession can change everything. It even changes how we see ourselves as we receive that total forgiveness, just leaving it all behind, unhitching the trailer and walking free. That's the joy and the liberation that awaits us. It awaits each of us if we just say yes to His invitation

How can anyone with a human heart, look into the eyes of the little Infant in the Crib, see those little arms craving to be taken to your heart, say sorry and turn away. Please treat yourself to accepting His invitation before Christmas has passed us by. Then your Christmas can really be a special celebration, a big yes to the personal invitation from the Lord to you

So, Christmas is a time of gift giving. Could the person whose birthday we are celebrating be the only one who doesn't get His Gift this Christmas. He has told us the gift He most wants, a little manger in our hearts where He can feel welcome and at home. He has told us how to make that little manager for Him; -by making a good confession. This week He's waiting for our answer; yes or no, to a very special invitation we've received. This is the best birthday present we can drop into those appealing outstretched arms of the Infant in the crib. This Christmas, take that little vulnerable Infant in the Crib in your arms. Receive this sacrament and welcome Him to the manger of your heart. Don't leave him with the memory that this was the Christmas, you forgot His Birthday present

The Immaculate Conception:

The special connection we have with Mary

The gospel for of today, the Feast of the Immaculate Conception lets us know that Mary has a very special connection with God, that Mary has a very privileged connection with Jesus, and we can all access that special connection. God called Mary to accept a very special role. Mary wasn't just at the manger on day one. She was also at His side through His ministry. Remember the marriage feast of Cana. She was also at His side on Calvary and on the cross. In an amazing gesture of generosity, Jesus gave us Mary His mother, to be our mother. Can you imagine any mother, who has a special connection, not using that to help her son or daughter? Can you imagine Mary our mother, not using her special connection with Jesus, to help us?

There's a lovely story told about a little dialogue that took place in Heaven. Jesus saw a few 'characters' that He hadn't been expecting, and He challenged Peter who oversaw the gate, demanding an explanation for their presence. And Peter's answer to Him was, 'look Jesus; I was helpless to do anything about it. We block and turn them away at the gate, but when we turn our backs, that mother of yours drags them in over the walls'

That is the mother, we all have that special connection with. That's the mother who can't refuse us anything we ask. If we aren't using our special connection with her, whose fault is that, certainly not hers. She's on hand, to even drag us in over the wall. How could any of us, ever be so foolish as to overlook or not appreciate, the special connection each of us can have with Mary

That Special Holiday

Advent; 'A time for finding and bringing home something we had lost'

Anne was blessed with a happy home and a devoted husband. Her business was doing well. But there was something missing. Happiness and fulfilment needed more than material security and a bulging bank balance. She felt they both needed a break from the 'rat race' they'd become immersed in. A total break for a few weeks might do them both the world of good. She was thrilled when Seamus was partial to her suggestion. A Caribbean cruise would put some distance between them and the Irish weather. Even better, he would organise it.

The flight to Miami went off without incident. This was their first real holiday together since the family had left the nest. The luxury liner had everything they could ask for. The Irish weather they had left behind, was now a distant memory. Seamus was enjoying his daily workout in the gym and Anne just loved her early morning swim.

Dinner together each evening was a special treat. The menu was a far cry from the fast food picked up rushing home from the office. Anne was beginning to wonder if she would even recognise her own kitchen when she got home!

Over dinner one evening, Anne seemed a little subdued and quieter in herself. Had it something to do with that phone call earlier that day. Seamus was concerned, but he respected her privacy and had no wish to pry. He would let it lie for the moment. But next morning, he knew he had to grasp the nettle. If there was something wrong, he needed her to share it with him. So, he braced himself to put the question. Which of the grandchildren is it, or is it one of their parents? Anne was taken aback at the question and reassured him that all was well with all the family. It's your finance company then, is it not? Seamus asked. I know you were worried about it last year, but you assured me that crisis had passed, all was well again.

Seamus didn't seem reassured, and she was now upset, because he was worried. So, she knew she had to have the conversation with him. If I was a little distracted last night, she said, it had nothing to do with that phone call that I took. Indeed, it had nothing to do with the family back home or with the business. It is just that I realised that soon we will have disembarked this liner and be heading home. I am so scared we are just going to revert to where we came from. I had begun to feel, that over the last few years, we had lost each other. During this holiday I got real glimpses of the Seamus I once fell in love with, and began to feel that maybe, just maybe, we had found each other again. I'm just so scared that when we go back home, we will slide straight back into the rat-race, that for these few weeks, we'd left behind

Anne was surprised, to discover that Seamus had been feeling the same as she was. He just couldn't pluck up the courage to put words on it. Though he really wanted to, he felt that if he broached the subject, it would have thrown a damper on their special holiday. He too had feared that what they had found in the Caribbean would be left there, that it couldn't be packaged and brought home. They realised they were on the same page. Something, very precious to them both had been lost, but found again.

Need I say, their holiday far exceeded the wildest dreams they had when setting out.

That's what Advent is inviting us all to do, – to take time out to 'do a little thinking', hopefully deciding the time has come to make a new beginning. For me, that new beginning is in my relationship with the Lord. You have made us for yourself O Lord, Augustine said, and our hearts will never be at rest until they rest in you

Advent is a time to realise, that on our journey through this life, the quantity can never compensate for the quality. To know that I am 'God's work of art', means I don't have to worry myself about what my critics think. To know that I am really loved by God as I am, is to be free to be myself, and that I don't have to find my value in the fickle esteem of others

On that first Christmas night, The Christ Child came to bring us that freedom, but He was told, there was no room in the Inn for Him. In a few weeks' time He will return, but with a difference. This time, He will be knocking, not at the door of an Inn in Bethlehem, but on the doorway to my heart. These few weeks of Advent are to ensure, that when His knock comes, there will be a room and a place for Him, because I've been doing some thinking lately and taking a good look at my life. I have re-evaluated my priorities and decided the time has come to make a new beginning in my relationship with people, but very specially in my relationship with my God. Christmas and New Year for us can be very different then, because like Seamus and Anne, we have decided to re-find something we may had lost, bring it home from the crib and have it on display, not in a crystal vase on the mantlepiece, but in the far more precious place, in each of our hearts

Advent

'The empty armchair'.

My friends, to appreciate Advent, to enter into the season which we are celebrating, it is a help to understand ourselves against the backdrop of the great canvas of history, seeing our 'little world' in the context of our Faith. To be Christian, is to believe in a God of infinite and of boundless love. To be Christian, is to believe in a personal God incapable of containing or controlling that love; a God whose compulsion is to share it. There being nothing or nobody with whom to share that love, our God creates.

God's infinite love bursts out into creation. That which He creates is a reflection of Himself, or as the Bible says, in the image of Himself He created us

Having created us, He had to find some place to put us. He placed us in a temporary little home we call, Earth. So, the reason we were created and came into being was, to be receivers of God's love. Our vocation is to be available to be loved by God. Early human history depicts us reneging on Him. But God was unwilling to lose us or give up on us. He made a promise to send His Son to bring us back. That promise of a Saviour, and the certainty that God would fulfil it, became the foundation and the backbone of the faith of God's Chosen People. They woke each morning, they lived each day, they closed their eyes each night in expectation, in expectancy, waiting for the Messiah. Parents handed on the expectation to their children. Grandparents handed on the expectation to their grandchildren. Each generation waited expectantly, hoping that promise would be fulfilled in their lifetime. All those welled up expectations were fulfilled on that first Christmas night; in Bethlehem.

But, from that promise at creation to its fulfilment in Bethlehem, straddled thousands of years and generations of families living in constant expectancy, living in active waiting, living in anticipation of it happening. 'Advent', is those thousands of years of expecting and waiting, compressed into a few short weeks of waiting and preparing, for us. We now, in these few weeks, are 'God's Chosen people', waiting and looking forward in expectation and in preparation of His birth among us.

There is a lovely symbol in a Church in Rome: It's an empty marble armchair surrounded by angels. All their eyes are glued to that chair in expectancy that at any moment, it will be filled. That armchair is the Christian symbol of Advent. But that armchair is far more than just a symbol. It is also an open invitation to all of us, to each create that vacant armchair, that special place of welcome, not in our church building here or not in the good siting room at home, but to create that vacant, empty, but well-prepared space, in each of our hearts between now until Christmas night. A space in our hearts that the Lord will recognize as His, when He comes among us on this Christmas night

Each of our homes will have its crib prepared and ready. But for that crib in our home to really be, what it is meant to be, it has to be a reflection of the crib in our hearts, that each of us have prepared for Jesus. When that is the case for each of us, we are really living Advent. When that is the case, we are really reflecting who we are, a truly 'Christian' family, a people of hope, a people of expectation. We are a people waiting together in vigil to light His Birthday candle, when the Baby of Bethlehem is born again in our Hearts and in our Family Homes on Christmas Night

Advent Wreath and its symbols

The Advent Wreath is in the form of a circle. A circle, having neither beginning nor end is the symbol God's love for each of us, which has neither beginning nor end. God says to each of us, I love you as you are, not as you want to be or could be, not as you might have been or should have been, not as others think you are, but as you are, with all your faults and failings, wherever you are at this moment, as you hear these words. That is you. That is the only you that exists. That is the only you available to be loved by me. I love you as you are at this moment and nothing you ever do, can or will ever, change my love for you. That's what we mean by saying God's love for each of us has neither beginning nor end, and is neither influenced nor changed by anything we do

The Wreath is decorated with evergreens. The message of Christmas is ever-green, the same for every generation. The message of Christmas is, God comes to our home so that He can bring us with Him to His Home. The evergreens on Advent Wreath are usually laurel and holly. The laurel is the symbol of the victory of Jesus over sin. The holly, a symbol of the price of that victory, its thorns reminding us of His crown of thorns. The red berries of the holly and red ribbon on Wreath are symbols of the red blood shed for us. Central to the Advent Wreath are the candles. The days are still getting shorter now. December 21st will be the shortest day of the year. Then the days begin to lengthen again. The sun will begin to rise a little higher the sky. In nature and in the world around us, light again wins its battle over darkness. Christianity saw the birth of Jesus as the real 'Coming of The Light', a Light that would overcome all darkness. So, they placed the Birthday of Jesus right here, at this point

There are five of candles on the Wreath. This weekend we light the first. God's chosen people knew a redeemer would come. The only question was when. Each generation hoped it would be in their lifetime. From the time of Abraham, they waited. From the time of David, they waited. The first candle we light this weekend symbolises the generations of waiting. Each weekend in Advent we will light another. As the time of Jesus' coming came nearer, God sent a special messenger John the Baptist, to prepare; 'a voice crying in the wilderness; prepare ye the way of the Lord '. Our second candle, which we will light next weekend, will represent John the Baptist. The third candle, the pink, will represent the person who played the most special role of all in the preparation for the coming of Jesus, Mary. Our third candle represents Mary. We want to prepare as well as Mary did, to welcome Jesus. The final candle we will light on the fourth weekend. We are now in the final stage of preparation. His coming is extremely near. That last purple candle represents our preparation. May the Light of the World come into each of our hearts, and may Our God shine through our lives and through us may He touch others. On Christmas night we will light the white candle, the Birthday Candle to celebrate that Jesus is among us. That's the night we will all ensure that there is a special place for Jesus, where He really wants to be, in each of our hearts.

Advent

The little baby says, 'You won't ignore me, will you'

It was my good friend, Fr Johnny Doherty, that I first heard use the expression, that I quoted earlier, "Jesus Christ didn't become man to start another religion. There was more than enough of them around already". He came for something else. What was that something else He came for?. Christmas holds the key. Today we will try find that key together.

Christianity, the faith of those who follow Jesus Christ, has many shapes and forms in our world today. But they all have one thing in common. At the core of all Christian religions is belief in Jesus Christ. That makes Christianity different from pre-Christian religions. Pre-

Christian religions might broadly be described as 'man searching for god' and trying in so many ways to find Him. Christianity turns that on its head. Christianity is not, us going in search of God. Christianity is God, coming in search of us; God coming in search of you and me. When we are searching for something that is lost, normally we need something to help us find it. Everyday examples are; you hear a noise outside at night you might need to turn on the light or grab a torch. Searching for coins in the beach, you might need to throw metal detector in the car. If you're hoping to catch a salmon in the river, you might provide yourself with a fishing rod and bait. If we were going searching in the dark of night for a missing person, we might use a whistle or call out their name, to make our presence known to them. And there's the crucial bit; something by which our presence can be recognised.

When we were the ones lost in the darkness, and when our God choose to go in search of us, He too needed some instrument, some signal, some way to make sure we recognized Him. What instrument did He choose; a little baby lying on the broad of its back in a manger, defenceless, helpless and vulnerable. A defenceless little baby couldn't pose a threat to anyone. A little baby calls, invites, attracts, pleads and craves for our attention. Bethlehem is the story of the extremities to which our God was prepared to go to, to unlock the gateway to our hearts, to find a language we would understand, find a signal we couldn't miss. His signal, a little baby in manger among the animals. The little baby's plea to each of us, "you won't ignore me, will you?" . Bethlehem: is truly the story of God's search for us, trying to tell us that He is crazy, totally crazy about each of us.

That's why, no Christian home can be without a crib. No Christian home can ever afford to miss the message God speaks to us in the crib. To get that message, to let it sink deep into our hearts, we all need to spend some time kneeling before that Crib. Its message is for each of us, 'God believes in me'. God is crazy about each of us. To touch our hearts, He became this helpless little baby in a manger

The Crib is the story of God, inviting, attracting, pleading, craving for our attention. Using an instrument,

He knows we surely can't resist, a little baby, arms outstretched towards us in a manger, so fragile, so vulnerable, so defenceless; utterly incapable of repelling or frightening us away; magnetic, to attract us and draw us closer to him, an irresistible appeal; not to our heads, but to our hearts

The manger in Bethlehem answers the questions we began with. Yes, it is true. Jesus didn't come to found another religion. He came to find us and draw us close to Him. He came to invite you and me to be His special friends. He came in the hope we'd welcome Him to our hearts. That's the message at the heart of Christmas. Would it be really special, if that too was the message at the heart of all our homes, this Christmas

Advent

Are you Jesus, the little boy asked?

It was a meeting of top executives in the New York Hotel. It was scheduled to be over by four in the afternoon, but it had run long over time. They all had connections home to catch. Trains don't wait, not even for top executives. Finally, it was over. They were racing against the clock to catch their connections. Taxis were already lined up, engines running. The station was only a ten-minute ride. But it was New York traffic, and they were against the clock. They made it to the station yard with just minutes to catch their train. So, they took off on foot, darting to and fro, in search of shortcuts through the crowds, trying to make it to the platform on time

It was then it happened. The little boy selling apples at the apple stall, had all his apples stacked up so neatly. They were like little mini- Egyptian pyramids. Someone crashed headlong into his table, the pyramids came tumbling down. Apples were hopping off the concrete and flying in all directions, as the crowd ducked and dived to avoid squashing them. As the whistle blew, they were barely inside their carriage door. They dropped into their seats to catch their breaths again. It was then they realised that one was missing. He must have stumbled in the stampede and missed the train. But nothing they could do now, the train was on its way

Their friend hadn't stumbled. He had turned back deliberately. In his mind's eye he could see a picture of that little boy. He could see him struggling against the tide of people, desperately trying to recover his precious apples. A pang of guilt had hit him. He had turned back and headed for the apple stand. He began to gather up all the ones he could. But he could see that so many of them were so badly battered that they were unsaleable. As he off loaded his armfuls on the table, he realised something else, the little boy was blind. He was totally helpless to undo the mess. It flashed across his mind how lucky he himself had been; all the precious gifts he had for his whole life enjoyed. The time lost at the meeting, the train he'd missed, all seemed so trivial now. He put his hand in his pocket, took out more than would have paid for all the apples, and pushed the dollars into the little blind boy's hand. He was stunned by what happened next. It was a reaction he could not have expected. The little boy held onto his hand and squeezed it. 'Are you Jesus,' the little boy asked?

If we live, as we are invited to live. If we are preparing for His birthday in a week or two, the way we are supposed to. If others notice they are being treated, the way they would expect that He would treat them. If those around us see a little difference in us, a little more thoughtfulness and a little more time for them, a phone call, to let someone know we feel their sense of loss, a hand shake they never expected, because it's been so long, a little uplift we've so often meant to give, but never did. If those around us are benefitting from these little changes, a little of the weight they felt may just be lifted. If a little chink of light creeps in and lights their darkness, they may never put it into words the way that little boy did, but we'll have helped them feel, a little of what he felt.

Christmas; the gift of peace for each of us

In the past week, the postman's often been at your door. How did you know that he'd come and gone? You knew by the evidence he left behind; the Christmas cards that came through the letterbox. Has the **Lord** arrived in our homes for Christmas? If He has, we'll know, just like we do about the postman, by the evidence He's left behind. What evidence does the Lord leave that He's around? Well, let's let Him speak for Himself. "My peace I leave you, my peace I give, a peace the world cannot give", That is His 'Christmas gift' to us. If He's already arrived at our place, we'll recognise that He has, by the gift He's left behind; His peace within us, His peace in our own hearts, His peace in our homes, peace within our families, peace with our neighbours and at peace with our God. Christmas is a good time to let His words change us. "If you are bringing your gift to the altar, Jesus tells us; and there remember that your brother has something against you, leave your gift before the altar, go home, make peace with your brother first, then come back and offer me your gift".

There's a man I always remember at Christmas. Joe is since long gone to his eternal reward. It is years since he shared with me a story; his memories of Christmas night in the yard of his local church; seeing two neighbours who hadn't spoken to each other in months, or maybe even in the year before, on Christmas night walk across the chapel yard and extend the hand of friendship to each other, because they couldn't live with the contradiction of entering the church on Christmas night, to welcome the coming of the Infant of Peace, while at the same time harbouring in their hearts a bitterness towards each other.

We know the postman has come by the evidence he left behind, the scattered Christmas cards on the hallway floor. We know that the Infant in the Crib has come to us, when the aroma of His peace permeates our life, peace with each other within our own family, peace with our neighbours and we have made our peace with our God. The message of the Angels on the first Christmas night; Glory to God on high and peace to people of goodwill is a message that can only be shared by first being lived. When it is being lived by us with each other, the evidence of His presence radiates in and from our lives. "Put Christ back into Christmas", they tell us. Christ has always been and always will be, in Christmas. But the evidence of His presence is more obvious and recognisable, when peace and harmony radiate from our hearts and in our homes, and then it is reflected in our lives. He is best recognised by those around us, when we ourselves have first welcomed Him and His presence is obvious in our lives.

The Nativity of the Lord

'Christmas is 'the story of a handshake'

I remember talking to someone in the lead up to Christmas one year. She said, "Christmas means nothing to me. Well, I did send few cards alright. But this year the Christmas tree is still in the attic. And if you happen to pass by my place this week, you won't see any lights on my roof or in the garden. I live alone. And I'll be having Christmas dinner on my own. But that's just fine with me. And then she said, but what makes Christmas for me is our mass on Christmas night. Our church is full to overflowing. All of us are there together. And we we're all there for the same reason. It is like a family wedding, you can feel it in the atmosphere, that special bond between us on Christmas night; all of us being one with one another".

Christmas Mass is like no other mass in our parish. That phrase 'all of us bonded together as one' on Christmas night reminds me again of that story of Christmas night, that I have shared so often. The people were gathered outside the church long before mid-night mass. The five-minute bell rang, and they're all heading towards to door, when a man walked across the yard of the church to extend the hand of friendship to his neighbour. The hand of friendship was accepted and shoulder to shoulder they walk into the church on Christmas Night. They hadn't spoken in the twelve months before. But they were unable face the 'contradiction' of being in the same church on Christmas night, while still holding that grievance against each other

And the man who shared that story with me, added. For those of us who saw it happen, and knew the background to their long running feud, it was the most powerful sermon we ever got on the message at the heart of Christmas. And the more I think about it, the more I realise how right he was. Because Christmas is the 'Story of a Handshake'

A God, who like the two neighbours on that Christmas night, couldn't live with the contradiction of the division between Him and us, extending His hand to offer us His handshake, so that He could walk shoulder to shoulder with us on life's journey on this Earth. Aware, that His extended hand of friendship could be refused or could be rejected by us, God went beyond even the limits of our imagination, to find a way that would make it next to impossible for us to turn down, His offer of that handshake. - by presenting Himself to us, as a helpless little infant in a crib. He knew better than any of us that babies have a power, that no adult has, the power to draw people, to them; the power to thaw even the most hardened heart

Haven't we seen it for ourselves in families who've been at loggerheads, how the arrival of a new baby changes everything, breaks down barriers that seemed unbreakable, mends fences that were un-mendable, how a new baby brings together families who were ripped apart. When God choose to reach out to us His hand of friendship, He choose a 'handshake' no human heart could turn down, the extended arms of that helpless little infant in our Crib

So, I think of that woman for whom Christmas is not about the decorations or the lights; but about our 'being Family' with one another on Christmas night. I think of those two men in the yard of the church before midnight Mass, who just couldn't live with the contradiction of kneeling in the same church on Christmas night, while there was such bitter division between them

I think of the little infant in the Crib tonight, our God, extending to us His arms in friendship, and like you I face the question; How do I respond to those little extended hands in the Crib tonight. Surely, I don't have the heart to turn them down.

Mary, the Mother of God

"Even Heaven can't resist a Mother's Prayer

As we all know, motherhood is at the heart of Family. There's a mother in our history who may be a model for us. Her name is Monica or better known today as St. Monica. In Monica's heart, as in the heart of so many mothers, there was some serious pain, not for herself but for her son, Augustine

He had reached the pinnacle of academic achievement, becoming a professor in Milan, but for his mother Monica, nothing he'd achieved could compensate for what he had lost. Augustine had abandoned his faith in God. Monica, who couldn't live with the prospect of Her son losing his immortal soul, got on her knees and stormed heaven for him. Through her sheer persistence, through her refusal to accept the loss of her Son to God, through her 'storming the gates of Heaven' for him, she is credited with her son Augustine's conversion. Augustine, returned to his faith again and is revered as one of our saints today. Even heaven cannot resist the prayers of a mother, who has a dream, - that no achievement on this earth could compensate for the loss of her son's immortal soul. How many are in heaven today because of the persistence and insistence of a mother's prayers?

Monica's pain is replicated for many parents in our day, who have to watch on, as a son or daughter takes the wrong road in life. Parents are watching a beautiful life becoming destroyed. It is my experience, that in those situations, parents will go to any length. Parents will go to any expense. Parents will lose the shirt off their backs to save their child. Parents couldn't sleep at night, if they believed that they had left any stone unturned, to save their son or daughter. I've never heard a parent in this difficult situation just say; Ah sure they're all doing it; that's the way life is these days. We did our best, brought them this far, it's their life now! Never have I seen a parent give up on their own. If there is a way to fix it, they'll find it, regardless of the cost to them

The story of Augustine is replicated in our own times. We human beings haven't changed that much with history. Temptations are as real today as they were in Augustine's day. But sometimes you wonder if some of our attitudes and priorities have changed a bit in the intervening years. When it is about the destruction of the physical body through the curse of addictions, whichever ones they may be, arguably we haven't changed. But when it is the immortal soul that may be at risk, do we get less worked up? Do we react very differently to how Monica did ?

"Oh, we're in the 20th. century now, and that's how life is". Tis not our job to pull them out of bed to go to mass. We can't drag them in and tie them to the seat. We did our best in rearing them, but now their life is theirs. And anyway, sure that's what they're all doing nowadays. We did our best and now we can do no more"

Now hold it a minute, before your tempted to hurl something at me. No one is asking that anyone be pulled out of bed, or that young people be dragged to church at the weekend or tied to a seat to be kept there. And let's be fair, I don't believe that any parent would say, it is not really my problem if they lose their immortal soul. If that's their choice, then that's their choice. I believe that deep in every mother's heart, there is a Monica. A Monica, who believes in the core of her inmost being, that nothing this world has to offer can compensate for the loss of an eternal life with God

God gave each of us an instinct, which we see in St. Monica, that we never give up our hopes and dreams, for our children. Regardless of what they have abandoned, we never abandon them. We can be as convinced as Monica was, that even heaven cannot resist the prayers of a mother who has a dream, that no achievement on this earth could compensate for the loss of her child's eternal soul. God gave each of us the instruments to realise that dream, the weaponry to win the battle between good and evil. That weaponry St Monica used with such effectiveness to bring her own son back to God. The weaponry I refer to is the weaponry of prayer. Only when our knees are worn can we say to God that we've done our part and no, there never comes a time to say we've lost.

I leave you with a famous line from her son, St Augustine. "Faith is to believe what you do not yet see; the reward for this faith, is to see what you believe."

What every mother wants but does not yet see, is all her family united with her one day in God's presence. The reward for this Faith, for those who persist in prayer is, one day to see 'what you believe and dream of', realised. That is the message of St Monica's life for all of us today. St Monica's prayer for all of us is that the dream of Mary, whose feast day we celebrate today, will be fulfilled in us. No doubt it will, if we too storm Heaven for those we love

Epiphany January 6

'Following the star'

Today we come together to remember the arrival of the Magi, the three wise men coming to Bethlehem with their gifts. Tradition tells us that they came from the East and that they made their way by following a star. It is reputed to have been a particularly bright star. Since stars are not normally visible in the daytime, it must surely be that they travelled at night, and only after a long journey through the darkness, found who they were searching for. Many of us can have a parallel experience today, struggling to find God in the darkness, in which we find ourselves

Lost in the darkness of the suffering or loss of a loved one.

Through the darkness of not being able to understand.

Through the darkness of tragedy that has suddenly struck

Through the darkness of disappointment or failures.

Through the darkness of being wronged and being hurt

Through the darkness of being misunderstood and isolated.

It's only in the dark that the stars shine. The darker the night, the brighter they appear. Of course, they are still there in the daytime. The fact that we do not see them does not mean they have gone away. So it is with the Lord, always present, a lot of the time unnoticed and unrecognized, as it were, but tangibly present in times of darkness to people of faith. Just as the ship needs the beacon to lead it ashore; Just as the aircraft needs the radar to lead it to ground; Just as the train needs its signals coming into the station; Just as the traveler needs his signposts to lead him to his destination, so all of us, travelers in what is sometimes called the valley of darkness, need a beacon. We need signposts to guide us home. In the language of today's feast, we need our 'star' to guide us, so that like the Wise Men so too we will find God in our lives. We have a star that does not deceive, a compass that does not lie, a light that shines at all times, pointing the way, and calling us to follow.

A light, we sometimes don't notice until darkness hits us; Christ, our Light; Christ, our morning star guiding us until we see before us the lights of our eternal port. As we begin a New Year together, let us make sure we keep our eye on that Star, so that we won't get lost should we find ourselves plunged into darkness

The Baptism of the Lord

Today is the feast day of the Baptism of our Lord. So, I would like to reflect with you on Baptism. It's not possible to speak on Baptism without highlighting the central role of parents, A very well-known speaker addressing parents began with these words. "I know nothing, he said, at which people work harder, or for which they make more sacrifices, than parenting and by and large they make a darned good job of it". From time immemorial, you parents are held up as the example of human unselfishness, as the ones who go without, so that your family can have. You haven't got that honour without earning it. Your role is crucial too in handing on faith. The way we do it is clearly set out. There is only one way, example.

I remember a parish where I ministered some years ago. There was a little community, of a different faith persuasion, based close by. Sometime, as we prepared for the celebration of a Baptism, I would invite parents to reflect on the following. If instead of bringing little Johnny here to our church today, you took your him along to the alternative available, and asked that little Johnny be enrolled in their faith family, I think you might be asked a couple of questions: Are you a member of our church yourself? If you explained that you were not, I expect you might be asked if you intended to join. If your answer to that question was, well I wasn't really thinking about that, I'm not sure they would see a point in enrolling Johnny. Because they are not in the business of collecting babies' names to have them on a register. Think about it. Would you buy a bike for your child unless you want him to cycle or enroll him in a swimming pool unless you intend him to swim, or in music classes unless you intend him to learn music? Similarly, enrolling your child in faith presumes that you wish your child to embrace this faith. Would this be a reasonable expectation to have, in the absence of your guiding example to support them?

And a word to you, if you are invited to be a sponsor at a Baptism. You have been chosen. You have been selected. You are being presented to the child as a model. Effectively, what we are saying to this little child is: When you are growing up, there will be many influences that will try to pull you this way and drag you that way. But we want you, to have a model of Christian living, that you will always be able to look up to and follow, especially when you want to know the right way to live. That person is your Baptism Sponsor. So, you are being presented to this little child, as a model to imitate. You are being invested with sacred trust. Unless you are honestly committed to living your faith, doing your best to follow the way of Christ in your own life, would you be honoring the trust placed on you to take on the role of sponsor in baptism? We know that we are shaped and formed by the influence of those closest to us.

Parents, you are given sacred trust. That trust is honoured by your example, how you live. Baptism is about initiating your child into a way of life, that is practiced and lived for them, by their parents. Sponsors are people who commit to being living examples of that way of life for the little child growing up. Baptism is a very special moment in the faith life of the child. To be invited to be a child's sponsor is a very special privilege

We thank God for the Christian faith of our families. We pray that our understanding of the Sacrament of Baptism will ensure that the faith we have received will be handed on in its richness and fullness to our children. I say all this to you today while acknowledging the words of that famous preacher, Chuck Gallagher

I know nothing at which people work harder or for which they make more sacrifices than parenthood, and by and large they make a darned good job of it". Thank God this is a statement we can all agree with. Thank God it is what we see every day in our community. Long may it be so. "Our children grow in the image of those they love". May they always be blessed in seeing in their parents and God parents; models and examples of how they are called to live

The Holy Family of Jesus, Mary and Joseph

Christmas is a time, perhaps more than any other during the year, when we appreciate and are conscious of the blessing that we are to each other in our own family, and of the blessing that our family is in our lives. It's very fitting that on this day so near to Christmas, we celebrate the feast of the Holy Family. As we celebrate that feast this weekend, our prayer today is one of thanksgiving, for what we mean and are to each other, in our own family.

Parents are the unsung heroes in of every family: We all know that. The real cost of what so many of us have received, is what our parents were prepared to go without, so that we might have. There is great wisdom in the advice to cherish our parents while they are with us, rather than having regrets about them when they're gone. I can still remember some lines of a lovely poem which a friend shared with me over forty years ago. I believe the original was written by Berton Braley. It expresses this so well.

If with pleasure, you are viewing,
Some good work that I am doing,
And you like me, or you love me, tell me now.
Do not withhold your approbation,
Till the preacher makes his oration
And I lie with snowy lilies o'er my brow.
For then, no matter how you shout it,
I won't hear too much about it
I won't see how many teardrops you have shed.
So if you like me and you love me, tell me now

[apologies to the author for my inability to quote his words accurately]

On this feast of the Holy Family, if you are blessed to still have your parents, tell them what they mean to you, while they can still hear it. They won't be able to smell the fragrance of the roses, when they're gone. So, if you like them and you love them, tell them now! Words of love and admiration, words of appreciation and affirmation spoken from the heart, are treasured long after the bouquets are binned and the chocolates consumed!

Second Sunday of Christmas

'If I have to ask the price, maybe it's not for me'

I wonder if you have seen the program on hairdressers a in West-Limerick town, that was screened some years ago. I was just thinking, if they went back to make such a programme, this time about weddings, and they chose to interview brides on their way into the church, these might be some of the questions they would ask

How could you possibly make this massive life commitment? What enables you to make this huge step into the unknown? The young couple wouldn't have the slightest hesitation in telling them and in telling the whole world, that because of their love for each other, they could face anything together. Without each other, life wouldn't be worth living. Only, with each other, could their dreams of happiness be fulfilled

At the heart of every marriage are two unique people, who have experienced the mystery of love, and have been captivated by their dream. Us together forever. You, you only, and you always. Their commitment to each other is total. The lifeblood of their marriage is their relationship; the total commitment of two people to each other, in love and trust, for the rest of their lives.

The relationship that is at the heart of every marriage, is the same relationship that is at the heart of real faith; a relationship of total trust in another person, a total commitment of two lives to each other. A commitment, that shapes and influences every choice, we make. Faith, without this personal commitment, is like a marriage without relationship. The externals may look the same but the core missing. It is of that kind of "religion without relationship" that Jesus said, this people honour me with their lips, but their hearts are far from me

In the Palestine that Jesus came to, I'm sure there were many things lacking. Religion wasn't one of them. They had their scriptures, they had their commandments, their priests, their prophets, their temples and their synagogue. If what Jesus came to do, was to start another religion, He didn't pick the best place to do it ! It would have been like bringing coal to Newcastle.

But Jesus did not come to start another religion. What Jesus did come to do was, to call us into a relationship, the same kind of relationship that's at the heart of a marriage. The core of it being, two people in love with one another. The core of any marriage is not the laws that govern it, but the love of the couple who are living it. The core of our personal faith is not a book of rules and regulations that govern it, but the personal love and trust, that for each of us is at the heart of it

I remember the Sacred Heart picture hanging on the kitchen wall at home and most said prayer we remember our parents pray was 'Oh, Sacred Heart of Jesus I place my trust in You. Oh, Sacred Heart of Jesus I place all my trust in You'. When it came to the crunch, their faith was not in rules or regulations; - but in a relationship they had with Jesus. So, I'm saying nothing new, just re-tapping into what was always true, that one-to-one relationship, always at the heart of Faith. Every relationship makes some demands and comes at some cost. But when 'my relationship' is everything, the price or the cost isn't even considered

I'm reminded me of the gentleman who decided to buy himself a Rolls Royce. He went along to the showroom, looked it over, loved it and then approaching the salesman asked; "How much?". "Sorry sir, the salesman said, if afraid that, if you have to ask the price, then this car is not for you!"

Faith is like that, a precious and priceless relationship of two people who are in love with one another, - the Lord and You. For anyone who needs to know the cost beforehand, maybe it's not for them. If you don't believe me, go back to the cameraman outside the church. Imagine him asking the bride on her way to the altar to put a price on what their relationship is worth to them. Not only could she not answer, but she also wouldn't even be able to comprehend the question.

So, it is with people of faith in their relationship with the Lord. Relationship is not calculated at a cost. Relationship is cherished as a privilege. So let it be with our Faith. When we cherish the privilege, we couldn't even contemplate thinking of the cost. Such things could never be packaged in the same box !

Christmas Reflection

This beautiful reflection is credited to the late Colm Mullan, R.I.P. of Derry.

The snow was falling since early morning. The driving wind had folded it into drifts. Darkness fell, but the snowstorm continued unabated. It was Christmas night. The people in the valley were getting ready for midnight mass. A mother tucked their warmest clothes around her little ones as they set off. Tonight, daddy would not be joining them. She tried to keep it from the children, not to ruin their happiness. But daddy doesn't believe in God, a God who made the universe becoming a little baby, that was too far-fetched for him

But Mary's heart was heavy. She loved him deeply. Her faith was so important to her, and she couldn't share it with him. Tom generally didn't interfere, but tonight, he could no longer hide his feelings. Believing in a fairy tale about God becoming a helpless little infant was one thing but throwing his children to the mercy of a raging blizzard two thousand years later, to celebrate the happening, was more than he could take! Mary's heart was heavy, as with the children, she set off. Tom settled himself down before the roasting fire, still wondering how his wife, in every other area such a sensible woman, could be so gullible to fairy tales.

Had he dozed asleep? He wasn't sure, but he knew he'd heard a thump. Then there was second, quickly followed by a third! It was the window, good God 'twas going to smash. Grabbing his lamp, he rushed outside. In the darkness there were feathers everywhere. He reached down and picked up a furry object. It was warm to touch, the broken body of a little bird. Fleeing towards the light in the hope of safety inside, they were crashing headlong off the glass, maiming themselves in their futile dash for shelter. Tom opened the garage door. He placed the lamp on the floor inside. He tried to coax and lure them in. He tried to drive them, to shout them, to shoe them in, but with no success! When he could no longer stomach the carnage against the glass, he gave up and moved inside, leaving the barn open and the lamp sitting on the garage floor. But the 'thumping' off the glass continued. How he wished he could communicate with them. How he wished he could speak 'their' language. If only he could find a way of giving them his message, in the barn they would be safe inside. Was his imagination playing tricks on him? For one fleeting moment he imagined, if only he himself could become a little bird, if for that single moment he could become one of them. Then he could safely lead them in. He could teach them that in the barn they'd be safe.

And then the penny dropped. That's exactly what God had done. He needed to talk our language to find a way to us. So, He became one of us, a little, baby in a manger, a fragile, vulnerable, defenceless little baby in the crib. It was as if a thunderbolt had hit him. In a flash of light, he grasped what God had done. To reach us, He had become a helpless infant in a crib. His mind boggled. But he knew he'd just got a 'tiny glimpse' of something, he knew, he could never hope to fully comprehend. As he headed down the valley that night, he was oblivious of the blizzard that was raging all around him. He didn't even notice the surprised looks his neighbours threw at him, as he pushed his way into the crowded church, already more than halfway through midnight mass. But he couldn't miss the expression on Mary's face, as he squeezed into the seat beside her. He didn't know that the reason his children kept glancing up at him, was that they had never seen such a radiant glow on daddy's face before. It was the best Christmas the family ever had.

For a moment now, can we all just step inside that story, reflecting on the immensity of what, for us, God has done and when we visit the crib this Christmas, let's just soak it in. In many hearts this Christmas, God is missing but not missed. The message of Christmas is that at the crib, that in God's heart no one is missing without being missed

[Thank you to Kevin Mullan, Derry]

'The Baby is Missing !'

Who is the greatest in the Kingdom of Heaven

It was Christmas morning, and he was on his way to the early Mass. He popped in to visit the crib and say and a prayer. Things didn't look right. And then it hit him, the baby was missing from the manger! But He was there when he'd locked up last night. Surely no one would steal the baby from the crib on Christmas morning! He had left his mobile in the house, but there was a landline in the sacristy. He headed for it. It was, as he rounded the corner by the Grotto, that he saw the little boy pushing along his shiny wheelbarrow

A child, with a wheelbarrow in church grounds, before the early mass on Christmas morning, on top of the baby gone missing from the crib. What on earth was going on?. When he got closer, he spotted there was something in the wheelbarrow. It was the missing baby. Trying to get his head around all that was going on, he asked the child what he thought he was doing on Christmas morning removing the baby from the crib. The little boy was excited telling his story. 'I asked the baby Jesus, if He would get Santa to send me a wheelbarrow for Christmas, he said, and I promised the baby Jesus, that if I got my wheelbarrow, He would be the very first person to get a drive in it himself. I got my wheelbarrow and now I am keeping my promise to baby Jesus!

And when they asked Him,

"Who is going to be the greatest in the kingdom?",

Jesus called a little child for them to see

And if you really want to be the greatest in the kingdom

Just like this little child, you've got to be"

The Tight Rope Walker

'Trust is not where I put my words but where I put my life'

The tight-rope walker had everyone holding their breaths, as he performed without even a safety net, in the circus tent. Once when the circus was here, he stretched the wire across a deep gorge a mile outside the town, As the crowd held their breaths and looked on, he walked across the gorge to the other side and back again, without a safety net in sight. Then to wild applause he announced, 'I will now walk across the wire again, but this time I will push this wheelbarrow across before me.'

The applause was deafening in anticipation of the treat. Just as he was about to start, he noticed the man enthusiastically leading the applause. He seemed to be a leader in the community. Addressing this gentleman, he said, 'Do you believe I can do it, Sir?'. 'Yes,' the man said,

'I am certain that you can do it.' Would you put your life on it, he asked. I would, the man said and if I had two lives, 'I'd put them both on it'. All right then, he said, I'll take your word on that. You are absolutely certain I can do this; You are so sure; you would put your life on it! You would put your life on it that I can do it without a safety net. If that is the case, the acrobat said, 'Hop into the wheelbarrow and I will take you for the drive across!'.

Need I tell you; The man declined, and hard to blame him. But the acrobat had made his point. Trust is not where I'm prepared to put my words. Real trust is where I'm prepared to put my life. That is the kind of trust we can have in God's personal care for each of us, the kind of trust that enables us to 'entrust' our lives to Him. Real faith can be translated into trust, which is childlike in its simplicity, but gigantic in its strength and depth. May it be the faith, with which all of us are blessed this Christmas.

Little Christmas

'They went home by a different way'

Christmas has been celebrated. We hope it was a very special time for each of you and for all your families. Little Christmas or, the feast of the Epiphany, traditionally pulls down the curtain on Christmas for another year. The visitors head home, some of them to the far side of the world. Family members return to their jobs. The schools return to work. Shortly the decorations will come down. They will be packed away for another year.

Doesn't it kind of mirror the first Christmas. The shepherds heard the angels sing. They said, Let's go to Bethlehem and see these wonders that are taking place. Having seen and celebrated, they returned home and back to their job; to minding their sheep

For us as for them, time now moves on. We too return to the things that occupied us before. Just a thought to take with us as we do. We are remembering at this mass the visit of the wise men. The gospel tells us that the wise men came to the crib, found the infant, recognised who He was, and paid their homage. They didn't stay around the stable or around Bethlehem. They too had to return home. But the gospel uses a lovely sentence about them. It says that; 'they returned home by a different way'. We've been to the crib. We too have seen the infant. We too have recognised who He is. We too have paid our homage. Wouldn't it be lovely if we too 'returned home by a different way' !

There is something very special about Christmas. There is a 'warmth' in the greetings we exchange with one another. There is an awareness, a caring and a concern for the less fortunate. There always seems to be just 'that bit more time' that we make for each other. Like the shepherds and the wise men, we too must move on now, wouldn't it be lovely if we brought with us some of that warmth, that softness, that concern and care, that 'time' we always found for each other at Christmas. If we brought all that along with us on our journey now, just think of the difference it could make to so many people in the year ahead. Then, just as it was said of the Wise Men that came from the east, it could also be said of us, that after seeing the infant in the Crib we too went home by a 'different way'

The Baptism of the Lord

The Rabbi said, 'Love him all the more'

One evening at a little post Baptism celebration, grandad related a story which he swears happened in Co. Clare. The baby's father went to the parish priest to arrange a Baptism. During the conversation, the priest enquired as to the name of the new baby. Admitting that he had already used up all the names traditionally used in his family, he suggested the priest might have a suggestion. Opening his breviary the priest checked the date. 'St Fursa, Bishop and Martyr'. That's it, the priest said; We'll call him Fursa. To which the child's dad responded, Ah Father, we'd better not, it might 'stick' to him!

In the old days non-practicing parents were scarce on the ground. Children were born into communities with a strong faith ethos. Prayer, in your own and in your friends' homes, was the norm. Weekly mass attendance was taken for granted. Sacramental attendance was dutifully observed. Much has changed and we recognize this today. The strong family and community supports to the faith have dwindled. Parents or godparents may be disconnected from church and faith practice. While the celebrant may not always be at ease in the situation, in which he finds himself, he is very much aware of the sensitivities involved; this is not the appropriate time or place to focus on any inconsistency. So, the priest can sometimes find himself in a dilemma. We owe it to new parents, to provide an opportunity for them in advance, to better understand their role and responsibility in requesting baptism and to raise with the priest matters they might like or need to discuss.

Appreciating this, many parishes have introduced some changes around baptism. Shortly after the baby is born, either parent approaches the priest. He provides the parents with a booklet in which the sacrament of baptism is very simply, but very beautifully, explained. The celebration of baptism is a special moment of grace for each family. Parents are called to bring their children to God. The reality often is that children, at such times, lead their parents back to God. Very often the baptism of a new baby is the opportunity and occasion of a new beginning for parents. It's a time of special grace, an invitation to those who may be away, to return home.

I remind you again of the story of a Jewish father, who was heart-broken because one of his family had abandoned the faith of his people, and as the father saw it, had slid back into a pagan way of life. He came along to the Rabbi and poured out the story of his heartbreak and maybe indeed of his anger. When finished, he asked the Rabbi "What should I do with him?", expecting, no doubt, advice that would confirm what he intended to do, to cast him out of the family. He was amazed at the Rabbi's reply. The Rabbi said, "love him all the more."

It is my hope and prayer, that we as a faith family, as a parish community, will always live by the Rabbi's advice. While of course we feel the pain and sadness within our faith family and will always be the poorer for the loss of any of our members, we must always remember that God's love far surpasses our perceptions and that god's ways are not always ours. When He chooses a moment of grace, be it baptism or another moment in their lives, to invite back some who have wandered, it is so important that we ensure that in their returning, they experience the truth of the Rabbi's words; that far from being judged, that they are loved all the more.

APPENDIX TWO

Holy Thursday; Good Friday; Holy Saturday

HOLY THURSDAY LITURGY

My contribution for Holy Thursday is set out in the form of a commentary, integrated into the Liturgy. I have always thought that it is important to unfold the story of Holy Thursday, as we journey together through the Readings. I have found it helpful to try to situate the Mass we celebrate today into the context of its 'Roots' in the Story of His Chosen People. We begin with a little introduction before the Readings

Introduction.

"I will be Your God and You will be my People"

These words are imprinted on every Jewish Heart

Commentary

They were God's Chosen People; and they knew it. Chosen by God out of all the nations of the world, miraculously delivered out of slavery in Egypt. Generation after generation they celebrated this identity and this delivery. Life came to a complete halt. They sat around together sharing their stories and their history. They celebrated their deliverance with a Great Meal. This Meal was called the 'Passover' Meal

Our first reading this evening explains.

The roots and origins of this Passover Meal

Goes into detail on how it was to be celebrated

On how it was to be passed on to each generation

What this Meal would forever celebrate.

What this Meal would forever signify for them

1st Reading & Responsorial Psalm

[After the First Reading and Psalm]

Commentary

Jesus took this Passover Meal which was at the very heart of the Jewish Faith, and which was steeped in symbolism for Chosen People. He made some changes. He became the Lamb that would be sacrificed, the Lamb whose blood, would save His people. He became the 'Food' that His followers would gather round the table of the Altar to share; –

The 'Mass' – became the New Passover Meal of God's People

Holy Communion', the food we would forever share

Jesus Himself the Food for Our Journey

And just as that First Passover for God's Family wasn't just an 'Event' that happened once but was repeated each year on its anniversary by God's Chosen Family, so, our Passover Meal, the Last Supper on that 1st Holy Thursday, wasn't a 'once off event' in the upper Room in Jerusalem. But each time we celebrate mass ['Our Passover Meal'], we relive together that 1st Holy Thursday night. It's not as if, we were at that Table with Jesus. It is that we actually are. Don't take my word for it this evening, just listen to these six lines from St. Paul

2nd. Reading ; [Commentary after reading]

'Until the Lord comes therefore, every time you eat this Bread and drink this Cup, you are proclaiming His death'.

....

Commentary

On this Holy Thursday evening, Jesus celebrated the First Mass, ordained His First Priests and He did all this during a Passover Meal gathered with God's People, united across the Land steeped in an awareness of

- God's closeness to them on this night
- God's presence with them on this night

WE find in the Gospel what Jesus now expects of US

Gospel Proclamation

[After the Gospel]

Jesus, taking a basin of water and washing His disciples' feet and saying to us; 'I have given you an example, If I who am the Lord wash your feet, you should wash each other's

So, our readings this evening open up for us the full meaning of the mass, and the reason we celebrate mass. We are now God's people gathered; - To recall the past, what Jesus has done for each of us, to celebrate in the present, - His Presence with us. To look forward to the future, Our Exodus, Our Passover to our Eternal Home with Him

We gather in the certainty that the mass we celebrate this evening is the mass Jesus celebrates with us this evening, asking us now to do for each other what He has done for us;

Wash each other's feet, – Not just tonight but always.

- To be at the Service of One Another

That's the Model of Service to one another we as followers of Jesus are called to, not just today but everyday

- Not just to admire and wonder at
- But to live and practice in our own lives

When what now seems extraordinary, becomes for us the ordinary, –as it certainly will, then we will truly be His Disciples

---

GOOD FRIDAY

The ceremony laid out below is based on a priest and two readers leading, with an organist and vocalist. Obviously very important that all can be clearly heard

Stations of Cross

Opening hymn: Faithful Cross by Tom Kendzia

1st Station of the Cross ; Jesus is condemned to Death

Priest;

In our world Jesus is condemned today.

"As often as you did it to one of these you did it to Me"

Reader One

Many who have done no wrong, are condemned. So often, we hear people say, 'What did I do to deserve this'. They have done nothing wrong, but they carry their Cross, The cross of silence, in their marriage. The cross of dreams, turned sour. The cross of guilt, placed on them by others. The cross of family or friends who do not understand, or (as they might feel), do not try to understand

There are subtle ways in which we condemn people. A quiet whisper in another's ear, about them

'Just between ourselves', as we would say; A pain-inflicting smirk delivered that cuts to the heart

Priest

Lord Jesus as we walk with you today, we see those who caused you pain. Help us this evening to see where we ourselves fit into this picture

Help us tonight, as we see those who caused you pain on Calvary, to reflect on where we are the cause of your pain today

Second Station: Jesus take up His Cross

Priest; He did no wrong. No deceit was found in Him. When insulted, he returned no insult. In His own body, He brought our sins to the Cross

(St. John): So they took Jesus, and carrying the cross by Himself, He went out to the place call the Skull, in Hebrew, Golgotha

Reader Two:

St. John says: 'Carrying the Cross by Himself'

It is cruel to have to carry a cross alone. Yet that is what many people have to face. Each cross is so much heavier, if we have no one to share it with. But we are neither meant nor expected to carry the cross alone. That's why God gave each of us family. That why God has called us to be a community with each other, to carry each other's crosses and to share each other's burdens

At this Station we remember those who today carry their cross. For some it can be a diagnosis of ill health. For some it can be their mental health. For some it can be constant anxiety. For some the fear of redundancy. For families, the fears and insecurities about their future

Priest.

Lord Jesus you were forced to carry the Cross by yourself. But we can help today to carry your cross, as those beside us, struggle to carry theirs. Help us to feel privileged, to be called to share in carrying the crosses of those in our family and community. When we carry theirs, we carry Yours.

Hymn: Behold the Cross by Bob Hurd

Third Station. Jesus falls the First Time

Priest ; After a brutal beating, Jesus' strength was at a low ebb. The weight of the cross was too much. He stumbles and then He was gone. When Jesus fell, He alone took the impact of the suffering and the pain. When we fail, very often it is others who suffer the impact and the pain

Reader One;

As individuals and as communities, do we place heavy crosses on the shoulders of innocent people? ,-

Crosses we can avoid making, but crosses they are defenceless against taking.

A major European Report has warned that time is running out to avoid the catastrophic consequences of Climate Change, more frequent and intense storms, droughts, heat waves, rising sea levels, out of control raging wildfires and destruction of our eco system. Three and a half billion people are living in circumstances that make them vulnerable to the effects of Climate change

But a liveable future is possible for all on this earth, if our generation acts decisively and changes the way we live. As one report put it, – Humanity is living on thin ice, and the ice is melting fast

Priest

Lord: The Cross that crushed you, was made by others

Your innocence did not reduce the pain but intensified it.

You told us that what we did to others, we do to You

Open our eyes to the consequences of how we sometimes live today

May our lifestyle today, not sentence innocent defenceless generations to come to the catastrophic consequences of Climate Change

Fourth station: Jesus meets His mother.

Priest

Mary must have remembered the words of Simeon

'This child is destined for the fall and the rise of many in Israel

And you yourself will be pierced with a sword

That the thoughts of many hearts may be laid bare.'

Reader Two:

Like mothers throughout the centuries, Mary stood next to her son in His agony. In the Garden the evening before, He had cried out to His father to take this pain from Him. Did He at this moment cry out to His mother to do the impossible for Him.?

We don't know. But we know he didn't have to, because all His pain was already being carried in her heart. How Jesus must have wished He could have spared her the pain. And like all mothers through the centuries how Mary wished she could have borne His pain for him.

We remember and carry in our hearts at this station, all mothers. We remember those who have stood by their child's graveside. Those who have experienced such total helplessness seeing someone they love being destroyed by addictions to alcohol or drugs or involvement in crime. Their sentence; - to watch in helplessness. -to carry the greater pain.

Priest.

Lord, we stand with your mother Mary, by your side today

We feel her pain of helplessness and powerlessness

We stand today with mothers who take her place

Who, in our world or our community, know your mother's pain

We thank you Lord for the gift of Motherhood, for all mothers.

We thank you especially for the gift of your own mother to us

Hymn: Stabat Mater (Chant)

Fifth Station: Simon helps Jesus to carry His Cross

Priest

'After mocking him, they stripped him of the purple cloak and put his own clothes on him. Then they led him out to crucify him. They compelled a passer-by, who was coming in from the country, to carry his cross; it was Simon of Cyrene, the father of Alexander and Rufus'.

Reader One:

It is not common today to become involved in the problems of strangers. You go to the help of someone being beaten up in the street only to find you get the anger of the gang vented on yourself. It is easier to ignore, to turn the eyes away. It's got nothing to do with me !!.

Who are the Simons in our world today ?

The people who give up their time to staff the food kitchens

The people who tired after a long day's work, pick themselves up to go and spend an hour with someone seriously ill or alone. The people with a job who are heartbroken for those redundant

The people who look beyond their own needs to the greater needs of others. A friend in need is a friend indeed. Those who stand by people who are demonised. Those who respect human dignity in whatever form. Those who distinguish between the sinner and the sin

<u>Priest</u>

Lord Simon's story touches all of us. We would like to think that we would have his courage to stand by you when you are demonised in our world. We would like to think that when it is not politically correct or socially acceptable to walk with you and be identified with you, that we would have Simon's courage. Lord, help us to be strong. Help us to know that we are not alone in these situations; that you are always by our side. Give us strength to help those that it is not popular to help. Give us strength to be good neigbours to each other, even when it comes at a price to us

Sixth Station: Veronica wipes the face of Jesus

Priest

In Jesus time women had their place in society defined for them. Convention ruled that they be in the background. It took some bravery for Veronica to step forward from the crowd. They were those who would have felt outrage at her daring. Jesus rewarded Veronica for her courage. Tradition tells us that He left the imprint of His face on the cloth she offered Him

Reader Two; Jesus left His mark on Veronica's towel. Veronica too left her mark on Jesus. We all leave our mark on people we reach out to help. The face of Jesus is imprinted, not just on cloth, but on every human face. Every one of us is made in His image and likeness. Who are the people who today reach out to wipe the face of Jesus in our society. We think of the nurse who sits by a dying bedside. We think of attendant's care in nursing homes. We think of family members who make huge sacrifices to be with their loved ones at the end of life

Whose face do I reach out to, to tenderly wipe. Whose tears do I extend a tissue to dry

When have I shown Veronica's courage in stepping forward. Am I tempted to say; 'Not me Lord, I couldn't to that'.

Priest

Lord, we pray for those who have graced our lives with compassion. We pray for those who have stepped forward and extended their hand, when they weren't sure it would be accepted.

We pray especially for those who have reached out to us and to whom we have not had the courage to respond. Lord, that I may have Veronica's courage to do what's right. Lord that I may see you in each distorted human body.

(Hymn: Were you There?)

Seventh Station; Jesus falls the second time

Priest

At this station we are tempted to focus on the weakness of Jesus. Unable to continue, he falls again. He must have been tempted to stay there, to die right there at that point on the hillside. But there is a more important focus. Though bereft of strength He was determined to rise again from his fall and face what awaited Him

Reader One.

Rising the second time takes a very special kind of courage. No matter how hard we try, we fall again. And as we do, the memories of our first fall push us down and weigh even more heavily on us.

We know 'what they'll say about us now;'- the unkind words that will be spoken. He got his chance, why didn't he take it ?. He has no appreciation of what people have done and suffered for him.

At our lowest, in our powerlessness we long for a word of affirmation, a word of recognition of the effort, a word of courage and encouragement. How often do we get the opposite. How often do we give the opposite to the one who is down again.

We remember here those who are so disappointed with themselves, those who are inflicted with the pain of self-rejection or self-disgust. We remember those in whose ears the words 'I told you so' echo once again and make them feel even worse than they already are.

Priest

Lord, we see you crushed, spread-eagled on the ground. We hear the murmuring in the crowd who are baying for blood. That was then, 2000 years ago. But we see you on the ground today in our own community, desperately struggling for the strength to rise up and face life again. We know that those in your shoes today realise they have a terrible hill to climb. We ask you to help us to be, encouragers, affirmers, givers of courage and of strength. May we never presume to judge, those whom we see to fall

Eight Station; Jesus meets the women of Jerusalem

Luke tells us that a large crowd of people accompanied Jesus, including women who mourned and lamented for Him. Jesus said to them; Weep not for me but for yourselves and for your children

Reader Two:

Women were central to the ministry of Jesus. Women were central to the support He had during his Passion. It was Veronica who stepped forward with the cloth. It was Mary who was there for Him at the 4th, Station. It was the women who are named standing by His Cross. It was the women who went to visit Him in His tomb. And yet women often feel excluded from His mission and His ministries today.

Some feel excluded by the church authorities. Some feel excluded by their own peers. It is not always popular or politically correct to be seen to be intimately associated with your church. And yet without you, where would our families, our society or our church be today. Your role is so crucial in handing on the faith in your own homes. How many of us first learned or first prayers from your lips.

Priest

Lord at this station we recognise the courage of these women reaching out to you in your suffering. Lord let us see in each woman's life a manual of unselfishness. May we not just admire their generosity. May we try to imitate it in our lives. May your Spirit guide your church so that all human dignity will be equally recognised and reflected in our ministry and in your mission in our world today

Hymn: Caoineadh na dTrí Mhuire (Traidisiúnta)

Ninth Station: Jesus falls the third time

Priest

We call this station: Jesus falls the third time. In other traditions it is called: Jesus falls the last time.

It is possible that Jesus fell far more than three times. He must have reeled and staggered and fallen many, many, times. Each time no doubt he was dragged back on his feet by the those who took pleasure in His every agony. What is really important is not the number of times Jesus fell, but whatever the number, He got up the last time. However intense the hardships, He would not give up.

Reader One:

In our time we know that many people experience intense hardships in life. Where do they get the strength to rise again and face tomorrow, we often wonder. People who have battled their whole life with alcohol and fall again. People who battle to overcome the scourge of drug addiction and once again find that it seemed all in vain. People whose determination and steel overcomes their battle for health, only to have their hope is shattered once again. People who overcome their fight with depression and emerge from the dark hole, believing that they have won the battle, only to find themselves back to where they started again.

Time and again people point to the courage they have seen in people who have found themselves in hopeless situations, but who have refused to give up and have had the courage to start all over again. Jesus gives us the example. Despite His pain and anguish, He continued to carry the Cross on His shoulders

Priest

Lord none of us know today, what is in store for us tomorrow. But what we do know is that there is nothing tomorrow can bring, that You and we can't handle together. Help us to realise always, however hopeless our situation seems, that you are with us. Inspire us to follow the example you gave us.

Tenth Station: Jesus is stripped of His Garments.

Priest;

Matthew tells us that after they had crucified Him, they divided His garments among them.

Reader Two:

To be stripped, is to have lost everything. We remember at this station tonight the suffering people of Gaza and Ukraine, stripped of everything by the aggression of their neighbour. As Pope Francis asked about the current war in Ukraine. What kind of victory is one that plants a flag on a “heap of rubble?"

‘A heap of Rubble’, that buries the hopes and dreams of ordinary innocent people like ourselves, who have done no wrong to anyone, that covers not just the hopes and dreams of a people, but in many cases also the bodies of fathers and mothers, Grannies, Grandads and innocent children. What kind of Victory is; -

"Mothers, mourning the murder of their husbands and sons ..

Refugees, fleeing from bombs, with little children in their arms

Young people, robbed of their childhood and of a future...

Soldiers, sent over a border, to kill their brothers and sisters".

Priest

Lord this evening we entrust into your care the millions of refugees who have been forced to flee the violence in their country, and the millions of others displaced internally. We entrust into your care all the innocent people trapped in war and in basements, who can find no escape

Be with them Lord in their Agony, bring an end to this horrible genocide. Change the hearts of stone that inflict such suffering on innocent people. Give them hearts of flesh instead, that they may see the horror of their ways and bring this dreadful suffering and loss of life to an end

Hymn: Behold the Wood of the Cross by Dan Schutte

Eleventh Station: Jesus is nailed to the Cross

Priest

When they came to the place called the Skull, they crucified him and the criminals there.

Isaiah said: Yet it was our infirmities that He bore, our sufferings that He carried. He was pierced for our offences, crushed for our sins. By His stripes we were healed.

With whom we die, is sometimes as important as how we die. Those who plotted the death of Jesus knew this. They hanged Him on a Cross between two criminals. In the eyes of those looking on, they wanted Him to be seen as the third.

Reader One:

To be nailed to a Cross is to have all freedom taken away. Jesus could not even move his little finger unless someone removed the nails that bound him. In our world today who are the people who are immobilised? Who are the people who are totally helpless to help themselves. Who are the ones who are now totally dependent.

We think of those who are old, sometimes confined to an institution, -totally dependent on others, even to feed them. Difficult as this may be for them, they often suffer a greater pain. They sometimes feel irrelevant, - having overstayed their time among us. A Filipino nurse, who come from a different culture, asked; Do we hide them away, because their presence reminds us of an uncomfortable truth that soon we will be in their chair?

Priest:

Lord, while treasuring the work of the caring professions. who so tenderly minister to our old and immobilised, may we never be happy that, in ensuring their physical needs are met, we have fulfilled our obligations to them. May their freedom and their dignity always be our most important concern.

Hymn: Into Your Hands by Carmen Scialla

Twelfth Station: Jesus dies on that Cross

Priest

When Jesus saw his mother there and his disciples whom he loved, He said to his mother 'Woman behold your Son' and to his disciple He said, 'Behold your mother'.

Reader Two ; Jesus action was a sign of 'letting go'. Words of someone who also learned the time for letting go;

"I remember the first morning I brought my mother into the emergency room. I made her promise to get well. Then came the moment when the doctor told us she would not recover but she would not die tonight. We should go home and have some rest. But I felt there was something else we had to do. We gathered around her bedside. Each of us told her how much we loved her. We prayed and then each of us told her it was alright.

We told her she could let go. Its O.K granny her granddaughter said to her, you can go now but hang on if you want to. We prayed again and then left the room. In thirty minutes, she was gone. "I am certain she was waiting for our permission and assurance that she need not fight death for our sake".

Priest

The words of Jesus to His mother just before he died were a sign of his 'letting go'. For so long he had struggled to hold onto life. Now the hour had come. He looked to those who would most feel His absence and entrusted them to each other. All of us will come to this moment. We don't know the day or the hour. Some will die with dignity, some will not. Some of us will fall asleep and not wake again. Others will journey through weeks maybe months of pain

Lord deepen our faith, that when that day comes that it will be our returning home to you. May our practice of 'letting go' in our everyday life prepare us for the final act of letting go that we must one day make. Deepen our faith that death is not a destination, just a gateway we pass through on our way home to you

Hymn: Jesus, Remember Me by Jacques Berthier (Taizé)

Thirteenth Station : Jesus is taken down from the Cross

Priest

Pilate was amazed that He was already dead. He summoned the centurion and asked him if Jesus was already dead and when he learned that he was he gave the body to Joseph

Reader One:

I wonder who broke the news to Mary.? Maybe her own eyes confirmed it for her. Maybe it was the lot of John, - His special friend. As we hear so often from those who have had to experience it, there is something unnatural for a mother to have to stand by the grave of her own child. We always expect it to be the other way round. But such pain is so often the lot of parents. Mary's son was just thirty-three. There are many in our parish who have had to stand in Marys shoes. We remember you very specially at this station and we now silently remember you in our prayer {short silence}. We remember in our hearts the parents of every little child, son or daughter, who has had to keep vigil by their graveside

Priest

God our father we stand by the Cross as Jesus dies for us. We stand with Mary in her pain. We stand tonight with all parents who have had to stand in Mary's shoes. We entrust all, who have to receive a body into your loving care. Give them the strength you gave Mary at the Cross.

Fourteenth Station: Jesus is laid in the tomb.

Priest

Now in the place where He was crucified there was a garden, and in the garden a tomb, in which no one had yet been buried. They placed the body of Jesus there.

Reader Two:

Every culture has its own way of dealing with death. But around death and burial there are always special rituals. The Jewish faith has a lovely ritual. During the period of mourning, they gather together and share their stories and their memories of the person who is gone. As they each tell their story and share their memory, all the goodness in the person, and the love in which they were held by so many, comes to the surface.

It blends into a beautiful image of the one who has just left them. In their own hearts that person's resurrection has already begun, as they re-live the goodness that was in them. Sometimes we have to let those close to us go, so that they can be with us in a new way.

As one family put it so beautifully, it was not my father's absence during those days after the funeral, but his presence with us in a new way, as we began to experience the influence he was having in our lives. That was what convinced us he was alive beyond the grave

Priest

Lord as we stand by your tomb this evening, we remember all those who will die today and tomorrow in our country and across the world. We thank God that He sent us Jesus to walk this road and bring us through death to Resurrection. We know the story doesn't end here nor did it begin here. Jesus spent 33 years among us.

We have just re-lived one journey that He made. He has taught us that there are many other facets to life, and He wants us to love life and value it. The more we do, the more we will look forward to a fuller and better life beyond the grave. While journeying with Jesus to Calvary we know that this is not the end but the beginning and together now, we look forward to celebrating His Resurrection together at Easter.

Hymn: All in the April Evening by Katharine Tynan Hinkson & Hugh S. Roberton

HOLY SATURDAY

Personally, I have found that unfolding the story, by using a linking commentary connecting the readings, works well for me. Others obviously will have their own style. I just offer this as an option.

Short Introduction before the Ceremony begins

Welcome to the Most important celebration on the Christian Calendar; -the Celebration of the Lord's Resurrection. Our Ceremony to-night will be in four parts. We begin with The Service of Light. From the Pascal Fire we light the Pascal Candle, symbol of Jesus rising on this Easter Night, the Risen Jesus, Light of the World, dispelling the darkness of sin and death

After our Service of Light, we will journey with God's People from Creation, through slavery and deliverance, to today. In the third part of our ceremony, we will light our candles again and renew our Baptism promises, our commitment to being faithful forever. We will conclude our ceremonies this evening as we celebrate our Mass of The Resurrection

So now we begin our ceremony

Father will now light and bless the Pascal Fire outside the main door. From the fire he will light the Pascal Candle. Raising the lighting Pascal Candle aloft, Father will

sing the two Words: 'Lumen Christi '[3times]. Our response to each is 'Deo Gratias' Father will then go directly into singing the EXULTET --the great Easter Proclamation that 'He is Risen'

Singing of The Exultet

After the Exultet has been sung

Commentary

As we move through our Celebration together tonight, I invite you all to enter into the atmosphere of what we have gathered to celebrate, by reflecting together on its meaning

Some people are blessed with a great memory. They can remember right back to their early childhood. But however good our memory may be, there comes a point, beyond which we can't reach back any further into history. To go, there, we need access to sources and records. We call it history, both oral and written. God's people have a Special Book of their story. We call it the 'Bible', "The Book of Our People". It is 'special' because it is ALL our story, -the story of OUR interaction with God and God's inter-action with US through the centuries. Tonight, we begin at the very beginning

A reading from the book of Genesis;

In the beginning God created the heavens and the earth. God said, 'Let us make man in our own image, in the likeness of ourselves,' And so it was. God saw all he had made, and indeed it was very good.

The Word of the Lord

Responsorial Psalm Ps 103 [sung]

Response :

Send forth your spirit, O Lord, and renew, renew the face of the earth.

Prayer

Commentary

And the' Good Book' says: In the image of God, He created us. To us He gave the fruitfulness of the earth. To His people He promised a land of milk and honey. The story of God's People is the story of God's goodness to them. It is the story of God inviting His People to trust Him, as they had never trusted anyone before. Sometimes, we think a lot of trust is asked of us. Let's hear what trust that was asked of Abraham!

A reading from the book of Genesis:

Reader:

God put Abraham to the test. 'Abraham, Abraham' he called. 'Here I am' he replied. 'Take your son,' God said 'your only child Isaac, whom you love, and go to the land of Moriah.

I will make your descendants as many as the stars of heaven and the grains of sand on the seashore. Your descendants shall gain possession of the gates of their enemies. All the nations of the earth shall bless themselves by your descendants, as a reward for your obedience.'

The Word of the Lord.

Responsorial Psalm

Response

Like the deer that yearns for running streams, so, my soul is yearning for you, my God.

Prayer

Commentary

Abraham's faith was tested. Faith will always be tested by life's experience. God's people were often tested in their history. A land of 'milk and honey' they had been promised. But that land of milk and honey was to become a land ravaged by famine. A famine, so terrible they had to go 'cap in hand' to Egypt in search of food. That food came at a price. They became slaves in Egypt

They did what we all do when we're in deep trouble. They turned to God. God heard their cry, as God always does. God responded, as God always will. Books have been written; Films have been made about what happened next, The Exodus; God's Miraculous Delivery of His People from slavery in Egypt. Let's just listen to our people's story

A reading from the book of Exodus;

The Lord said to Moses, 'Why do you cry to me so? Tell the sons of Israel to march on. .... they put their faith in the Lord and in Moses, his servant. It was then that Moses and the sons of Israel sang this song in honour of the Lord:

Responsorial Psalm Ex 15 [sung]

Response

I will sing to the Lord, glorious his triumph!

Prayer

Commentary.

Sing a great song of thanksgiving to God, they did!. But how quickly they forgot all about Him when they got their 'milk and honey back'. In times of disaster, they went scurrying to the Lord

But when everything was going 'so so', again they quickly moved Him on to the Back Burner

God gave us too a beautiful world. But a world that is being ravaged today by Climate Change

Rising sea levels, wildfires and destruction of His Eco System. Hunger, wars and misery in our world are not God's judgement on us, but the consequence of our misuse of His Gift. He is calling us to turn back to Him today. Yes, indeed our God is rich in forgiving

He treats us very differently to the way we treat Him

His thoughts are not our thoughts. His ways are not our ways

(***Quick gathering together of what we have shared***)

We began with the Story of Creation. God made each of us in His Own Image, presenting us with all we could ever need. The Chosen People saw disaster at first hand. The Land of Milk and Honey became a land of Famine. They were pounded in slavery into the Egyptian mud. But when they turned to God, they were to discover that even the laws of nature would be suspended to save them. -The story of the Miraculous Exodus from Egypt

The message that jumps at us out of the pages of our history is; God's love is greater than we can ever grasp. We may fail Him, but He will never fail us. Faith will be tested, but the purpose of the test will always the same. God is trying to draw us closer. God is asking us to trust totally. Like God's People, emerging from the Red Sea to dry land, emerging from slavery to freedom, emerging from darkness to light, let us join now in our Great Hymn of Praise and thanks to our God

Gloria in Excelsis Deo

Commentary

The Epistle of our mass to-night draws together the meaning of all we have been remembering and re-living, these last days: Jesus died and rose to life again. It will be the same for all who are joined to Him. God will bring them with Him through death to Resurrection. We are joined to Him by our Baptism. So, we will be joined to Him in His Resurrection

Epistle: A reading from the letter of St Paul to the Romans

When we were baptised in Christ Jesus we were baptised in his death; in other words, you too must consider yourselves to be dead to sin but alive for God in Christ Jesus. The Word of the Lord.

Responsorial Psalm :

Response > Alleluia, alleluia, alleluia!

GOSPEL (Year b)

When the Sabbath was over, Mary Magdalene, Mary the mother of James, and Salome bought spices When they heard that Jesus was alive and that she had seen him, they did not believe it.

The gospel of the Lord

After the Gospel.

My Dear Friends. We have heard the story. We have lived it together these days.

God calls us. God shows us the Way. He invites us to come follow. He shows us to where.

But He leaves us free to choose. Those who say yes are showered with blessings in this life and welcomed to everlasting happiness in the next.

But God invites. He doesn't force His Way on anyone.

The 'Way' to God Is the Way Jesus has mapped out for each of us. He tells us: I am the Way the Truth and the Life. No one can come to the Father except through me. The way of Friendship with Jesus is the opposite, to the way of sin.

We each must now choose for ourselves which road we take.

We've heard the story. We face the choice.

We each have to make our own. No one can make it for us.

At our Baptism, someone else made the choice for us. We are now about to be invited to take ownership of that choice ourselves. In a moment we will all take a Candle in our Hand. We will be invited to accept that Light into our Heart and commit ourselves to live by it, as we renew together and take ownership of our Own Baptism Promises

Father will now bless The Baptism Water and invite you, holding your candle to seal your Baptismal Commitment. This is the Water that will be used in all Baptisms during the Easter Season.

Printed in Dunstable, United Kingdom

65496011R00318